SPANISH DRAMA BEFORE LOPE DE VEGA

SPANISH DRAMA BEFORE
Lope de Vega

A REVISED EDITION

BY

J. P. WICKERSHAM ⌞James⌟ CRAWFORD

with a Bibliographical Supplement
by Warren T. McCready

GREENWOOD PRESS, PUBLISHERS
WESTPORT, CONNECTICUT

Library of Congress Cataloging in Publication Data

Crawford, James Pyle Wickersham, 1882-1939.
   Spanish drama before Lope de Vega.

   Reprint of the edition published by the University of
Pennsylvania Press, Philadelphia.
   Bibliography: p.
   Includes index.
   1. Spanish drama--To 1500--History and criticism.
2. Spanish drama--Classical period, 1500-1700--History
and criticism. I. McCready, Warren T. II. Title.
[PQ6104.C7 1975]   862'.009   74-15215
ISBN 0-8371-7814-2

First Edition, 1922
Second Edition, 1937

Reprinted with corrections
and Bibliographical Supplement, 1967

To

MAY WICKERSHAM CRAWFORD

*This little book is affectionately
dedicated*

CONTENTS

PREFACE

THE original edition of this little book was printed in
1922. For a number of years it has been out of print
and this has led me to prepare a revised version.

While the general plan has remained unchanged, a number of modifications has been made in the arrangement.
The bibliography has been brought up to date, and a rereading of the plays has yielded, I hope, fresh points of
view and, now and again, a new fact.

Notes for the eight chapters are included at the close of
the text. A selective list of books on the drama before
Lope as well as a list for each dramatist or anonymous
play will be found in the section of Bibliography.

I appreciate very much the help that I have received
from reviews of the first edition, particularly the one by S.
Griswold Morley.

Joseph E. Gillet, to whom the study of the Spanish
drama before Lope owes so much, has kindly allowed me
to see two unpublished articles and texts, and I am also
grateful to H. J. Chaytor of St. Catharine's College, Cambridge University, for having sent me in manuscript an
edition of an inedited Spanish play of the sixteenth century.

Finally, I am much indebted to an old colleague, M. Romera-Navarro, for his kindness in having read the manuscript and to a younger colleague, Gregory G. LaGrone, for
help in the reading of the proof.

J. P. W. C.

NOTE TO THE 1967 EDITION

The University of Pennsylvania Press wishes to thank Professor Warren T. McCready, of the University of Toronto,
for his generous help in preparing the Bibliographical
Supplement.

THE SPANISH DRAMA BEFORE ENCINA

ALTHOUGH material is almost entirely lacking for a study of the liturgical drama in Spain, the close relationship that existed between the ritual of the Spanish church and that of other countries of Western Europe, and particularly of France after the eleventh century, allows us to assume that in Spain, as elsewhere, the religious drama developed from the tropes attached to the Introit of the Magna Missa of Easter and Christmas. To the study of the origins of the medieval liturgical drama, the portions of the Peninsula where Spanish was spoken during the Middle Ages contributed only two eleventh-century texts from Silos and one of a somewhat later date from Huesca of the Easter tropes, and only one eleventh or twelfth-century Christmas trope of a primitive type from Huesca.[1]

In spite of this noteworthy lack of liturgical texts, Spanish literature may claim the honor of possessing in the *Auto* or *Misterio de los Reyes Magos* one of the earliest plays in a modern tongue. This composition consisting of about 147 lines—owing to metrical difficulties it is not possible to speak more precisely regarding its length—was found in a manuscript of the Chapter Library of Toledo and is now preserved at the Biblioteca Nacional of Madrid. On scribal and linguistic grounds Menéndez Pidal ascribes the text to about the middle of the twelfth century,[2] but the unique manuscript probably belongs to the early part of the thirteenth. It was performed to celebrate the festival of the Epiphany, probably in the city of Toledo.

In the main the *Auto* agrees with the biblical narrative or liturgical texts, but it differs somewhat in details. The play opens with three monologues, amounting to fifty-one lines, in which the author adds some original features in his description of the Wise Kings by telling of their doubts as to whether the new star in the heavens really betokens the Saviour's birth. The next scene, in which the Magi confer with one another concerning the meaning of the new star, is not found in any liturgical text. Furthermore, the gifts of the Magi are spoken of as a means to identify the Christ Child.

We next find them appearing before Herod who, on learning of their mission, bids them find him so that he may go to worship him also. When left alone, Herod becomes the ranting tyrant who appears in so many later plays, and summons his scribes and astrologers to interpret to him this mystery. They fall into a dispute and the play abruptly ends. We may assume that at least one scene, namely, the adoration of the Christ Child by the Magi, has been lost.

In only two elements does the *Auto* differ from the liturgical texts or from general theological tradition independent of the liturgy: the dispute between the scribes (136–147) and the Magi's decision to offer their gifts as tests of the identity of the Christ.[3] As to the first point, the manuscript ends abruptly and its meaning is at times not too clear, but there is nothing contrary to accepted theological tradition. The second point is that instead of regarding the gifts as symbols of faith in the threefold nature of Christ, the author of the *Auto* uses them as tests as to whether the Christ Child is king or God or mortal. This trait is found in a single verse of a hymn explaining the motive of the Three Kings' visit, preserved in a manuscript of the twelfth century: *Ut probetur, deus esset an homo*, and in a group of French manuscripts called the *Évangile de l'Enfance* of the latter twelfth or early thirteenth century based upon an apocryphal Gospel of pseudo-Matthew, and the French versions of the gift motive have verbal similarities with the Spanish *auto*. It is likely that the latter derives ultimately from a liturgical Epiphany play from France with the addition of an uncommon explanation of the gifts which came from one or more of the narrative poems of the *Gospel of the Infancy*.

The author handled his material with independence, originality, and dramatic sense. It is written in the main in couplets of nine-, fourteen-, and seven-syllable lines, reminding us in its rich metrical structure of the variety of versification which characterized the plays of the Golden Age.

An oft-quoted law of the *Siete Partidas* gives us valuable information concerning religious plays in Spain about the middle of the thirteenth century.[4] After prohibiting certain abuses that will be discussed later, the law expressly declares that members of the clergy are permitted to present (*fazer*) plays (*representaciones*) that deal with the birth of Jesus, the announcement of the angel to the shepherds, the Adoration of the Magi, and the Resurrection. Such Christmas, Epiphany, and Easter plays were allowed with reasonable restrictions, and their function as a vehicle of religious instruction is clearly recognized. The words of the text indicate that these plays took place both inside and outside of churches, they contained dialogue and were accompanied by a crude attempt at acting. The ban laid by the law upon the performance of such plays for the sake of gain seems to prove that at times the performances must have been given in Spanish.

The history of the religious drama during the two hundred years that followed upon the *Siete Partidas* is shrouded in almost complete obscurity. Not a single Castilian play is known to have been composed during those two centuries that witnessed the unfolding and culmination of the French medieval religious drama. Furthermore, even the allusions to dramatic performances that have been discovered refer almost exclusively to Catalan and Valencian territory. For early examples, a document of the year 1360 tells us that it was customary for the canons of the Cathedral of Gerona to represent the Three Marys, probably the *Visitatio Sepulchri*, on Easter; a primitive Christmas representation is first mentioned at Valencia in 1432, and dialogue is first referred to in a document of 1440.

Plays dealing with the incidents of the birth and death of Christ were destined to have strong competition in the new Corpus Christi festival, which began to be celebrated throughout Western Europe in the first half of the fourteenth century.   Instead of the church serving as a setting, as had been done for the Easter and Christmas plays, Catalan and Valencian documents emphasize the procession held on Corpus Christi, in which religious bodies and guilds escorted the Host through the streets.   Sacred scenes or tableaux were sometimes presented on that day in the open air, as for example, the *Sacrifice of Isaac* and the *Dream and Sale of Joseph* by the beneficiaries of the Gerona Cathedral in 1360.   It is likely that the above scenes were chosen to explain their symbolical relationship to the Eucharist. References to the Corpus procession at Valencia date back to 1355.   This ceremony became increasingly important as a municipal festival.   At the beginning of the fifteenth century, pageants called *entrameses* and *roques* were constructed to carry singers and musicians, dressed as angels, patriarchs, and saints, about the city.   These pageants were only moving shows and probably employed dialogue solely to supplement the living picture.[5]   We have no evidence that pageants were similarly employed in the Castilian-speaking portions of the Peninsula before the latter half of the fifteenth century, at which time they formed part of the Corpus procession at Seville.   The miracle play consisting of many pageants was the form employed in Valencia and Catalonia, in counter distinction to the *auto,* which is a Castilian product.   In Castile and Andalusia we have documents which, although scanty in number, prove the continuity of tradition in the religious drama until about 1500 or later which made the church and not the streets the center of dramatic activity at the Corpus Christi as well as at Christmas and Easter.

A passage in the *Crónica del Condestable Miguel Lucas de Iranzo* " gives us an idea of the religious shows at the homes of noblemen in the fifteenth century. On Twelfth Night, 1462, the visit of the Magi bringing gifts to the Virgin and Child was represented at his palace at Jaen, and we are told that this ceremony took place each year. Two years later an entertainment was held in church at Christmas which presented the birth of Jesus and the adoration of the shepherds. The brief descriptions do not allow us to judge whether dialogue was employed, but they give evidence of a practice that was to develop into drama in the hands of Encina.

About three hundred years separate the *Auto de los Reyes Magos* and Gómez Manrique's *Representación de Nuestro Señor,* the earliest extant example of the *Officium Pastorum* in Spain. An uncle of the famous poet Jorge Manrique, Gómez Manrique was a gallant soldier and an important figure in the political life of his day, as well as a gifted poet. His *Cancionero* is made up almost entirely of lyrical verse. His Christmas play was composed to provide entertainment for the nuns at the convent of Calabazanos where his sister was mother assistant, and its date may be fixed between 1467 and 1481. It presents in simple, unaffected style and with a spirit of true devotion the familiar incidents of the Christmas story. It is worthy of note that after the shepherds proclaim the child as the Redeemer, Gabriel, Michael, and Raphael offer to him the tokens of his Passion, the chalice, the pillar and cords, the scourges, the crown, the cross, nails, and lance, a bit of symbolism that we find again in the sixteenth-century *Aucto de las donas.* A charming lullaby written on a popular air and sung in chorus by the nuns concludes the little piece. The versification of the *Representación de Nuestro Señor,* with its variety in the strophic form and its attempt to make it flexible to accord with each character is noteworthy and is thought to be evidence of early popular usage in the drama.

This little play shows slight progress, if any, in dramatic art over the *Auto de los Reyes Magos*. Dialogue is introduced only in a brief scene when the shepherds discuss the meaning of the angel's song. For the remainder of the play, each character merely recites a stanza or two and then withdraws. While it preserves no liturgical elements and is completely secular, the tone throughout is devout. Manrique also wrote a brief composition for Good Friday which was evidently performed. Based upon the *Planctus* and therefore rather lyrical than dramatic, the Blessed Virgin, St. John, and Mary Magdalene tenderly mourn the death of Jesus on the Cross.

A better idea of the sort of Christmas plays of the time which served to entertain an audience of peasants and tradespeople is a brief extract of Fr. Iñigo de Mendoza's *Vita Christi*, first published about 1480. These *coplas* were not intended to be acted, but the poet probably borrowed these features from popular performances which he had witnessed. After explaining the mysteries of the Incarnation and Annunciation, the devotional tone abruptly changes on reaching the incidents of the Nativity. Four shepherds are terror-stricken by the appearance of a figure that seems to fly through the air. While they are still disputing, the angel appears again, announces the birth of the Redeemer of mankind and bids them worship him. The shepherds make ready to obey, and in the distance they see a strange light and they hear the gentle voice of the Virgin singing to her new-born Child. Gifts are taken to do honor to the Child and his Mother, and one of the shepherds describes the song of the angels at the manger.

The scenes are in dialogue form, and the author's comments serve to show their relationship to each other. The rustic language employed recalls the *Coplas de Mingo Revulgo* as well as the shepherds' speech that we find in the plays of Encina and other early dramatists. Apparently, even at this time, the shepherd was the chief comic figure in the secularized religious drama. In the mingling of sacred and humorous elements, as well as in the use of rustic language, Íñigo de Mendoza was a precursor of Encina.

Judging from an expense account of a Christmas representation presented in 1487 at the Saragossa Cathedral, costumes and scenic effects were not wholly disregarded. An ox and an ass were represented at the manger; the prophets were provided with wigs and the angels with gloves, and a winch was used for the Virgin's chair. The Chapter paid five florins to the stage-director and two florins to the man, woman, and child who played the parts of Joseph, Mary, and Jesus. We do not know whether there was any dialogue, nor whether the platforms mentioned in the text were stationary or carried through the streets. In the same account we read of an *entremés* of shepherds on the festival of Holy Innocents, undoubtedly humorous.

The aforementioned law of the *Siete Partidas* that gives us our first definite information concerning religious plays, and another following closely upon it, furnish interesting facts regarding certain festivities that were in vogue at the time. These were called *juegos de escarnios* and were attended by so many abuses that ecclesiastical officers and judges were ordered to suppress them. The festivities were held in churches and elsewhere and the general public was admitted.

Later Spanish documents that are more specific, for example, the data mentioned in the Council of Aranda (1473), make us believe that these festivities were related to the New Year revels held by the sub-deacons in cathedrals and collegiate churches under the name of Feast of Fools, and to the drolleries held on the days of St. Stephen, St. John the Evangelist, and the Holy Innocents by the deacons, priests, and choir boys.[7] Documents of the fifteenth century give considerable facts concerning the mock ceremony of the Boy Bishop at Gerona and Lérida, and we have a fairly complete account of the custom at Seville in the first half of the sixteenth century. One of the commonest features on these occasions was the farcing of cer-

tain portions of the Office.   This consisted in the addition
of a trope and of a few words, at first in Latin, and later
in the vernacular.   Such a combination was called *farsia,
farsura, epistola farcita,* or *farsa,* and the later use of this
word to designate a comic scene indicates the character that
it must have early assumed.   Church Councils and Cathedral Chapters protested time and again against the *ludi
theatrales, larvae, monstra, turpia carmina* and *derisorii
sermones* that were introduced as a part of these post-
Christmas revels, but the lower clergy cheerfully risked a
fine for the pleasure of conducting the services, and the
onlookers crowded the churches to see the fun.[8]

The whole question of the origin of comedy in Spain is
beset with difficulties.   We know that the reign of the
Roman mime did not come to an end with the fall of Rome,
nor was his voice silenced by the vigorous protests of
Church Fathers and Councils throughout the Middle Ages.
The frequent references to him and to the *joculator* of a
somewhat later date are ample proof of his success as an
entertainer.   We first hear mention of *juglares* in a Spanish
document of the year 1116, and the same word is used in
the *Siete Partidas* of the following century, as well as *reme-
dadores* and *bufones.*   Their presence was indispensable at
weddings and festivals, and their accomplishments consisted in singing, playing musical instruments, exhibiting
trained animals, performing acrobatic feats and buffoon-
eries.   A study of the early sixteenth-century plays furnishes valuable information regarding the repertory of
these entertainers.

There is abundant documentary evidence [9] that the Royal
Entry and other festivities were celebrated by municipalities
with processions and games of various kinds.   We are
told, for example, that when Alphonso XI made his entry
into Seville in 1327, there were masquerades (*máscaras*),
representaciones which doubtless referred to pageants or
floats without action or dialogue, triumphal arches, and
knightly games.   The initiative for these pageants rested

with the municipalities, assisted by the guilds and brother-
hoods.

A procession held at Saragossa in 1399, in honor of the
coronation of Martin I, included a pageant which represented a castle bearing four sirens, a child dressed in white
who represented the King, and many angels who sang in
praise of him. During the banquet which followed, a masquerade was performed which required considerable scenery,
and indicates the tendency toward symbolism in such entertainments. In the procession held in the same city in 1414
to celebrate the coronation of Ferdinand of Antequera, a
mock siege was represented, followed by a castle-pageant
bearing on the tower four maidens symbolizing Justice,
Truth, Peace, and Mercy. This pageant is of especial interest because of its early use of allegory. The songs used
on this occasion were for a long time incorrectly ascribed
to Enrique de Villena.

The *Crónica del Condestable Miguel Lucas de Iranzo*,
covering the period from 1450 to 1471, gives an excellent
idea of the diversions of a nobleman of his time. After a
dinner given to celebrate his marriage in 1461,[10] gentlemen
of his household entered, wearing masks and representing
that they had been freed from captivity in order to attend
the fiesta, and they executed a pantomimic dance. More
interesting is the masquerade performed before Lucas de
Iranzo two days after Christmas in 1463. Some knights
dressed in Moorish costume and acting the part of escort
to the king of Morocco, challenge the Christians to a cane
tourney, promising to renounce their Prophet in case of
defeat. We can readily surmise the outcome which results
in the complete rout of the Moors and the pouring of a
bucketful of water on the king's head as a symbol of
baptism.

Among the works of Gómez Manrique, we have the text
of a simple masquerade written to celebrate the birth of his
nephew. Here Justice, Prudence, Temperance, Courage,
Faith, Hope, and Charity recite stanzas endowing the child

with the virtues they represent. More elaborate is the masquerade written by Gómez Manrique in 1467 at the command of the Infanta Isabel to celebrate the fourteenth birthday of her brother Alphonso, who had been proclaimed king of Castile in 1465 as a result of the rebellion against Henry IV. After a laudatory introduction in which it is explained that the Muses have come to honor the young king, nine ladies of the Court, including the Infanta Isabel, prophesy happiness, liberality, power, and success in love for the youth who was to die the following year without having occupied the throne.

The dialogues and debates which appear in the *Cancionero de Boena,* and more especially in the *Cancionero de Hernando del Castillo,* are non-dramatic, but a few of these themes were contributing factors in the creation of the courtly drama in the early sixteenth century. The *reqüesta de amores,* a sort of pastoral, was dramatized by Encina and many others, and the well-known *disputa* of the seasons is found in two plays by Gil Vicente. Of like nature is the charming *Diálogo entre el Amor y un viejo* which was first printed in the *Cancionero General,* Valencia, 1511, without the name of the author. It was first ascribed to Rodrigo Cota by Francisco del Cantc in 1569 who not only attributes to him the *égloga que dicen de Mingo Revulgo* but *el primer auto de Celestina.* The fact that the *Diálogo* was written about a century before Cota's authorship of the piece was mentioned and that he guessed incorrectly about the paternity of the first *auto* of the *Celestina* should not make his opinion final. Cota was a contemporary of Gómez Manrique and Antón de Montoro who mention him in their verses, and the fact that in the introduction to the *Tragicomedia de Calisto y Melibea* (1502) the authorship of the first *auto* was ascribed to Juan de Mena or to him may give some idea of the vogue he enjoyed. Written in seventy nine-line *coplas,* an old man, disillusioned with life's pleasures, has retired to a lonely spot where he hopes to find rest for his tortured spirit. When Cupid intrudes

upon his privacy, he bids him angrily to withdraw, for he
has already brought him untold misery. The tiny god
humbly pleads his cause, alleging all the blessings that he
confers upon men. The poor fellow is deceived by these
specious arguments and offers to become once again the
servant of Love, whereupon Cupid brutally ridicules his
pretensions, makes sport of his infirmities and promises
him still greater suffering.

As far as the origins of the piece are concerned, it is likely
that the author read Juan de Mena's *Coplas contra los
pecados mortales,* especially the debate between Reason and
Lust,[11] and by changing the abstract theological figures into
a dispute between an old man and Cupid, he had the ingredients of a play which he found in the line: *Hago al viejo
que remoce.* Moratín speaks of the dialogue as a play with
action, and the text with its introductory material postulates
some scenery. The author had evidently read Ovid, and
one *copla* beginning *Al rudo hago discreto* was borrowed
from the *Ars amatoria.*[12] It influenced especially Encina's
Representación del Amor and in a less degree his *Égloga de
Cristino y Febea.*

II

JUAN DEL ENCINA

IN his famous *Loa de la comedia*[1] in which Agustín de
Rojas outlines the early history of the drama, the horor
of being the first Spanish dramatist is ascribed to Juan del
Encina. While this may not be literally true, we must
concede to Encina the title of founder of the Spanish drama.
The fact that no less than seven editions of his *Cancionero*
appeared between 1496 and 1516 is proof that his plays
as well as his lyrical verse were read and admired, and
there is no question that his religious and pastoral dramas
were accepted as models by other poets for half a century.

Encina was probably born in 1468 at Salamanca. His
father, Juan de Fermoselle, was a shoemaker who saw his
other sons do well in the priesthood, law, and as professor
of music. Records show that Juan was a choir boy in the
Cathedral in 1484, and by 1490 he had discarded his
father's surname and is mentioned as chorister with the
name of Encina. It is possible that the latter was his
mother's name and that a budding humanist should prefer
to be called Encina, with all its Virgilian connotations, to
the unpoetic name of his father.[2]

He studied at the University of Salamanca where he
took his baccalaureate degree and received minor Orders.
He studied with Nebrija whom he eulogizes in the introduction to his own *Arte de la poesía castellana*. A considerable portion of his lyrical verse dates from his student
days, since he states in the dedication of his *Cancionero* to
Ferdinand and Isabella that his poems were composed between the ages of fourteen and twenty-five.

While at the University he won the favor of its chan-
cellor, Gutierre de Toledo, who was probably instrumental
in securing for him a post in the service of his brother

Fadrique Álvarez de Toledo, Duke of Alba. He entered the latter's household in the autumn of 1492 and remained there at Alba de Tormes until at least the year 1498, as musician, actor, and playwright.

His first two plays were presented on Christmas, 1492, in a hall of the Duke of Alba's palace. The first, which serves merely as a prologue to the Christmas play which followed, is a sort of " disguising " which presents two shepherds who extol the virtues of the Duke and Duchess, and discuss the author's own personal affairs. The protection offered to Encina by the Duke had aroused the enmity of less fortunate rivals. In the play Juan, who seems to be Encina 1 imself, complains that his verses are circulating in corrupt form and promises an edition of his works which will silence all detractors. One of these rivals was the poet Lucas Fernández, and Juan speaks with contempt of his pretensions to enter the service of the Duke. The pastoral form of this " disguising " was probably suggested by Virgil's *Eclogues,* and to these Encina was also indebted for his use of the word *égloga* to designate his plays.

Before Encina, a *lenguaje villanesco* had been used in the *Coplas de Mingo Revulgo* (1464 or before) and in the shepherd's scene of Fray Íñigo de Mendoza's *Vita Christi.* In the *Coplas de Mingo Revulgo* the rustic language was seriously employed to give local color to a dialogue between two shepherds in their defense of the people against Henry IV, but later it was used for comic relief. Not much is known at present in regard to the origin and diffusion of the so-called dialect of Sayago,[3] but it was doubtless due to Encina's influence that the rustic speech became the rule in later pastoral and religious plays.

The play which followed is a primitive example of the *Officium Pastorum* and represents a blending of the Christmas liturgy and the Gospels. The interlocutors are four shepherds, Matthew, Mark, Luke, and John, who have just heard the news of Christ's birth. In simple language they discuss the fulfilment of the prophecies, each of the

shepherds employing the phraseology of the corresponding
Gospel. Singing and dancing, they set out to worship the
Child, and the play ends with a charming carol. While
this composition has little dramatic value, it is attractive
for its simplicity and its devotional spirit.

The *Representación a la muy bendita pasión y muerte de
nuestro precioso Redentor* was presented in the chapel of
the Duke of Alba's palace on Good Friday of the year 1493
or 1494. Two hermits who have learned of the Crucifixion
of Jesus seek the sepulchre and meet Veronica who relates
to them the Saviour's Passion, according to the Gospel accounts, and shows them the cloth on which Christ's features
were imprinted. They kneel in prayer and an angel appears who explains in simple language the doctrine of the
Resurrection. A *villancico,* in which happiness is promised
to the afflicted, concludes the play.

The *Representación a la santísima resurreción de Cristo,*
presented in the chapel at Easter, 1493 or 1494, is a primitive form of the *Officium Peregrinorum.* As Joseph of
Arimathea kneels before the open grave, Mary Magdalene
relates to him that Jesus had appeared to her as a gardener.
Luke and Cleopas then enter, saying that the Saviour had
appeared to them on the road to Emmaus and had even
broken bread with them. These faithful disciples explain
devoutly the significance of the Resurrection for mankind,
and an angel bids them be of good cheer since Christ has
risen from the dead. The incidents are merely related and
in the latter play particularly, there is a considerable didactic element which was to become more prominent in the
plays of Fernández and of Sánchez de Badajoz.

The two Carnival eclogues were performed at the palace
of the Duke of Alba on Shrove Tuesday of the year 1494.
The first, which merely serves as a prologue to the second,
is a colloquy in pastoral style between two shepherds, Bras
and Beneito, in which they extol the virtues of the Duke and
lament his rumored departure to serve in the army against
France. Another shepherd announces that peace (Sep-

tember, 1493) has been signed between the two countries, and the play ends with a *villancico*.

The second Carnival eclogue presents four shepherds who are testing the capacity of their stomachs in anticipation of the fasting that begins on the morrow. One of the shepherds gives a highly humorous account of the defeat of Carnival by Lent, which recalls the thirteenth-century *La Bataille de Caresme et de Charnage*[4] and also *La pelea que ovo don Carnal con la Quaresma* of Juan Ruiz, and going back ultimately to Prudentius' *Psychomachia*. This little piece ends with a *villancico*, which has much in common with some of the Goliard songs, is unsurpassed among Encina's lyrics.

The *Égloga representada en reqüesta de amores*, performed in all probability at Christmas, 1494, is conceived in an entirely different spirit from the plays already examined. While the pastoral element in the aforementioned plays springs from a desire to give a realistic representation of everyday life, the theme of the *recuesta de amores* is distinctly aristocratic.

The shepherd Mingo courts the shepherdess Pascuala and urges her to accept his love. His plea is interrupted by the appearance of a knight who soon pioves to be a rival. He sneers at Mingo's pretensions; the two suitors abuse one another and finally Mingo suggests that the shepherdess choose between them. The knight agrees to this, and Pascuala expresses her preference for him, on condition that he become a shepherd. The courtier gladly accepts the terms, offers Mingo his friendship, and the play ends with a song.

The *recuesta de amores* theme, or *pastourelle*, is found occasionally in the courtly literature of the fifteenth and early sixteenth centuries. Encina himself is the author of a sort of *contrasto* between a shepherd and knight, printed in the *Cancionero musical*, and this eclogue represents the same sort of transition from lyric poetry to drama as we find in the thirteenth-century French *Jeu de Robin et Marion* by Adam de la Halle.

The second *Égloga en reqüesta de amores,* with the same characters as the above, was performed after an interval of a year, probably at Christmas 1495, and consists of two scenes. In a brief prologue, the timid Mingo offers to the Duke and Duchess his collected works (which were printed in 1496), and in rather awkward fashion we are informed that a year has passed since the incidents described in the preceding play. The knight, now known as Gil, wearies of pastoral life and longs to return to the palace with Pascuala. The latter dons the robes of a lady and amazes Mingo and his wife by her beauty, which Mingo ascribes to the power of Love. Gil urges Mingo to accompany them, but the shepherd hesitates, alleging his ignorance of courtly manners and his delight in the simple joys of pastoral life, which he describes in verses that reveal true poetic feeling. The idea of becoming a gentleman, however, tickles his vanity, and with keen satisfaction he puts on his best clothes and adopts the airs of a courtier. The play ends with a song in praise of all-powerful Love. Here the well-known *débat* on the relative advantages of city and country life is combined with the theme of the power of Love which was frequently treated in the fifteenth-century *cancioneros* and ultimately is derived from Ovid's *Ars amatoria.*

These two compositions cannot be considered popular in any sense of the word. We are not dealing here with real shepherds, but with shepherds portrayed in accordance with an aristocratic literary tradition. We have abundant evidence of the contempt of the *cortesano* for the *villano* which was so frequently expressed in the courtly literature of the day, and the dramatic basis of these plays, performed before an audience of gentlefolk, lies in the portrayal of the shortcomings of rustics to meet aristocracy on its own level. The situation also gave the author an opportunity to satirize pleasantly some of the affectations in manners and language imposed by fashion.

In addition to the eight plays already mentioned, Encina's *Cancionero,* which first appeared at Salamanca in 1496, contained other compositions.   His *Arte de la poesía castellana* considers the theory and practice of verse-writing as understood at the close of the fifteenth century.   In his paraphrase of Virgil's *Eclogues* he uses freely his original in order to make it applicable to the historical events of his own time, but in spite of this medieval conception he anticipated Boscán in his insistence on the necessity of combining *el ingenio* with *el arte.*[5]   As a poet, he is esteemed for the musical qualities of his work rather than for the content, and he is at his best in pastoral lyrics.

The *Representación del Amor,* first published in the 1507 edition of the *Cancionero,* has an especial interest because of its performance at Salamanca or at Alba de Tormes in 1497 before his patron, Prince John of Castile, and of his bride, Margarita of Austria, whose marriage had been solemnized at Burgos on April second of that year.   To celebrate this happy occasion Encina chose the theme of the omnipotence of Love, treated in burlesque fashion, with a shepherd as the victim of the tiny god's shaft.   Cupid enters, armed with bow and arrows, asserting his power over all mortals in terms that closely resemble the boasting loquaciousness of Amor in the *Diálogo entre el Amor y un viejo.*   He meets the shepherd Pelayo, who failing to recognize him, asks by whose permission he hunts on forbidden territory.   Pelayo refuses to heed Cupid's warning and is laid low by an arrow.   The shepherd, Juanillo, finds Pelayo suffering keenly from his wound, the nature of which the unfortunate victim is unable to understand, even when Juanillo explains that it was caused by Amor, but to Pelayo, the word Amor suggests only *morder* or *mortaja.*   A knight who joins them adds his testimony to the anguish caused by Love.   In the charming song *Ojos garzos ha la niña,*[6] with which the play ends, the poet probably referred to the newly-married Princess, who was to become a widow a few months later.

Two separate editions of the play were published in the first half of the sixteenth century, Lucas Fernández alludes to it in his *Farsa o cuasi comedia del soldado,* and the plight of Pelayo became popular in Spanish and Portuguese songs.[7]

Another Christmas play, often styled *Égloga de las grandes lluvias,* was performed in 1498, probably at the Duke of Alba's palace. Four shepherds, seated around a fire, talk of the heavy rainfall and floods that have caused severe losses. They begin to play " odd and even " but the game is interrupted by the angel's song, announcing the birth of Christ. They do not understand at first: one of the shepherds confuses the word *Salvador* with *saludador.* Finally they take their simple gifts and set out to visit the manger. Here we have a crude attempt at realism which almost completely overshadows the sacred scenes.

Reference is made in the play to the post of choirmaster in the Cathedral which had become vacant. The shepherds discuss who the lucky appointee will be, and when Anton suggests Juan, Miguellejo objects that they will probably prefer some outsider. Documents show that in 1498 Encina and Fernández were numbered among those who solicited the appointment. Fernández was able to count on the support of influential friends and relatives, and the question was finally referred to a commission of the Chapter which decided that the salary attached to the post should be divided among three choristers, one of whom was Lucas Fernández. Encina's disappointment over his failure to secure the place, coupled with his feeling that his services were not adequately appreciated by his patron, led him to leave Salamanca.

An anonymous and undated Christmas play entitled *Égloga interlocutoria* has also been attributed to Encina by several critics. Like Encina's second Christmas eclogue, with which it has a number of verbal similarities, this play presents four shepherds who have heard the news of Christ's birth. Unlike the former play, however, the shepherds show little interest in this announcement, and are completely absorbed in their petty quarrels and their desire for amusement. They gamble for a while, and the play ends quite abruptly with a eulogy in *coplas de arte mayor* of the Duke and Duchess. It has been noted [8] that this play has the same incidents as the *Égloga de las grandes lluvias,* arranged in reverse order. It shows carelessness in workmanship and is far inferior to any play printed with Encina's name. It has been argued that it was written in haste by Encina for a Christmas celebration; that its author did not intend to publish it, and that its preservation was due to an actor who wrote it out from memory. It is difficult to decide whether this be true or whether someone unscrupulously pilfered from Encina's *Égloga de las grandes lluvias* after the latter had left Salamanca.

In the plays already examined, Encina shows no influence of foreign models. His indebtedness to Virgil is limited to his use of the word " eclogue " to designate plays where shepherds appear, and to the pastoral form in the prologues to the first Christmas and Carnival plays. The religious compositions represented an attempt to adapt the liturgical drama to the requirements of a small audience in a private house or chapel, while the two *Églogas en reqüesta de amores* and the *Representación* dramatized themes found in the lyric poetry of his day.

We do not know the exact date of Encina's first visit to Italy. It is likely that he took letters of introduction from the Duke of Alba to the Pope, who was born a Borja of Valencia, but it is certain that he found that Rome appreciated his talents better than Salamanca. On the twelfth of May, 1500, he obtained benefices to certain churches in the diocese of Salamanca where he is mentioned as " *dilectus filius Johannes del Enzina, clericus salamantinus,*" etc., and " *continus comensalis noster* " of the Pope. On September 25, 1502, he got square with Lucas Fernández by obtaining the post of *cantor* for which he had applied

in 1498, but there is no evidence of his return to Spain at
that time.   The Chapter would not yield, however, and we
do not know how the matter was settled, but inasmuch as
Fernández lost his position later, it is possible that Encina
received the post and also the emoluments.

It was during his first visit to Italy that an edition of
Encina's *Cancionero* appeared at Salamanca in 1509 with
two new plays, the *Égloga de tres pastores* and *Auto del
Repelón*.   The first of these, as its name indicates, is a
pastoral composition, but it has little in common with the
poet's earlier plays of shepherds.   Fileno is driven almost
to madness by the indifference of his sweetheart, Cefira.
Unable to get sympathy from Zambardo, who falls asleep
over the recital of his grief, he then confides in his friend
Cardonio.   The latter counsels moderation and then a sort
of *contrasto* follows, in which Fileno attacks women with
the bitterness shown by Boccaccio in his *Corbaccio,* to which
he himself refers, while Cardonio eulogizes women and
their virtues.   As soon as Fileno is left alone, he curses
Cefira for the suffering she has caused him, takes leave of
his flock and stabs himself.   When Cardonio returns, he
finds him lying on the ground, his body stained with blood.
He mourns tenderly the death of his friend, calls Zambardo
to aid in the burial, and inscribes an epitaph over his tomb.

The play is composed in eighty-eight octaves in *coplas de
arte mayor,* Encina's first and only attempt to use this meter
for dramatic compositions.   It shows more power and
seriousness of purpose than its author had shown before.
Love is here no trifling matter as in the two eclogues *en
reqüesta de amores,* but a consuming passion that drives the
hapless Fileno to his death.   It is the first tragedy of the
Spanish theatre, and holds the same position in the drama
as the *Cárcel de Amor* of Diego de San Pedro in Spanish
fiction, with which he was acquainted and had used.   Juan de
Valdés spoke approvingly of it in his *Diálogo de la lengua,*
although he preferred the *Égloga de Plácida y Vitoriano.*

The *Égloga de tres pastores* shows a great advance in dramatic art over earlier Spanish plays, but at least one episode is a reminiscence of his own Christmas eclogues, namely, the opening scene in which Zambardo falls asleep while Fileno is mourning over his unrequited love for Cefira. The dispute between Fileno and Cardonio regarding the relative virtues and imperfections of women is the first example of a theme that occupied the attention of poets, misogynists and philogynists of the fifteenth and sixteenth centuries, and which occurs later in the *Farsa del Matrimonio* of Sánchez de Badajoz, the *Comedia Tibalda* of Perálvarez de Ayllón and other plays.

The latter part of this play dealing with the suicide and burial of Fileno is a close adaptation of the second eclogue of the Italian poet, Antonio Tebaldeo.[9]   Born at Ferrara in 1463, he served as tutor in poetry to the princess Isabella d'Este until 1494 or 1495 when he went to Bologna and later to Mantua. . Toward the end of 1499 he returned to Ferrara, was later secretary to Lucrezia Borgia, and we find him at Rome in 1513.   He lost his books and property in the sack of Rome (1527) and he died in 1537.

His early verses were published in 1498 or before without the poet's knowledge.   These consist of four pastoral eclogues, epistles in *terza rima* and about three hundred sonnets, which are characterized by exaggeration and abuse of rhetorical figures to gain an unexpected effect.   At the turn of the century Tebaldeo's popularity was almost as great as Sannazzaro's himself, and three editions of his verses were printed in 1498 or before, three editions in 1500, and at least fourteen editions between 1501 and 1550.

His second eclogue consists of 151 verses in *terza rima*. Here the lovelorn Damone refuses the proferred sympathy of his friend Tirsi, explaining that he wishes to bear his burden of grief alone.   When Tirsi withdraws, the shepherd declares that he is ready for death since Amarilli turns a deaf ear to his wooing.   As he stabs himself, he bids a tender farewell to his flock, now left without a shepherd, and with his last breath pardons the maiden for her cruelty. When Tirsi returns, he sees his friend lying in a pool of blood with a dagger in his heart. He tenderly mourns his death, prepares the body for burial, and composes an epitaph for his tomb.

It is interesting to note the changes made by Encina in adapting this eclogue. He expanded the 151 lines of Tebaldeo's original to 704 lines. Rossi defined his four pastoral eclogues as *destinate alla recitazione;* but Encina, however crude his technique, had in mind a play to be acted. Tebaldeo's eclogue has brevity and unity of purpose; Encina's play has an additional character and is diffuse. Tebaldeo's poem is deadly serious; Encina realized this danger, and he adds Zambardo for comic relief. He closely followed his original in describing Fileno's death and burial.

As for the date, it is possible that a highly laudatory reference to Oriana in three stanzas may be proof that he had read *Amadís de Gaula,* the earliest known edition of which was printed in 1508. The first dated edition of Encina's play was published in the 1509 *Cancionero.*

The *Auto del Repelón,* first published in the same volume, is the only play of Encina that deals entirely with farcical material. It describes the hair-pulling, whence the title, and other tricks played by Salamancan students on two shepherds, Johan and Piernicurto. They are very much frightened, but they pluck up courage in the course of time, and on meeting a lone student they proceed to drub him unmercifully. The play ends with the singing of a *villancico dos por dos,* that is, the two shepherds, the student and Juan Rabé who appears unexpectedly from nowhere, but whose voice is required to make up the quartet. It may be regarded as a precursor of the *pasos* of Lope de Rueda with the important difference that it seems to be a separate entity and not merely a part of a longer play. In the absence of any data regarding its date of composition, I think it is likely that it was written before Encina's first trip to Italy, and that it was probably performed in the palace of the Duke of Alba where the tricks played on peasants by Salamancan students must have amused the aristocratic audience which was gathered there.

The new Pope, Julius II, was as kind a patron of Encina as Alexander VI. In spite of the fact that he was not an ordained priest, he received an appointment from the Papal Nuncio to an archdeaconship and canonship at Malaga and took possession toward the end of 1509. He was evidently regarded as an important person since he was employed by the Chapter on various missions. However, his relations with it were somewhat strained, chiefly because he had not taken Orders, and also because of frequent absences from his post. On May 17, 1512, he obtained permission to go to Rome, and probably remained there until July of the following year. He was there when Julius II died and when the son of Lorenzo the Magnificent was elected to the Papacy on March 11, 1513.

We know that he had returned to Malaga by August 1513, but in March of the following year he announced his intention of going back to Rome on some pretext or other. The objections of the Chapter were overruled by a Bull of Leo X who continued to extend to him papal favor, and shortly after his return to Spain, he got a summons in May 1516 from the Bishop of Malaga to appear at Valladolid under penalty of excommunication. We do not know the reason for this nor the outcome, but apparently he was still supported by the Pope, for he was appointed to the lucrative post of *subcolector de espolios de la Cámara Apostólica* which permitted him to absent himself from Malaga. At the end of 1517 or at the beginning of 1518 he made his fourth journey to Rome. He was bordering on fifty and he determined to cast aside worldly affairs, take Orders and make a pilgrimage to the Holy Land. Accompanied by another pilgrim, Don Fadrique Enríquez de Ribera, Marquis of Tarifa, he started off in July 1519 and a little over a month later reached Jerusalem where Encina said his first Mass. He gives an account of this journey in his

Trivagia o vía sagrada de Hierusalem, printed at Rome in 1521.

Returning to Rome, he probably remained there until 1523 when his name first appears as prior on the minutes of the Chapter of the Cathedral of Leon. He died toward the end of 1529 or at the beginning of 1530 and was buried in the Cathedral of Leon, and four years later his body was moved to Salamanca.

Two plays by Encina, namely, the *Égloga de Cristino y Febea* and the *Égloga de Plácida y Vitoriano,* were not included in any edition of his *Cancionero,* and the dates of printing are unknown. The first presents, with pastoral setting, the conflict between asceticism and worldliness, and the triumph of the flesh over the spirit. The shepherd Cristino is weary of life and determines to do penance for his sins. In spite of the protests of his friend Justino, he departs to don the garb of a hermit. Cupid is furious on learning of his disloyalty and bids the nymph Febea to bring the shepherd to his senses. A brief talk with Febea suffices to prove to Cristino that the Church is not his vocation, and he promises Cupid to discard his cassock provided that he be granted the love of Febea. Cupid agrees to these terms, but warns him not to repeat his experiment. By this time Cristino realizes that a hermitage is only suitable for centenarians and that, after all, there are more good shepherds or courtiers in the world than friars.

The background is undeniably Italian from the viewpoint of the characters. Cupid is shrewder, more mature than he was in the *Representación del Amor,* and the nymph, Febea, is wholly pagan. The anticlerical satire with its blatant insistence on the demands of the flesh is expressed by Justino and Cristino. While I admit for the play an Italian background, I do not think that its source can be found in any particular Italian play as has been suggested by Mazzei.[10] We have already seen that a dialogue between Reason and Lust in Mena's *Coplas contra los pecados mortales* developed into a primitive play, *Diálogo entre el*

Amor y un viejo which was used in Encina's *Representación
del Amor*. It is probable that by reading a later and amplified version of the *Diálogo,* published by Miola,[11] in
which a beautiful woman is introduced as the companion
of the other two characters, he determined to write another
play with the figure of the lady added, and Cupid in the
earlier *Representación* becomes Lust in the *Égloga de Cristino*. It is tempting to suppose the play contains autobio-
graphical features. Cristino, feeling old and weary, quotes
from the book of Psalms: " In the morning they are like
grass which groweth up," etc., but he acknowledges that if
he had suffered so many pains in God's name as he did for
love affairs and for masters, he would now be canonized;
and the doubts that assail him are expressed, half seriously,
half jestingly. When Cristino asks what will the people in
the village say of him, for to change one's mind is a bad
thing, it is possible that he had in mind a forgotten resolu-
tion to take Orders. As for the date, we can only say with
certainty that it was written before the publication in 1514
of Fernández's *Farsa o cuasi comedia del soldado,* which
refers to it.

A play by Encina was performed at Rome on January 6,
1513, at the house of Cardinal Arborea before the Spanish
ambassador and an audience composed of distinguished
members of the Spanish colony and *demi-mondaines*. A
letter to Francesco Gonzaga, Marquis of Mantua, describes
it as dealing with *le forze et accidenti di amore,* which
might refer to another performance of the *Representación
del Amor* in the opinion of Senhora Michaëlis de Vasconcellos, or to the *Égloga de Plácida y Vitoriano* as is the
opinion of most critics. The *Égloga de Cristino y Febea*
might also qualify because its theme deals with the power
of Love, but a phrase of the letter, referring to the author
qual intervenne lui might possibly have in mind the recitation of the prologue of the *Égloga de Plácida*. Nothing is
known of an edition printed at Rome in 1514, save that it

was mentioned by Moratín, and the two early extant editions bear neither place nor date.

The *Égloga de Plácida y Vitoriano* is much longer and shows a more complex plot construction than any other play by Encina. It opens with a prologue recited by a shepherd who, addressing the *compaña nobre,* and especially *nuestro amo* (probably Cardinal Arborea), gives an outline of the plot and asks for silence. The eclogue or comedy (both terms are used) consists of thirteen brief scenes, two of which, the sixth and tenth, are of the nature of *pasos* and were introduced for comic relief. A *villancico* is sung at the close of the sixth scene.

In a game of hide-and-seek which promises to end in tragedy, Plácida mourns because she believes herself abandoned by her lover Vitoriano, and when she withdraws the latter appears, complaining that he has been unable to forget her. He seeks counsel from his friend Suplicio who urges him to forget the old love by embarking on a new venture, quoting from Ovid's *Ars Amatoria,* and suggests that he pay court to Flugencia. He does so, but while the lady makes fun of his promises of undying affection, she gives him reason to hope that his desires will be gratified.

The next scene, partly derived from the *Celestina,* has little connection with the rest of the play. Flugencia meets Eritea, an infamous hag, and they discuss magic love-potions and other practices suitable to her trade. After they leave, Vitoriano tells Suplicio that nothing can make him forget Plácida, and he goes alone in search of her. A brief scene follows between two shepherds who talk about the strange conduct of the two lovers, and agree that love often makes city folk ridiculous. Plácida reappears with the requisite tears and laments, and finally she stabs herself. Then Vitoriano sees the body and he desires to take his life, but his friend warns him that by doing so, he would lose his soul besides, and only consents to leave him alone on the promise of doing himself no injury.

This scene is followed by the *Vigilia de la enamcrada muerta,* a sacrilegious parody of the *Officium Defunctorum* in which Cupid is invoked, which recalls the *Liciones de Job* of Garci Sánchez de Badajoz and other compositions of the *Cancionero General,* and also Juan Ruiz's burlesquing the Divine Office in the *Libro de Buen Amor.* We need not wonder that the play was placed on the Index of 1559. The desire for comic relief explains the next scene in which two shepherds express doubts concerning Sulpicio's good faith and show scant interest over Plácida's death. Desiring to die without confession, he commends his soul to Venus—a grotesque conglomeration of the sacred and profane—but she stays his hand, assuring him that Plácida is not dead and offering to restore her to her lover if he will have faith. She is brought back to life through the good offices of Mercury, and the play ends with singing and dancing. Following the text, there are ten songs which are not Encina's work, and also a farced version of the *Nunc Dimittis* by the dramatist Hernán López de Yanguas.

While this play has rather a series of disconnected episodes than a well-knit plot, it shows a decided advance over Encina's earlier compositions. The *dénouement* brought about by the intervention of a classical goddess is characteristic of the Italian pastoral drama. At the same time, one scene shows evidence of Encina's familiarity with the *Celestina,* and the burlesque scenes in which shepherds serve as a foil to the extravagance of the protagonists recall the poet's own eclogues *en reqüesta de amores.*

From the standpoint of structure, the play is notable because in it probably for the first time in the Spanish drama we have well-defined beginnings of the prologue or *introito,* later named *loa,* and the *paso* or *entremés.* The prologue, which should not be confused with the prose *argumento* meant to be read, consists of eleven eight-lined stanzas of *pie quebrado,* spoken by a shepherd Gil Cestero. It was probably written in Italy, and the same may be said of the prologues of Torres Naharro with which it has so much in common, but it does not derive anything from the Italian drama; as a matter of fact, most of its elements are found in Encina's plays or in his lyrical verse. His greeting, *Dios salve, compaña nobre,* resembles *Dios salve, buena gente,* of the first eclogue, and the references to Cardinal Arborea and the Duke of Alba are very similar. He gives his name and his trade, and talks about his relatives and acquaintances, and this becomes a convention in later comedy. He devotes eight *coplas* to explain the plot; over long, one may say, but Encina doubtless regarded it as necessary in order to acquaint his audience with the sequence of events.[12] Juan del Encina and Torres Naharro were both living at Rome in 1513. If it were a question of imitation I think it is probable that Torres Naharro imitated Encina because the latter's one prologue is primitive in type, while Naharro's are more complex. Possibly there is no interrelationship between them, but they go back originally to a dramatic monologue recited by a clown in shepherd's dress.

Encina must have been familiar with the word *entremés* in other connotations as, for example, an elaborate dish, a platform on which allegorical figures were carried through the streets in procession, and courtly mumming and dancing, but the term was unknown in a dramatic sense until about the middle of the sixteenth century.[13] The word *paso* came into general use as a dramatic form at about the same time. The truth is that Encina did not apply any term to the comic scenes in his *Égloga de Plácida y Vitoriano* because the thing was so new and unplanned. In writing the *Égloga de tres pastores* he used Tebaldeo's dramatic poem, but to avoid the danger of his audience falling asleep over too much rhetoric, he introduced a " sleeping-scene," borrowed, not from an Italian author, but from his own earlier plays. In a longer play, the *Égloga de Plácida,* he felt the need of using the comic relief scene three times; no great innovation it is true, but developed by his contemporaries, particularly by Torres Naharro, and by his successors, the new form was established with the name *paso* or *entremés*. In attempting to determine the priority between Encina and Torres Naharro in writing passing scenes or rudimentary *entremeses,* we can only repeat what has been said in regard to their relative claims to being called the author of the first Spanish prologue. Torres Naharro may have seen or have read the *Égloga de Plácida* and have imitated Encina in writing the shepherds' parts, but I believe that he followed the tradition of popular Spanish comedy of which we know so little, and that independent of Encina but with the aid of his popularity, Naharro was the chief contributory force to the development of the *entremés.*

The measures used by Encina are *coplas de arte mayor,* octosyllabic *coplas de pie quebrado* of five-, seven-, eight- and ten-line strophes, and octosyllabic *coplas* of eight lines and of nine lines. No notable change is seen in the strophes of the earlier and later plays. On the basis of the strophic form Encina did not write the anonymous *Égloga Interlocutoria.*[14]

Encina is also known as being the outstanding musical composer of his generation,[15] and about eighty of his compositions with their music are preserved in the *Cancionero musical,* edited by Barbieri. It cannot be surprising therefore that all of his plays, with the exception of the introduction to the first Christmas eclogue, the *Égloga de las grandes lluvias* and the *Égloga de tres pastores,* conclude with a *villancico* or *cantorcillo,* usually accompanied by a dance. The second *Égloga en reqüesta de amores* and the *Égloga de Plácida y Vitoriano* are divided by a song. In the majority of cases the text is included, and the music of some of them can be read in the *Cancionero musical.* Most of these songs were sung by four persons and this fact seems to have determined the number of characters in many of the early plays. If it were necessary, a boy could sing the soprano's part in this quartet.

All forms of dramatic entertainment known in Spain in the fifteenth century found literary expression in Encina.

His practice of combining recitation with song was continued by Fernández, Vicente, and other poets, and leads directly to the *zarzuela* with Calderón. The numerous editions prove that his innovations awakened interest, and his influence upon the development of religious, festival, and pastoral plays cannot be questioned during a half century. Later on his plays and lyrical verse were forgotten, and he was remembered only for the *Almoneda* and *Disparates* which he had written in a hilarious mood.[16] In *El sueño de la muerte* we can get some idea of what his name connoted to Quevedo's contemporaries.

Soy yo, dijo, el malaventurado Juan del Encina, el que habiendo muchos años que estoy aquí, toda la vida andáis, en haciéndose un disparate o en diciéndole vosotros, diciendo: "No hiciera más Juan del Encina; daca los disparates de Juan del Encina. . . ."

Los disparates de Juan del Encina is listed in Correas' *Vocabulario* of proverbial phrases. It is the irony of fate that the founder of the Spanish drama, and the outstanding musical composer of his time should be known a hundred years later chiefly as the author of the first nonsense verses in Spain.

III

RELIGIOUS DRAMA BEFORE LOPE DE RUEDA

L UCAS FERNÁNDEZ had many things in common
with Juan del Encina: he was a fellow Salamancan
and Encina's junior by about six years; both studied for
the priesthood; both were musicians and were interested in
play-writing, and we need not be surprised that they were
rivals. The three uncles of Fernández were priests of
much influence; Martín González de Cantalapiedra is remembered as professor of music at the University from
1465 until his death in 1479, and his brother, Alfonso,
after the death of Lucas' parents in 1480, became for him
a real father. Lucas received his baccalaureate from the
University and was ordained a priest, but he also showed
great interest in music and in writing plays.

We have already seen the rivalry over the post of *cantor*
of the Cathedral occasioned by the death of Fernando de
Torrijos in 1498, for which Encina and Fernández were
the outstanding candidates. The former lost, at least for
the time being, and went to Rome, while Fernández was
given part salary and a little later full salary for the post,
but in 1502 by pulling wires in Rome Encina got the appointment. Litigations continued until 1507, and at that
time Fernández was no longer *cantor* of the Cathedral.

Documents show that he took part in the Corpus Christi
festivities in 1501 and 1503. On the death of his uncle,
he obtained the benefice of Alaraz, near Salamanca; in 1522
on the death of Encina's brother, Diego de Fermoselle, he
was appointed to the Chair of Music in the University and
while occupying this post he died in 1542. His six plays
and a brief *Diálogo para cantar* were printed at Salamanca
in 1514 and were not republished in full until 1867, al-

though Gallardo reprinted three of the secular pieces in 1835 and 1859 in *El Criticón.*

In addition to a Passion play which we shall take up later, Fernández wrote two religious plays, the *Égloga o Farsa del Nascimiento de nuestro Redemptor Jesucristo* and the *Auto o Farsa del Nascimiento de nuestro Señor Jesucristo* which deal with the Nativity. The term *farsa* is an unusual word at that time and seems to have been limited at first to Castile if we can believe a statement made by Villalón in his *Ingeniosa comparación entre lo antiguo y lo presente* (1539): "*en las representaciones de comedias que en Castilla llaman farsas. . . .*" The *Auto o Farsa* shows in its general plan a marked resemblance to Encina's *Égloga de las grandes lluvias* with a homely scene of everyday life which introduces the Nativity. In the latter part the shepherds talk learnedly of the Redemption and of the prophets who had foretold the coming of Christ, and they depart for the manger, singing in praise of the Child. It is written in octosyllabic *coplas* of nine lines.

Meredith [1] has proved, in my opinion, that the *Égloga o Farsa del Nascimiento de nuestro Redemptor Jesucristo,* which opens with a monologue of the boasting shepherd Bonifacio and continues with a dialogue between the latter and Gil, is taken from Encina's first eclogue. Bonifacio's first speech is a witty burlesque of the *cancionero* literature of his day, and in certain respects anticipated the *introito* of Naharro. Fernández built his play proper upon the second eclogue of Encina. After the hermit Macario enters, the shepherds make fun of him, ridiculing him as a seller of indulgences, but another shepherd confirms Macario's message that Christ has been born of a virgin at Bethlehem. After many questions which might properly suggest themselves to simple folk, Macario explains the Incarnation and Redemption. The shepherds then depart for the manger with their simple gifts, and the play ends with a *villancico.* It is written in *coplas de pie quebrado* of ten lines.

A reference to the Jubilee Year in the latter play shows that it was written about 1500, and the former seems to be still earlier. Since we know that at this time Fernández held the office oi *cantor* of the Cathedral, it seems obvious that the plays were performed under the direction of the author and in the vicinity of the church. The phrase *cantar en canto de órgano* has been at times misunderstood as proving that the play was given in church; this is, of course, erroneous and refers merely to polyphonic chant.

Few men can be said to have created a national drama, yet the title of creator of the drama in Portugal belongs unquestionably to Gil Vicente, the artist who wrought in gold so bea :tiful a thing as the Belem monstrance. Before his time we know of the courtly mumming, and we also have references to the religious celebrations which were held on Christmas, Easter, and Corpus Christi, but both secular and religious drama were in an undeveloped state, and his extraordinary production was due almost entirely to his own originality and artistry.

On June 7 or 8, 1502, Gil Vicente, dressed as a herdsman and accompanied by about thirty courtiers in similar costume, entered the apartment of Queen Maria in the palace of Lisbon and offered congratulations to her, King Manuel, Dona Leonor, the King's sister and widow of John II, and other members of the royal family on the birth of Prince John. He tells of the rejoicing in Portugal and the Spanish Court over the happy event, and prophesies that the child will some day reign as John III. His companions offer simple gifts, and then all withdraw.

This composition, called *Monólogo del Vaquero* or *Auto da Visitação*, was a primitive type of masquerade and was written in Castilian as a compliment to the Queen, who was the third daughter of Ferdinand and Isabella. A series of marriages between Spanish princesses and members of the Portuguese royal family had made the Spanish language fashionable at Lisbon where the Court, and court poets as well, were practically bilingual. This explains why Vicente

felt free to write plays in either language, as determined by
the circumstances attending their performance, and also to
assign Castilian parts to some characters and Portuguese
to others in the same play.   The reading of Encina's first
eclogue suggested the form of the *Monólogo*,[2] and he also
imitated him in the use of the *sayaqués* dialect to represent
rustic speech in his early plays in Spanish.

It appears that prior to 1502 Gil Vicente was in the service of Dona Leonor, widow of John II, and his position as
court entertainer seems to have been determined by the success of his first attempt at play-writing.   Dona Leonor was
so delighted that she requested the performance should be
repeated at the following Christmas matins, but he deemed
the little monologue unsuited for such a performance and
wrote a new play, the *Auto pastoril castellano,* written, as
its name indicates, in Castilian, and this was likewise presented at the royal palace.   Until the time of her death in
1525, he wrote religious plays for her as well as comedies
and farces.   He continued to write plays from 1526 to
1536, but most of these were comedies, farces, and court
festival plays.

The transition from monologue to dialogue marks an
advance in the poet's dramatic art.   The action is developed by the six characters introduced, and the lyrical gift
in which he excelled is seen to better advantage.   The
shepherd Gil, who prefers a quiet nook on the hillside with
his flock to the games of his comrades, was doubtless performed by Vicente himself.   His conversation with another
shepherd is interrupted by the arrival of the newly married
Silvestre who recites at length the pedigree of his bride and
the objects that constitute her dowry, which proves that
Vicente was acquainted with Fernández' *Comedia de Bras-
Gil y Beringuella.*[3]   After playing various games, they go
to sleep and are awakened by the angel's song.   The scene
at the manger is tenderly portrayed, and the play ends with
a paraphrase of a part of the *Song of Songs* and the prophecies concerning the birth of Christ.

Dona Leonor was again pleased by the entertainment and requested that another play be written for the following Twelfth Night. Her gracious enthusiasm must have been embarrassing to the poet, for the interval was too short to allow him to finish the play that he had in mind. Perhaps the scene in Fernández's *Égloga o Farsa del Nascimiento* in which two shepherds make fun of the hermit Macario suggested to him the introduction to the new play, the *Auto de los Reyes Magos,* in which the Wise Men appear at the very close and sing a *villancico.*

In the *Auto de la Sibila Cassandra,*[4] performed at the convent of Xabregas before Dona Leonor at Christmas matins, probably in 1513, Vicente attempted to write a Prophet's play with a pastoral setting. It is well known that the Erythræan Sibyl appeared in the pseudo-Augustinian sermon *Contra Iudæos, Paganos et Arianos* as one of those who foretold the coming of the Messiah. A part was used in many churches as a lesson for some portion of the Christmas offices, and the Sibylline verses were often sung at matins on Christmas. Three of the twelve Sibyls known to the Middle Ages were introduced in this play, namely, the Erythræan, Persian, and Cimmerian as the aunts of a new Sibyl to whom he gave the name of Cassandra. Originally in the medieval legend Cassandra was the queen of Sheba.

Cassandra is courted by Solomon, but she brusquely repels his advances, and finally declares she will wed no man because she is the virgin in whom the Son of Man will become incarnate. The Sibyls confirm this prophecy of Christ's birth, but Isaiah objects that the humility prophesied of the Virgin Mother ill accords with Cassandra's presumption. The Erythræan Sibyl recites a version of the *Fifteen Signs of Judgment Day,* which well illustrates Vicente's critical spirit in using medieval material. Curtains are drawn aside revealing a back-scene, and four angels, the Sibyls, and the Prophets worship the Christ

Child. The play ends with a charming *cantiga* set to music by the author himself.

This play offers the first example of religious symbolism in the drama wnich attained well-nigh perfection in Calderón. In spite of the disparate elements of which it is composed, it has real dramatic interest, but long after the details of the plot are forgotten, our memory is haunted by the lovely lyrics that constitute its chief charm.

The date of the *Auto de los Quatro Tiempos,* written in Castilian like the preceding, is problematic. The rubric of the play in Vicente's *Copilaçam* of the first edition (1562) states that it was performed before King Manuel at the Alcaçova palace, that is, in 1505 or earlier, but some critics think it was written later, and Bell assigns it to 1516 on various grounds.[5] The Christmas play is almost entirely secularized. It opens with the coming of angels where they sing a part of the *Te Deum* in praise of the Christ Child. Winter then appears, weaving his complaints of cold and rain like a chaplet for a dainty little popular song, a few lines of which are sung at the end of each strophe. Spring then presents herself, singing in the same fashion one of Vicente's most charming lyrics that presents with rare beauty popular motives. The gaunt figure of Summer follows; Autumn also joins the group, and Jupiter calls upon the Seasons to accompany him to worship the newborn Creator. On reaching the manger, they sing a French *cantiga,* and present their homage and gifts to the Christ Child. David, dressed as a shepherd, recites farced versions of parts of Psalms CXXI, LXXXIV, and LI and the canticle *Benedicite omnia opera,* and closes with the chanting of the *Te Deum.*

These latter portions of the play give it a liturgical character that is not found in any Christmas play written in Spain at that period. At the same time the sacred element merely affords a setting for a version of the *débat* of the seasons which is related to the medieval *Conflictus hiemis et veris,* and which goes back ultimately to the folk dances that celebrated the death of winter.

Of much less consequence is the *Auto da Fe,* written in Castilian and Portuguese, and performed at Almeirim before King Manuel at Christmas matins, 1510. Two shepherds are dumbfounded by the magnificence of the festival, and the allegorical figure of Faith then appears who explains the doctrines of the Redemption. Three other Christmas plays, the *Auto pastoril portuguez, Auto da Feira* and *Auto da Mofina Mendes* are composed entirely in Portuguese and therefore fall outside the limits of this study.

The metrical forms employed in Gil Vicente's forty-four plays are distinguished by the variety and fluidity of strophe. He uses only the eight- and twelve-syllable line, with or without the *quebrado,* but he shifts the strophic structure when he thinks best. Morley [6] thinks that the fluctuating strophe continues with Vicente a popular tradition met with in medieval literature and in Gómez Manrique, but scarcely found in Castile after 1500.

The traditions of the Spanish religious drama were carried to Italy in the early years of the sixteenth century by Torres Naharro. His *Diálogo del Nascimiento* was written in Rome, and its date lies between 1512 when the battle of Ravenna is referred to, and 1517 when it was published with other plays in the *Propalladia.* The prologue is recited by a shepherd who gives a humorous and not too decent account of his courtship and marriage, and concludes with a brief summary of the plot.

Two Spanish pilgrims meet on Christmas Eve on their way to Rome, one coming from Jerusalem and the other from Santiago. The latter extols the success of Spanish arms, but his companion is weary of incessant warfare which ill accords with the angel's message of peace. He then narrates incidents of the Nativity, some of which are derived from the *Legenda Aurea,* and they then discuss theological questions, such as the relative gravity of the sin of

Adam and Lucifer, and the reason why the Son was chosen
as a Redeemer instead of some other person of the Trinity.
The prophecies are related in some detail, and also the
Annunciation, which bears a strong resemblance to Gil
Vicente's version of the same scene in the *Auto da Mofina
Mendes* (1534). The play comes to an end with the
shepherds singing the *romance " Triste estaba el padre
Adán "* which for years remained a favorite, and is the
earliest example of a *romance* used in a Spanish play. It
is impossible to say with certainty what relationship exists
between the play proper which is serious except for the
prologue, and the humorous, indecent *Adición del Diálogo*
which follows. Two shepherds, skilled in sophistry, ask
the pilgrims absurd questions and riddles,[7] engage in a contest of abuse and recite a sacrilegious farced version of the
Ave maris stella, with which the play ends. It might appear that the new part was introduced before the singing
of the *romance* three or four days after Christmas of the
same year or later with the object of reproducing, at least,
the burlesque spirit of the Boy Bishop revels.

The play is lacking in dramatic interest because the author
aims to commemorate rather than to represent the Nativity.
The prologue and the serious portion, consisting of two-thirds
of the play, is written in five-line strophes of the *arte mayor*
line which may have been original, or may have been borrowed from Vicente's *Auto das Fadas*.[8] The comic *Adición*
is written in octosyllabic *coplas de pie quebrado,* and is
indebted to Fernández's *Égloga o Farsa del Nascimiento*
in the questions asked of the pilgrims as well as certain
other resemblances. After all, compared with the dramatic
power of some of Naharro's secular plays, it is only an
interesting curiosity.

The influence of Encina and Fernández is still more evident in the *Égloga en loor de la Natividad de Nuestro
Señor,* of Hernán López de Yanguas, probably written before 1518. Four shepherds have heard the news of Christ's
birth and discuss like theologians the fulfilment of the

prophecies. We do not need the marginal notes to recognize his dependence on the Bible, including such unpromising dramatic material as the *Liber Generationis,* which is translated in full! It is probable that the comment made by Valdés in his *Diálogo de la lengua* concerning Yanguas, "Que muestra bien ser latino," was not intended as a compliment from the standpoint of Spanish style. A fragment of an anonymous play in *arte mayor,* and written shortly before 1521, was printed by Cotarelo y Mori, but owing to its incomplete state it is difficult to classify.[9]

The *Farsa nuevamente trobada* by Fernando Díaz shows no advance over the Christmas plays of Encina and Fernández. Composed like the aforementioned in *coplas de arte mayor,* it presents the conventional quarrel between shepherds, an angel who explains the Redemption, the gifts at the manger, and a song in conclusion. Preserved in an edition of 1554, it must have been written in 1520 or before.

The *Farsa a honor y reverencia del glorioso Nascimiento de Nuestro Redemptor Jesuchristo y de la Virgen gloriosa madre suya* of Pero López Ranjel, printed about 1530 or before, shows little advance over the Christmas plays of Encina which he undoubtedly knew. Gillet has likewise edited the *Auto cómo San Juan fué concebido* by Esteban Martín (or Martínez), printed at Burgos in 1528. It was performed on an open-air stage on the day of St. John the Baptist. Following closely the first two chapters of Luke, the devotional note is sustained until the confinement of Elizabeth where the midwife furnishes harmless amusement for the audience. This is the earliest play in which the *bobo* or dunce appears with that name. Other plays belonging to this early period that deal with incidents of the Christmas story are the *Auto nuevo del santo nascimiento de Cristo Nuestro Señor* by Juan Pastor, printed at Seville in 1528 and an Incarnation play entitled *Triaca del alma* by Fray Marcelo de Lebrixa, with only female parts, and written for performance by nuns. These two plays have not been reprinted.

The outstanding figure in the Spanish religious drama of the first half of the sixteenth century is Diego Sánchez (or Sánchez de Badajoz) whose twenty-eight plays were published posthumously by his nephew about the year 1554 with the title *Recopilación en metro*. Little is known of his life, save that he was curate at Talavera, near Badajoz, from 1533 to 1549 and died in the latter year or the year following. His dramatic activity extended approximately from 1525 to 1547. His plays, all of which bear the name *farsa*, are difficult to classify. It appears from internal evidence that twelve of these were performed on Christmas, ten on Corpus Christi day, two on saints' days, and four on other occasions.

Limiting ourselves for the present to the Christmas plays, only two, namely, the *Farsa de la Salutación* and *Farsa de los doctores*, deal with incidents of the Christmas story. The first presents with the simplicity of biblical accounts the Annunciation to the Virgin, with an unusual change of metre; the second shows the youthful Jesus teaching the doctors in the temple, with the addition of incongruous elements.

Theology is more prominent in the *Farsa de la Natividad* and *Farsa Teologal*. In the former, a boasting shepherd recites the prologue which recalls some of Torres Naharro's *introitos*, and then maliciously starts a quarrel between a parish priest and a friar regarding the relative joy of the Virgin at the Nativity or Incarnation, which is settled by the allegorical figure of Learning. This dispute seems to be a burlesque of scholastic argumentation in general, and probably refers to some over-animated controversy with which the clergy of Badajoz were familiar. In the *Farsa Teologal*, the shepherd-prologuist tells a ribald story of the consequences of marital infidelity, which was included in a briefer form in Timoneda's *El buen aviso y portacuentos*.[10] In the play proper, the ignorance of the same shepherd offers an opportunity for a theologian to explain at length the doctrine of the Redemption. With the seri-

ous part out of the way, the author was left free to entertain
the audience with a comic scene of rude horseplay in which
he excelled. The shepherd devises a sort of jack-o'-lantern
which frightens a young negress. A soldier then enters,
boasting of his prowess on many a battlefield, but he faints
away when he sees the lantern, and on recovering his senses,
calls for a priest to hear his confession. When the priest
comes, the braggart has recovered somewhat his composure,
and explains that his weakness has been caused by severe
toothache. A French dentist is summoned who is led by
professional zeal to extract not only one, but two perfectly
sound teeth before the soldier's pleas for mercy are heeded.
The incident is worked out with such completeness that we
must regard it as a primitive *paso,* and in its dramatic interest, it is entitled to rank with the best short compositions
of Lope de Rueda.

Two of the plays of Diego Sánchez performed at Christmas, namely, the *Farsa de Salomón* and *Farsa de Tamar,*
deal with Old Testament themes. The first presents the
familiar story of the decision rendered by Solomon in a
dispute between two women regarding the ownership of a
child, which is explained by a friar according to an interpretation of St. Augustine. The following scene shows
that an ignorant shepherd was sometimes able to protect
himself when imposed upon. The *Farsa de Tamar* treats
a salacious incident from Genesis and ends, strangely
enough, with the announcement of the birth of Christ.

The Morality play, which was so popular in western
Europe during the fifteenth century, was apparently unknown until later in the Castilian-speaking portions of
Spain, and we know of one text, the *Mascarón,*[11] of that period from Catalonia. In the following century on the other
side of the Peninsula, we find Gil Vicente writing Moralities
such as *Auto da Alma,* the trilogy of the Two Boats, and
the *Sumario da Historia de Deos.* In the first gropings
toward allegory in the non-Catalonian portions of Spain,

allegorical figures were introduced to teach theology, but the allegory or morality play came later.

Four plays of Diego Sánchez, performed at Christmas, contain allegorical characters in teaching theological doctrines. The *Farsa Moral* begins with the defeat of Wickedness by the Cardinal Virtues, and ends with a final victory over the former as a consequence of Christ's birth. One of the best plays of Diego Sánchez is the *Farsa Militar* which presents a friar who, after successfully resisting the temptations of Lucifer, World and Flesh, falls a victim by reason of an insidious appeal to his vanity, but he ultimately vanquishes his enemies by confession, contrition, and penance. It contains a passing scene which recalls Timoneda's *Passo de dos ciegos y un moço,* and ends with a scene in which the inability of a deaf man to understand the announcement of Christ's birth furnishes the chief comic element. An alternative ending is also given in the printed version where there is a reference to the battle of Mühlberg in 1547. The play does not appear to be anti-clerical in spirit, but is rather a warning that even the most virtuous must be constantly on their guard against temptation. Theological abstractions become excessively wearisome in the *Farsa racional del libre albedrío,* but on the other hand a Prophet's play, the *Farsa del juego de cañas,* delights us with a lyrical spirit which resembles Gil Vicente. It has been called the earliest *zarzuela.* The *Farsa de la ventera* is a secular farce with only the slightest relationship to Christmas. This little play gives evidence of the poet's intimate knowledge of picaresque types, and of his ability to construct a comic scene with real dramatic interest.

Each play by Diego Sánchez is preceded by a prologue [12] recited by a shepherd who at times is an uncouth rustic amusing the audience by his ineptitudes, and then suddenly he is the theologian explaining some abstruse point of doctrine; the prologue of Sánchez is in turn a comic monologue and a sermon. Rude beginnings of this amalgamation between the fun-maker and the theologian have been found from Íñigo López de Mendoza, and the idea of disguising the moralist and the priest was no novelty. At times he boasts of his skill in sports, games, or music, or relates with salacious and even obscene details some incidents of his domestic life, such as the prologues to the *Farsa Militar* and the *Farsa Teologal*. On the other hand, the prologuist of the *Farsa de Tamar* condemns in unmeasured language the veiling of the face by women, and in the prologue to the *Farsa de Salomón* the author bitterly protests against selfish lust for gold and the inequalities between rich and poor, which is also treated in the *Farsa de la Fortuna o hado*. So far as the form of the prologue is concerned, Sánchez followed Torres Naharro in general without adding any new features. He was also acquainted with Encina, Fernández, and Vicente.

In nearly all of these early Christmas plays, the shepherds have an important rôle. Employed at first to give a rustic setting to the Nativity scene, both entertainment and a pretext for instruction were obtained from their ignorance of sacred symbols and dogma. For Sánchez's religious theatre, the Pastor carried the chief burden, for to him was entrusted the prologue, half-comic and half-serious; the drolleries and the sermonizing. Usually represented as a glutton, he has no desires beyond a well-filled stomach. He is impertinent and makes sport of everything, sacred and profane. In seeking an explanation of theological doctrines, he serves as a connecting link between the audience and the serious characters, because he looks at everything from the same standpoint as the humblest peasant among the spectators.[13]

In addition to the shepherd, other figures were frequently used for comic effect by Sánchez and some of his contemporaries. As in other countries, the devil appeared in many Spanish plays of the period,[14] conventionally costumed with horns, tail, and cloven feet, and was brought to terms by the Pastor, as in the *Farsa de los doctores*. The braggart soldier,[15] who resembles somewhat the Plautine *Miles*

Gloriosus, but seems to be a product of Spanish conditions, had a distinguished but infamous career in the sixteenth-century drama, and sometimes appeared in Christmas plays as in the *Farsa Teologal.* The negress slave, speaking an almost incomprehensible jargon, also was a favorite figure. The futile effort of the shepherd to teach the Creed to one of those poor creatures in the *Farsa Teologal* will be long remembered.

In all these comic incidents the shepherd [16] holds the central place, and in time a short comic scene with dramatic unity might develop within a serious play. This stage is reached, for example, in the *Farsa Teologal.* Their popularity was so great that they were introduced into religious plays that had no relationship with Christmas, and into the secular drama as well. Later on, these brief comic scenes with dramatic unity will be called *pasos* and *entremeses.*

Judging from the number of extant plays, Good Friday and Easter contributed much less than Christmas to the creation of the religious drama. The earliest, after Encina, is Lucas Fernández's *Auto de la Pasión,* printed with his other works in 1514. Here St. Peter, bitterly regretting his denial of Christ, is joined by St. Dionysius to whom he tells the incidents of the Passion. St. Matthew adds further details and the three Marys enter, chanting their laments in the form of a *planctus* of marked liturgical character. The Crucifixion scene is tenderly described, following at times literally the Gospel account, a Crucifix is displayed and all kneeling chant a stanza of the *Vexilla Regis.* Jeremiah mourns the suffering Christ in language borrowed in part from *Lamentations,* the Descent from the Cross is narrated, and all kneel before the monument or tomb, singing in polyphonic chant in honor of the Crucified One.

The liturgical element is more pronounced here than in any other Spanish play. It has little dramatic quality, since the incidents are narrated rather than represented, but it is impressive and pleasing by its use of sacred lyrical texts, the *planctus* of the three Marys, and the considerable musical element. It was performed by members of the clergy on Good Friday at the Cathedral of Salamanca.

A Passion play and an Easter play, printed at Burgos in 1520, have recently been edited by Professor Gillet. The *Tres Pasos de la Pasión* deals with the sentence of death decreed by the prophets on Christ; the latter appears for a moment to bid farewell to his Mother, and leaves her with St. John. In the next scene Mary and John are standing at the foot of the Cross, and Nicodemus appears, who suggests that they go to Pilate to secure the body of Christ.

In the *Égloga de la Resurrección,* the prophets, including the Erythræan Sibyl, sing their prophecies of deliverance; the newly risen Christ appears; he goes to limbo and presents the liberated souls to Mary who gives them her blessing. Both these little plays were written by the same unknown author, and were performed in the hall of a lady to whom they were dedicated. Singing plays an important part, especially in the *Égloga,* and they were probably written to illustrate the author's ideas on music.

We also have a primitive form of the *Officium Peregrinorum* in Pedro Altamira's *Auto de la Aparición que Nuestro Señor Jesucristo hizo a los discípulos que iban a Emaús,* printed at Burgos in 1523, according to Moratín who copied fifty-two lines in his *Orígenes.* It has been recently edited from a Burgos 1603 (or probably 1553 according to Morley's conjecture) [17] edition where Pedro Altamirando (*sic*) appears as the author. It is written in *coplas de arte mayor,* and it deals with the appearance of the Risen Christ, as recorded by the Gospels. The play is impressively simple, and may have been given in church at Easter time.

It is a noteworthy fact that there is scarcely a trace in Spain of the composition of plays embracing in a cycle the chief incidents of sacred story from the Creation to Easter, such as we find in France and England. This offers additional proof in favor of the independent development of the Spanish religious drama. It is regrettable that the

seventeen plays, called *Autos Cuadragesimales,* written by
Vasco Díaz Tanco [18] for performance on Sundays in Lent,
Thursday and Friday of Holy Week, and Easter have not
been preserved. These dealt with incidents of the Ministry
and Passion of Christ, and are the only evidence that we
have of such serial performances in Lent. Since the author
refers jokingly to his advanced age in the prologue to his
Jardín del alma cristiana (1552), stating that they were
written in his youth, we may ascribe them to a period from
1520 to 1530. This bizarre figure was born in Frexenal
in Estremadura, and was captured by the Turks, as he
himself tells us in his *Palinodia* (1547). He was something of a poet, a great traveler, an historian, and a printer.
We know merely the titles of thirty-odd religious and secular plays from a list which he gives in *El jardín del alma
cristiana.* In addition, we have copies of the three *Ternos*
(collection of three plays), with explanatory material, preserved at the Biblioteca Nacional and at the British Mu-
seum, but the text of the plays was not included.

The Assumption of the Virgin was celebrated throughout Spain with great ceremony, but the first extant Castilian play on this subject is the *Farsa del mundo y moral,*
written about 1518, and first published in 1524 and frequently reprinted. Composed in *coplas de arte mayor,* it
deals with the vicissitudes of the shepherd Appetite, who
finally triumphs with Faith as a guide, much to the discomfiture of the World with his promises of honors and wealth.
The author, Hernán López de Yanguas was born about
1470 in the province of Soria, was a schoolmaster and took
Orders. He wrote pedagogical books such as *Dichos de
los siete sabios de Grecia;* a dialogue in verse entitled *El
Nunc Dimittis trovado* in which the familiar liturgical lines
are applied to a lover taking leave of his lady, and four
extant plays including the Christmas piece already referred
to, and two others which will be studied later.

It is probable that the festivals of certain saints were
occasionally celebrated by the performance of appropriate

plays, but the only example in the first half of the century
is the *Farsa de Santa Bárbara* of Diego Sánchez. It was
doubtless performed at Badajoz, where she was held in
especial devotion. This brief play presents an angel who
tells of the suffering of the young martyr while the devil
acts as prosecutor of her case. A shepherd, losing patience,
drives him away, and Christ and the angel crown her.

There is no definite proof that the festivities celebrating
Corpus Christi day in the fifteenth century had a definite
relationship to the doctrine of Transubstantition, but I
think it is sure that incidents were selected from the Bible
which had more or less analogy with the symbolical meaning
of the Eucharist. We have documents attesting Lucas
Fernández's [19] participation in the Corpus Christi entertainments at Salamanca, but to claim that in 1501 he presented on such an occasion his *Comedia de Bras-Gil y
Beringuella,* a betrothal play, simply because the document
says that there were three shepherds and two shepherdesses
taking part, which was the number in the *Comedia,* and
furthermore at Corpus in 1505 that he used Encina's *Representación del Amor* with a new title *Auto del Dios de Amor,*
is, it seems to me, far from the truth. It is true that
Vicente's *Auto de San Martín,* usually regarded as the
earliest *auto sacramental* in Spanish, was performed on
Corpus Christi in 1504 and contains no reference to that
festival, but since it is incomplete, it does not offer conclusive evidence that a play, totally unrelated in subject to the
Eucharist, might be used for a Corpus celebration.

The Spanish people were not so theologically minded
during the early years of the sixteenth century as they became later on, but the explanation of the Eucharist was
more abstract and presented graver difficulties than the
doctrines underlying Christmas and Easter. Of such a
character is the *Farsa sacramental* by Hernán López de
Yanguas, first printed about the year 1520, which is one
of the earliest Castilian Corpus plays dealing with the
Eucharist. Here with the setting of a primitive Christmas

play, after the manner of Encina, the significance of the Eucharist is explained by an angel to four shepherds, Jerome, Augustine, Gregory, and Ambrose. We find here the tendency toward allegory and theological symbolism which was destined to play so important a part in the development of the *auto sacramental*. Closely resembling the foregoing is an anonymous *Farsa sacramental,* written likewise in *coplas de arte mayor* in 1521. This presents a conversation between three shepherds and the allegorical figure of Faith who explains to them the doctrine of Redemption and the mystery of Transubstantiation.

The Corpus Christi plays of Diego Sánchez show a wider variety of material and a notable advance in dramatic construction. Four of these, namely, the *Farsa de Isaac, Farsa de Abrahám, Farsa de Moysén,* and *Farsa del Rey David,* treat Old Testament stories which have a close symbolical relationship with Christ's sacrifice. The first presents the substitution of Jacob for Esau in receiving Isaac's blessing, and ends with the explanation that the blessing bestowed upon Esau represents the freedom from the supremacy of Judah given to all peoples by the coming of the Messiah. The *Farsa de Abrahám* is an insignificant play containing a symbolical explanation of the Eucharist. In the *Farsa de Moysén,* St. Paul interprets the symbolical relationship of portions of the Old and New Testaments and expounds the meaning of the Corpus festival. The *Farsa del Rey David* establishes the symbolical connection between David and Christ.

A friar teaches the significance of the Eucharist in the *Farsa del Santísimo Sacramento,* with the same setting as the Christmas plays of Encina and Fernández. The *Farsa de la Iglesia* contains a dispute between Church and Synagogue, and includes a comic scene in which a shepherd attempts to baptize a Moor, a scene which is found in many later *comedias de moros y cristianos.* The *Danza de los Siete Pecados* represents the defeat of Adam by the seven

Deadly Sins, and finally his realization of God's mercy as revealed by the Eucharist.

The *Farsa del Molinero, Farsa del Colmenero, Farsa del Herrero* ana *Farsa de San Pedro* offer concrete proof of the participation of the trade-guilds in the Corpus plays. In some of these, a eulogy or defense of the particular trade forms the most important element, and the portions referring to the Eucharist are insignificant. The two unattached *introitos, Pescadores de tierra de Badajoz* and *Herradores* of Sánchez, belong here, and also probably the anonymous composition in dialogue, *Égloga sobre el molino de Vascalon.*

After th⌣ prologue to the *Farsa de Santa Susaña,* the shepherd-prologuist and a gardener engage in a dispute regarding the relative value of idleness and industry. In the course of his argument, the latter makes a defense of his own trade, which closely follows the form of *loa* that was frequently used in the time of Agustín de Rojas. After the introductory part, the play proper is intended to illustrate the evils of slander, and the material is taken from the familiar story told in the thirteenth book of Daniel. The characters are vividly portrayed, with an intensity rarely found in these early plays, and the interest is well sustained through a series of dramatic situations.

It is likely that most of the plays of Diego Sánchez were performed at Badajoz in the presence of the Cathedral Chapter. After his death, documents show that the *Farsa de la Iglesia* was given at Seville on Corpus in 1560, and it is likely that on the following year the *Farsa Moral* and *Farsa Militar* were given on the same day and city with the titles *Rey Nabucdonosor* and *La soberbia y caída de Lucifer.* It has been noted that he preserved medieval dramatic traditions better than any other play-writer of his time; it is probably due to this cause that his versification shows so little variety. Also in the *Farsa de la Salutación* the meter changes in that the Virgin and the angel use *quintillas* while the shepherds use *redondillas dobles:* a change that recalls the adaptation of meter which we find in Gómez Manrique's *Representación,* and which was to become one of the cardinal traits of the dramatists of the Golden Age.[20]

The sale of Joseph by his envious brethren, the incidents of his sojourn at Pharaoh's court, and the death of Jacob, one of the most dramatic stories found in the Old Testament, is the theme of the *Tragedia Josephina* by Micael de Carvajal. Born at Plasencia in the opening years of the century, documents reveal him to us as wasting his own substance and his wife's dowry as well, but not a record has been found touching upon his studies, his travels, his books or his friends. His death occurred sometime between 1575 and 1578. Judging from his dedicatory letter to the *Josephina,* he had always been disinclined to print his works—his spiritual daughters as he called them—but he realized fully the dangers of such a practice.

Fernando Colón purchased a copy of the edition of Salamanca (?) 1535, as recorded in his *Abecedarium,* but nothing further is known about this edition. Professor Gillet has edited the recently discovered edition of Seville 1545, consisting of 4,256 lines in *redondillas dobles* and divided into five acts or *partes,* and follows, so far as is known, the edition of 1535 with certain changes. The editions of Palencia 1540, which Cañete edited in 1870, and Toledo 1546 are progressively shorter; the author himself having made cuts in the text, particularly in the last two *partes* or acts, which have been reduced from five to four.

The name "tragedy" suggests classical influence, and the chorus of three maidens who sing at the close of each of the five *partes* or acts has the same source, but in other respects the *Josephina* has little in common with Seneca. An unusual feature is the prologue recited by Envy, which is probably classical in inspiration or may have been suggested by the opening of the *Moralité de la vendition de Joseph,* a part of the *Mistère du Viel Testament.* The story in the main is based on the book of Genesis, but there are a number of analogies on non-biblical details between the *Moralité* and the *Josephina* which suggest a common narrative source, possibly of Jewish or Mohammedan origin.

The tempo of the play at the start is slow and measured —too measured, one may say—and the figures are all hewn out of the same block—Joseph, his scheming brethren, Jacob, and Putifar—until Zenobia appears, at which the audience must have rubbed its eyes and suddenly become attentive and thoughtful, and the same thing happens to the reader of today. Zenobia is the only actually living thing on the stage and we miss her presence keenly, but we realize that Carvajal was only describing on Corpus Christi day the youth of Joseph with all its humiliations and shame to prefigure the life of Christ, and he did not care or did not dare to pay too much attention to the elemental Zenobia.

Sebastián de Horozco's *Representación de la parábola de Sant Mateo,* performed on Corpus at Toledo in 1548, is based upon the parable of the Vineyard. It has no clear relationship with this festival, and its interest lies in the portrayal of characters taken from everyday life. The two peasants, two ex-soldiers just released from Algerian prisons and now reduced to beggary, two starving solicitors for religious Orders, an old farmer and his dolt of a son who are engaged, one after another, for work in the vineyard, furnish a social background which shows unrelieved misery of the common people. Horozco was born in the early years of the century; he was a lawyer and served as counselor of the Holy Office. He acted as the reporter of great events or occurrences of Toledo, and his *Relaciones,* some of which have been printed, are interesting. He is likewise the author of a collection of *refranes,* and a *Cancionero* which was first published in 1874. Writing in the old-fashioned *coplas españolas* exclusively, he is at times gay, at times lewd, satirical, and witty, but rarely dull. In the *Cancionero* there are five short plays, but unfortunately only the one mentioned above has the date and the occasion of its performance.

More important is Horozco's *Representación de la historia evangélica del capítulo nono de Sanct Joan* which deals with the healing of a blind man by Jesus. In the opening scene we have virtually a dramatization of the last part of the first chapter of *Lazarillo de Tormes*. A blind beggar accuses his guide named Lazarillo with pocketing food intended for himself. He has stowed something away, but his master detects it by the odor. "It is bacon," he declares, "I smell it." While they are disputing, Lazarillo lets him strike against the corner of a house, and when the beggar crie out in pain, he says grimly, "Since you smelled the bacon, why didn't you smell the corner?"

In France one of the earliest farces, *Le Garçon et l'Aveugle*, was written on much the same theme, and was performed at Tournai about 1270; the same pair appeared in French religious and secular plays in the fifteenth century, and in the sixteenth it is also found in German and English stories, and Shakespeare refers to it in *Much Ado About Nothing*. The two early Spanish versions have so many similarities that Cejador [21] believed that Horozco also wrote *Lazarillo de Tormes*. We know very little about chronology because the dates of both works are uncertain; however, they have one highly important divergence. In the novel, it is a post which is responsible for laying low the blind beggar and for the escape of Lazarillo, while in the play the blind man's striking the corner of the street is only accidental, and is almost immediately followed by his meeting with Jesus. If the two versions are interrelated by more than a common source, it seems to me that Horozco's play is the borrower.

The beggar is led before Jesus, who anoints his eyes and promises that he will recover his sight if he bathes in the pool of Siloam. This is followed by a comic scene to which the author gives the name of *entremés,* one of the earliest examples of the term to denote a dramatic com-

position inserted within a play. Here an impecunious
lawyer is introduced who insists on taking all his client's
money as a retaining fee and for other expenses. The
humor is clever and amusing. The beggar returns with
his sight restored, and he falls to his knees, worshiping the
Saviour.

Of much less interest is Horozco's *Representación de la
famosa historia de Ruth* which presents Naomi and Ruth
returning home, and the latter harvesting in the fields of
Boaz. The text is incomplete, and there is no clear allusion to the sort of festival on which it was performed.
All of Horozco's five plays are written in old-fashioned
coplas.

We must return once more to Portugal and to Gil Vicente
to find the most important Morality plays, so the poet calls
them, composed in the Peninsula in the first half of the
sixteenth century. His trilogy of the Boats, performed on
Christmas 1516 and 1518, and sometime in Holy Week
1519, have as skippers of the two boats an angel and a
devil who judge men and women according to their deserts
in life, and who award them punishment or salvation.
The concept on which these plays are based has little to do
with the medieval Dance of Death, but Gil Vicente was
acquainted with the *Danza de la Muerte* and used it. The
Auto da Barca do Inferno was composed in honor of the
poet's patroness Dona Leonor and was performed in the
royal apartments. It was written in Portuguese and was
printed in 1517 or a little later. It presents among others
a usurer, a peasant, a friar of the Court, the Celestinesque
bawd, and a lawyer, who are claimed by the devil on the
boat which is about to set sail for hell. Each appeals for
the right to be saved, but all are rejected except the simple-
hearted peasant and the four knights who had fallen on
African battlefields, and to these latter the poet pays eloquent tribute. The figure of the angel who grimly lays
bare the souls of these persons, exposing their meanness,
greed, deceit, and lust is a powerful conception unsurpassed

in the Peninsular literatures in the sixteenth century. At
the same time, his use of irony and satire is often highly
amusing.

An anonymous Castilian adaptation of this play, which
closely follows its Portuguese original, was published at
Burgos in 1539 with the title *Tragicomedia alegórica del
Parayso y del Infierno*. The rôles of several characters,
particularly the nobleman, the usurer, and the magistrate,
are considerably amplified. It is very probable that a
Spanish follower of Erasmus revised Vicente's play, making
certain additions of an anti-clerical nature as, for example,
the usurer's purchase of a papal Bull for two *reales* which
will save him. At the same time he gave evidence of
having read Alfonso de Valdés' *Diálogo de Mercurio y
Carón*.

The *Auto da Barca do Purgatorio* is written in Portuguese, and therefore falls outside the limits of this study.
In the *Auto de la Barca de la Gloria,* composed in Castilian
and performed in 1519 in the presence of King Manuel, the
devil insists that Death shall bring men of high estate who
had escaped judgment in the two other plays. In accordance with these orders, representatives from the State and
Church, including the emperor and the pope, are brought
before the boatman of hell, who acts as prosecutor. With
uncompromising severity, their sins are set forth and the
torments that await them are graphically described. They
remind him of their exalted station in life, and he accuses
them of having been false to the responsibilities entrusted
to them. Even the pope is not spared, who is charged with
lust, pride, and simony. Their appeals for mercy are un-
heeded by the angel, and only by the intervention of the
Risen Christ at the close of the play can they obtain salvation. In these plays the poet shows himself an ardent
champion of social justice and of a high moral code among
all members of the clergy. It is possible that these plays
suggested to Lope de Vega certain features in his *auto, El
viaje del alma.*

The *Coplas de la Muerte*, printed about 1530, presents a personified Death who knocks unexpectedly and is given a cool welcome when the knight is ordered to follow him. When a bribe is ineffectual, the victim thinks of his will and of his wife and children. Death gives him leave grudgingly to make necessary preparations, and the unhappy man then commends his soul to God. In spite of the Christian ending, the brief play or poem has a Jewish background.

Among the sixteenth-century survivals of the *Danza de la Muerte*, first to be mentioned is the *Farsa de la Muerte* of Diego Sánchez. The play was written to be performed on Easter, and the date was probably 1536. There are four characters, the shepherd who recites the prologue and who comments upon the action, and an old man, a gallant, and Death. The old man's energy is spent; he welcomes Death while the shepherd shows consternation. The gallant is laid low by Death's arrow; the old man and Death fight together and fall, and the shepherd draws lessons from their fate. Incidentally, in the closing lines he praised the masons who presumably formed the guild who provided the money or the actors for the play!

The second survival of the theme of the *Danza de la Muerte* is Horozco's *Coloquio de la Muerte con todas las edades y estados* and was probably written toward the close of the first half of the century. Death summons six victims representing the ages of man and fifteen estates from the pope to the friar. Horozco's conception is thoroughly medieval and his tone is serious and devout.

We have already seen that by the year 1360 the representation, probably by tableaux, of certain sacred scenes formed a part of the Corpus Christi procession at Gerona. Documents for the Castilian-speaking parts are both of later date and less specific, but we can say that throughout Spain the Corpus festival had acquired considerable importance by the latter half of the fifteenth century. It became a municipal as well as a religious gala occasion and was supervised by the mayor and councilmen who insisted upon edifying spectacles or performances. Until the middle of the sixteenth century, the duty of organizing and paying for the *carros* or pageants generally fell to the lot of the various guilds. As examples, the *Farsa del Herrero* of Diego Sánchez contains a reference to the presence of smiths in the procession, and the rubric of the *Farsa de Santa Susaña* by the same author informs us that the play was performed on a *carro* that represented a garden.

It has been recently discovered by Shoemaker [22] that in the fifteenth and sixteenth centuries Spain followed the well-known medieval stage practice of France and other countries with respect to the multiple stage. As was to be expected, in the fifteenth century it was used chiefly in Eastern Spain and was generally, if not exclusively, employed in religious plays.

In the Castilian plays of the sixteenth century, there was a vertical multiple stage with generally two levels to represent heaven and earth, and a horizontal multiple stage with simultaneous settings. Almost all the plays which require the vertical or horizontal multiple stage technique are religious. The multiple stage was simplified in the course of time, but continued to be used on the *carros* of the *autos sacramentales* not only in the last half of the sixteenth, but in the seventeenth and eighteenth centuries as well.

IV

FESTIVAL AND PASTORAL PLAYS

WE have already seen that the Royal Entry and important political events were frequently celebrated in the fifteenth century by processions and allegorical pageants. With the courtly masquerade as a contributing factor, these developed into festival plays by a process analogous to that of the gradual transformation of the Corpus Christi shows into religious drama. One of the earliest examples of this new type is an *Égloga* by Francisco de Madrid,[1] written toward the end of 1494 and in *verso de arte mayor*. It deals with the invasion of Italy by Charles VIII and the consequent repudiation by Spain of the treaty of alliance with France. The interlocutors are three shepherds, two representing Charles and Ferdinand, and a third who tries to make peace. We do not know where this play was presented nor on what occasion, but its relationship with later compositions on political subjects is clear. Of the same type is Martín de Herrera's *Istorias de la divinal vitoria y nueva adquisición de la muy insigne cibdad de Orán*, celebrating its conquest by the Great Captain and printed in 1510 or 1511. As part of the festivities, Herrera wrote an *Égloga de unos pastores* which was presented at Alcalá, but the only known copy of the book is incomplete and does not include the *Égloga*.

Of greater interest is Torres Naharro's *Comedia Trofea*, performed at Rome in March or April 1514 in honor of the important mission led by Tristão da Cunha [2] which had been sent by King Manuel to negotiate with Leo X for a subsidy to be used in extending Portugal's colonial empire in Asia. It is not known under whose patronage the play was written and performed, but it is evident that Torres Naharro attempted to present the Portuguese claims in the most favorable light. Preceded by a comic prologue and composed of five acts of *coplas de pie quebrado*, the play consists of five loosely connected scenes, almost totally devoid of action. The extravagant praise of Manuel the Fortunate, recited by Fame in the first act, and the presentation by the interpreter of the twenty pagan kings who joyfully and ingenuously offer allegiance to such an exalted monarch, remind us of earlier masquerades, and an attempt is made to enliven these rather dreary narrative portions by the introduction of farcical scenes of shepherds. It is difficult to determine whether, for its form, the author was indebted to Italian festival plays of the same type as Sannazzaro's *Il Trionfo della Fama,* presented at Naples in 1492 to celebrate the capture of Granada, or whether it represents a logical development of Spanish allegorical pageants and masquerades.

It is true, as Menéndez y Pelayo said, that inspiration was lacking to Torres Naharro in this play, and that his failure was as complete as the shepherd Mingo's attempt to vie with Fame and to fly with a pair of borrowed wings. At the same time, the *Comedia Trofea* has a vast amount of historical interest, for it recalls the details of that mission which was to show in concrete form the glories of the newly won Portuguese empire. The play serves, too, as a record of the glorious achievements of Portugal in its heroic age. We must regard as literally true the statement made by Fame in the first act that Manuel was lord of more lands than Ptolemy had described. Surely the King's inordinate vanity must have been tickled by all this flattery, even though as a play the *Comedia Trofea* is far inferior to Gil Vicente's *Exhortação da Guerra* which Manuel had witnessed the previous year at Lisbon to celebrate the departure of an expedition against Azamor.

The eventful visit of Charles I to Valladolid was celebrated by the performance of an *Égloga Real* in December 1517, composed by a schoolmaster who signed himself "Bachiller de la Pradilla." With a prologue reminiscent of the *Égloga de Plácida y Vitoriano,* four shepherds who are floridly eloquent discuss glibly Roman mythology and the greeting which awaits Charles. The shepherds' parts are recited in *coplas de pie quebrado* while the rôles for the Infante and for the Four Estates are given in the more dignified form of *coplas de arte mayor.* The play voices their fervent desire that he succeed to the throne, and contains a prophecy of his future greatness. History tells us that in this first meeting with the Cortes, Charles did not receive such unanimous support from his subjects. There were many causes for friction and dissatisfaction, and he was not actually recognized as joint ruler with his mother until he had promised to maintain Castilian privileges and to exclude foreigners from office. Written in stiff, pompous language, it is chiefly interesting as an attempt to glorify the future Emperor by a biased presentation of facts. According to the author's own words, he composed it first in Latin, presumably in prose, and later " converted " it into Spanish verse.

Certain resemblances in style have led Señor Cotarelo to identify the Bachiller de la Pradilla with Hernán López de Yanguas.[3] As a matter of fact, their work is not dissimilar. On the other hand, how can one explain his use of this pseudonym, especially in reference to a Court play such as the *Égloga Real?* In the latter we have mention of a composition written by him at Vitoria in Latin and Castilian in honor of the parents of Charles, and he also adopted a like procedure in writing an eclogue, which has not been preserved, in honor of the election of Juan Ortega as Bishop of Calahorra. He was one of the first pupils of Nebrija at Salamanca, and was professor at Santo Domingo de la Calzada near Logroño when the *Égloga Real* was written.

Another composition which is interesting primarily because of its international significance rather than because of its real value is the *Coplas sobre la prisión del Rey de Francia* by Andrés Ortiz, written shortly after the battle of Pavia (February 24, 1525) and, at all events, before the ignominious captivity of Francis at Madrid. It is not certain whether this composition was actually presented or was a broadside telling of the Emperor's victory, but in the latter case the author followed the same procedure as in Encina's fifth eclogue. Most of this composition is in *coplas de arte mayor*, but there is also a *romance* narrating the battle of Pavia, an early example of the use of this meter in a play.

Another play which is chiefly of historical interest is the *Farsa sobre la felice nueva de la concordia e paz e concierto de nuestro felicísimo Emperador . . . e del cristianísimo Rey de Francia* of Hernán López de Yanguas, written to celebrate the Peace of Cambray, August 15, 1529, between Spain and France. Spain had reason to rejoice over this treaty which imposed humiliating terms upon Francis and made Charles sole arbiter of the destinies of Italy. However, although the note of rejoicing is present, the play seems to have been chiefly inspired by a profound sense of relief at the cessation of warfare. War, who appears dressed as a pilgrim, tries to justify herself, but Peace and other allegorical figures paint in vivid colors the havoc which she causes in the world. Satisfaction over the Ladies' Peace was of short duration, for Spanish troops were still fighting on other battlefields, and only a few years later war once again broke out between Spain and France.

Turning from the celebration of national events, we meet with a curious play which shows clearly the society and social usages of Valencia in the time of the viceregal court of Germaine de Foix. A second wife of Ferdinand of Aragon who died in 1516, she married the Elector or, as he was called at Valencia, Marquis of Brandenburg, in 1523. In the following year or the first months of 1525 a play was presented before the Queen and her husband called *Colloquio en el qual se remeda el uso, trato, y pláticas, que las damas en Valencia acostumbran hazer, y tener en las visitas que se hazen unas a otras,* included in his *Obras,* posthumously printed in 1562, by Juan Fernández de Heredia.

Perhaps in imitation of Torres Naharro's *Serafina,* Castilian and Valencian were employed in the *Colloquy,* and the lovesick Portuguese was added to this linguistic medley. The lady on whom the calls were made was a typical provincial Valencian who quarreled with the duenna Guzmana, who was very mindful of the fact that she was born in Castile. The portraits are very well done, and so is the figure of the Andalusian maid who arranges her mistress's hair for the reception, and the chaplain who flirts with Guzmana in delivering his message. The trivial conversation at the party is true to life, and when the herald interrupts these frivolities by the summons to a duel, the reader should not be unduly perturbed, for he should be sure that everything is bound to turn out happily. The *Colloquy* was written with grace and wit, and the poet gave it a note of reality which is rarely met with at that time.

Fernández de Heredia and his long-suffering wife Doña Hierónima have a prominent part in Luis Milán's *El Cortesano,* printed in 1561 when the principal actors were dead and well-nigh forgotten, but it gives an admirable picture of the viceregal court of Germaine de Foix and her third husband, the Duke of Calabria. Noted musician and performer on the *vihuela,* the author was also a witty versifier, and his *Courtier* is a highly diverting imitation of Castiglione's *Il Cortegiano* where the platonic gravity of the court of Urbino was replaced by the frivolity of the court of Germaine de Foix and her Neapolitan husband.

Included in *El Cortesano* is a courtly masquerade called *Farsa de las galeras de la religión de Sanct Joan* presented at the Royal Palace of Valencia whose date falls between 1530 when Malta was given to the Order of St. John, and 1558 when the Queen died. In this little entertainment, eight knights of St. John successfully engage in turn eight Turks who had captured their sweethearts on the high seas.

Knights and ladies then joyfully celebrate their reunion. The Turks apparently bear no ill will for their defeat, and dance a ballet. This is followed by a tourney, after which all persons taking part present themselves before the Duke and announce their intention of returning to Malta.

Entertainments of this sort, with their mingling of recitation, pantomime, singing, dancing, and fencing were frequently presented at many of the Italian courts in the closing years of the fifteenth century, and it is natural to suppose that these elaborate festivities were introduced in Valencia by the Duke of Calabria or by his associates. There is a May song, for example, which comes from a well-known Italian *Maggio*. Other masques of less dramatic character, such as that of the Greeks and Trojans, are also described in the same book.

No other literary form is so completely dependent upon patronage as the festival play. The most gifted poet might display his imagination and fancy in writing a play to celebrate some event, but he could not produce it without the encouragement and financial aid of a wealthy patron. We must explain the retardation in the development of the festival play in Spain by lack of royal patronage. The Emperor was not a man of letters and gave no encouragement to play-writers. Philip II was more interested in theology than in the theatre, and not until the reign of Philip IV did royal dramatic entertainments on a lavish scale come into vogue.

Happily, the external conditions that encouraged the festival plays in Italy were present at the court of Manuel I. The Portuguese Crown was enormously wealthy, and the King was also a patron of literature and took pride in having about him men of letters. Furthermore, his vanity led him to encourage and support entertainments which should carry his name throughout Portugal and to foreign lands as well.

Nothing, then, was lacking except the poet, and he appeared in the person of Gil Vicente whose genius was peculiarly suited to these court entertainments. From 1502 until 1536 Vicente was virtually poet laureate. During Manuel's reign the majority of his plays were written to celebrate religious festivals, but to this period also belong compositions like the splendid *Exhortação da Guerra* and *Auto da Fama,* inspired with patriotic fervor, and he also wrote some delightful comedies and farces. With the accession of John III to the throne in 1521, the religious plays were not wholly discontinued, but the festival entertainments acquired a more important place in the court life. From that time, Gil Vicente occupied a similar post to that held by Ben Jonson at the court of James a hundred years later. A royal wedding, or a betrothal, or the birth of a prince or princess, or a royal entry, could only fittingly be celebrated by a play written in honor of the occasion by the illustrious poet. Not only was he the author of these compositions, but stage director and sometimes an actor as well. It is regrettable that documents have not been discovered that would allow us to visualize these splendid spectacles with a basis of fact, but the texts themselves furnish proof that these plays were presented with a magnificence that charmed the eye as well as the ear.

Limiting ourselves for the present to the festival plays, the *Exhortação da Guerra, Auto da Fama, Cortes de Jupiter,* and the *Auto da Festa* are composed wholly or almost entirely in Portuguese, and therefore fall outside the limits of this study. The tragicomedy of the *Fragua de Amor,* in Castilian and Portuguese, was written to celebrate the betrothal in 1524 of John III to Catherine of Castile, sister of the Emperor. Here the winning of the Infanta's heart is described as the conquest of a castle by Cupid, who in spite of its bodyguard of Virtues, has succeded in nailing in its center the arms of Portugal. Venus then appears in search of her missing boy, but her anxiety is relieved when she learns of the new laurels he has won in Spain. The ultimate source is, of course, the first *Idyl* of Moschus, but Gil Vicente had probably read *Amor Fugitivus* in Politian's

Latin version, and he was likewise indebted to Pontano's
Latin epigram on the same theme.⁴ The setting also re-
calls Ben Jonson's charming masque *The Hue and Cry after
Cupid.*

A castle is then introduced, and the four Planets construct a forge of Love which has the power to restore youth
to the aged and to endow the homely with beauty. A
Negro is the first applicant for treatment; he comes forth
from the forge completely white but keeping, much to his
disgust, his peculiar manner of speech. The crippled figure of Justice with crooked staff and broken scales then
presents herself and asks to be straightened before the new
Queen comes to Portugal, but she is told that she can only
be refashioned when deprived of some of her ill-gotten
gains. The courage of the poet did not desert him even
when flattery in the King's presence would have been more
welcome than criticism. The next candidate is a friar who
has had enough of monastic life and wishes to become a
young gallant. With this change effected, the play ends
with apparently a promise of a second part.

The *Templo de Apolo,* written chiefly in Castilian, was
performed at Almeirim in January 1526 to celebrate the
betrothal of the Princess Isabel, sister of John III, to the
Emperor Charles, and her departure for Spain. In the
prologue the poet briefly refers to his recent illness, which
may have led the writer of the rubric of this play in the
Copilaçam of 1562 to apologize for certain imperfections
in his work, and then tells in burlesque form a vision he
had had when he believed that death was imminent, a
humorous travesty of the *Infierno de los enamorados*
theme. Apollo then appears and preaches a burlesque
sermón de amores, which, we shall see, was a prominent
feature of many betrothal and wedding plays. Various
allegorical figures, dressed as pilgrims, are refused admittance to the temple of Apollo by the doorkeeper, but are
finally admitted on showing proper credentials which include lavish praise of the Emperor and future Empress.

After so much rhetoric, we welcome the appearance of a poor peasant, named Janafonso, speaking Portuguese, who applies for admittance to the temple. The doorkeeper refuses to allow him to enter, but he pleads his case so valiantly and so playfully that Apollo allows him to come in. It has been held by many scholars that the rôle of the Portuguese peasant Janafonso was borrowed from the poet's own *Auto da Festa,* but it has been proven, I think, by internal evidence that the *Templo de Apolo* was earlier than the *Auto da Festa.* The figure of Janafonso was needed in the former play as a comic relief to so much grandiloquence. The poet liked him so well that he was taken over and used in the hastily written *Auto da Festa.*[5]

The *Nao de Amores,* written in Castilian and Portuguese, was performed at Lisbon in January 1527 in honor of Queen Catherine. There is real beauty in the romantic conception of the Prince of Normandy who must win the maiden Fortune to prove his love for Fame, the lady of his heart's desire, and who constructs a ship of Love, with Cupid as captain, to bear him on his quest. The boat is described with a wealth of symbolic imagery which recalls the earlier poem *La Nao de Amor* of Juan de Dueñas. With its motley assortment of passengers who embark to seek Fortune, the *Nao de Amores* may be regarded as a playful pendant to the *Barca do Inferno* and others of the trilogy.

The *Comedia sobre la divisa de la ciudad de Coimbra,* performed in that city in 1527 in honor of the King, and written in Castilian and Portuguese, proposes to explain in whimsical fashion the meaning of its coat-of-arms. Its fantastic plot is derived in great part from the romances of chivalry. As an excursion into archæology and legendary lore it is an answer to Sâ de Miranda's *Fabula do Mondego* which is conceived in the same vein.

The *Triunfo del Invierno,* written in Castilian and Portuguese, was performed in 1529 in honor of the birth of the Infanta Isabel. The author recited the prologue in

which he contrasts the good old times of the past with the
sadness of the world at present, and says that after having
written of the triumph of winter, later on he will compose
the triumph of spring.   Using as a background the well-
known medieval debate of winter and spring, the former
hears complaints of the hardships that peasants and sailors
suffer because of snow and icy water—disconnected scenes
linked together by lyrical songs; and then recites a *romance*
addressed to the King in which high praise is given to the
royal family.   It is probable that the *Triunfo del Invierno*
ended here—995 verses—and later, on the occasion of
some Court festivity, he began to write a play about spring
which would afford a contrast to which the author alluded.
This is obviously unfinished, consisting only of 230 lines,
but though brief, it has lyrics of great beauty.[6]

The *Auto da Lusitania,* written in Portuguese and Castilian, was performed at Lisbon in 1532 in honor of the
birth of Prince Manuel.   The introduction gives an interesting picture of a Jewish family in the capital.   The play
proper deals with the courtship of the maiden Lusitania
by a Greek knight, Portugal, who finally wins her hand in
spite of the pretensions of Mercury, whose suit is encouraged by Venus who speaks Spanish with an Andalusian
accent!

The most interesting scene is an interlude that shows
two devils taking notes on the conversation between a rich
merchant named Todo o Mundo and a poor fellow called
Ninguem.   Owing to these strange names, the devils gain
an equally odd impression of the state of this world, for
they learn that Everybody seeks honor and that Nobody
seeks virtue, Everybody desires Paradise and Nobody pays
his debts, and so on.   The jest is found as far back as in
the ninth book of the *Odyssey,* and it appears in the English
Nobody and Somebody, the French *Aucun et Tout le
Monde,* the *Entremés del Mundo y No Nadie,* Ulrich von
Hutten's *Nemo,* and other medieval and Renaissance writ-

ers.[7] It must be conceded that he gave it an effective setting and handled it with skill.

From its very nature, the construction of the festival play was often loose. Occupying a middle place between the pageant and real drama, it depended for success upon scenic effects, music, songs, and dances as well as upon the beauty of the lines. It contained more recitation than action or dramatic conflict. We cannot, therefore, judge Gil Vicente as a dramatist by his festival plays. In them we find wit, grace, good taste, and a charming lyrical note. It is in his comedies and farces that he displays his skill in dramatic construction, his keen powers of observation and broad human sympathy.

Both in the circumstances attending their performance and in subject matter, the festival and pastoral plays have much in common. The latter were entertainments for aristocratic audiences on the occasion of betrothal, wedding, or other festivity. They represented courtly traditions, and when rustic scenes were introduced, it only served to contrast the delicate sensibilities and polished speech of gentlefolk with the ignorance and rude language of shepherds.

Lucas Fernández's *Comedia de Bras-Gil y Beringuella* presents the *recuesta de amores* theme as played by peasant folk, and causing, doubtless, much hilarity from the aristocratic audience. The shepherd pays court to the shepherdess and is accepted as her betrothed, but her grandfather refuses to permit of their engagement because of Bras-Gil's lack of funds and of influential relatives. This objection is waived when the shepherd gives evidence of respectability by reciting a farcical list of his kindred and friends; in return the grandfather promises a formidable array of livestock and household utensils for the girl's dower, and the groom follows suit with an equally long list of wearing apparel for the bride. As a burlesque on courtly practices it is highly diverting, and we shall see that many wedding or betrothal plays were written in Spain in the first half of the sixteenth century which contained a comic pedigree of the groom and bride, the girl's dowry and the man's gifts. It was Lucas Fernández's first play, and since the author gave evidence of familiarity with Encina's *Égloga representada en reqüesta de amores,* it probably can be ascribed from 1498 to 1500. The metrical form is in *redondillas dobles.*

Based also upon the aforementioned play of Encina, Lucas Fernández wrote another play called *Farsa o cuasi comedia,* the theme of which is the rivalry between a shepherd and knight for a maiden's love. In this case she is a gentlewoman, and the farcical element consists in the inability of a poor lout to share the refined feelings and to understand the conventional language of the aristocracy. As she repels his advances, the thought occurs to her that like Doña María Coronel she might at least commit suicide, which proves that she knew intimately the novel *Cárcel de Amor.* In other pastoral plays a lady is similarly exposed to impertinent proposals from boorish shepherds. Because of the content and of two *villancicos* in praise of Love with which the play ends, it was undoubtedly written for performance at some betrothal festivity. It was probably composed about the year 1500.

Love among shepherds is again the subject of Fernández's *Farsa o cuasi comedia del Soldado.* It begins with a take-off of the preparations for suicide as found in Encina's *Égloga de tres pastores.* "Ya no soy quien ser solía," says Pravos, repeating the beginning of an old-time popular song, and with rather rhetorical outburst on the lips of a shepherd he takes leave of his flocks and of all that he used to love. The soldier enters and he learns finally from Pravos that he is in love, the same disease which has caused the death of Fileno and occasioned no end of trouble to Pelayo, Bras-Gil, Mingo, and Cristino. In spite of his long-standing rivalry with Encina for the position of choir master of the Cathedral and the latter's ultimate victory, there is not a trace of animus in his mentioning Encina's

five plays, the *Tres Pastores, Representación del Amor,*
two plays *en reqüesta de amores,* and *Cristino y Febea,*
along with one of his own, even though he did not take
Fileno's death with all of the seriousness which its author
might have expected.

He talks to his companion Pascual, but like Bras in
Encina's *Representación del Amor,* he cannot understand
what is wrong. The soldier, who is acquainted with the
courtly conceptions of the time, does what he can to explain what love is, but Pascual irritates him with his impertinent interruptions. Finally they fall into a heated
discussion; the shepherds maintain that military service is
only suited to idlers, rascals, and thieves, while the soldier
affirms that the army supports justice and order. Peace is
restored at last, and Pascual goes in search of Antona,
Pravos' sweetheart, who after some hesitation accepts his
hand. Pascual receives from each a promise of marriage,
and the play ends with a song in praise of Love. The
mock ceremony in the last scene and the text of the song
allow us to assume that it was performed to celebrate a
betrothal in the household of some nobleman. References
to Encina's *Égloga de tres Pastores* show that this play by
Fernández must have been written after 1509.

There is no clue to the date of composition of the brief
Diálogo para cantar, printed with the other six plays in
1514. There are only two characters, Juan Pastor, a lovesick shepherd, and Bras who had loved, had lost and had
recovered. As a play, it is not worthy of comment, but
from the standpoint of musical history it is very interesting,
for it was sung on the popular air *Quién te hizo Juan,
pastor,* and therefore it is our first printed text in the history
of the *zarzuela.*[8] Unfortunately, the music of this little
piece has not been preserved.

The *Égloga de Torino,* included in the novel *Qüestión
de Amor,* which was first printed at Valencia in 1513, forms
a connecting link between the Spanish and Italian pastoral
drama at the beginning of the sixteenth century. It was

frequently reprinted in Spain and was translated into French, but while Juan de Valdés in his *Diálogo de la lengua* gave grudging approval to the prose portions, he did not like the verse. Croce, who has identified successfully most of the characters in this *roman à clef*, conjectures that the author hides himself under the name of Vasquirán, that is to say, a certain Vázquez who wrote the *Dechado de Amor* (1510?), published in the *Cancionero General*. An imitation of the *Thirteen Questions* in Boccaccio's *Filocolo*—a bit of casuistry used by Tansillo's *I Due Pellegrini* and a little later by Garcilaso de la Vega in his first eclogue—gives the title to his novel, which has as background aristocratic society at Naples between the years 1508 and 1512. The departure of Flamiano for Ravenna and his death there in April 1512 is its last chapter. Written in prose and verse, it consists of unconscionably long letters, joustings and the like, and an eclogue which was performed before the mistress of the festivities, young Bona Sforza, daughter of the Duke of Milan and later queen of Poland (1518), and the other characters. As for the name *Égloga de Torino*, it comes from Ettore Pignatelli, nicknamed Torino (an abbreviation for Ettorino) who served, in the manner of those times, the fair and intelligent Bonita.[9]

The first part of the eclogue is based closely upon Encina's *Égloga de tres pastores*. Fileno's suicide, a martyr to Love, was in Torino's mind, but he was unable to carry out his purpose owing to the appearance of two companions. These fail to understand, as did Pelayo in Encina's *Representación del Amor*, the nature of Love's pains. Benita (Bona Sforza) then draws near and, on hearing the subject of their discussion, bids Torino cease his importunities, but the lover declares that he is powerless to banish her from his thoughts. Except for the *villancico* at the close of the play, it is written in *coplas de arte mayor*, suggested to the author by Encina's *Tres Pastores*. The origin of the eclogue is undeniably Italian, and the author got from Italian literature the practice of introducing real persons under a semi-veiled name, but for the rest of the play he followed in Encina's footsteps.

A somewhat similar close imitation of Encina's *Égloga de tres Pastores* is the recently reprinted *Égloga de Breno y otros pastores compañeros suyos* by Salazar, about whom nothing is known except the surname. Like Fileno, Breno is sick for love of Silvana and proposes to die, while his two companions are at a loss to understand in what respect the illness of love can differ from other physical ailments. When Breno leaves to carry out his fell purpose, a shepherd announces that Silvana is about to marry Cerdano, and further details are given in regard to the bridegroom's distinguished ancestry. They finally find Breno, not dead but in a faint, and he tells them of a vision he has had of the famous lovers of ancient times across the Acheron.

This little piece, written in ten-line *coplas de pie quebrado,* is a wedding play written to celebrate the marriage of Don Juan de la Cerda (Cerdano), second Duke of Medinaceli, to whom the play is dedicated, to Doña María de Silva y Toledo (Silvana), daughter of Don Juan de Silva, third Count of Cifuentes, in December 1511.

An anonymous *Égloga pastoril,* composed in five-line *coplas de pie quebrado,* is evidence that the plays of Encina were known and imitated at Valencia in 1519 or the beginning of 1520. The author was a Valencian, and the play was probably performed to celebrate the escape of the city from the dangers of plague and from a threatened incursion by a Moorish fleet. The solemnity of the verses that describe the abandoned state of the city, which recall the famous *coplas* of Jorge Manrique, ill accords with the burlesque account of the grief of the shepherd Climentejo over the marriage of his sweetheart to a rival and the cure of his malady effected by the village conjuror. The play is uneven and lacks coherence, but it is worthy of note that the earliest extant example of the secular drama at Valencia borrowed its form, chief incidents, language, and versification from a Castilian poet.

To approximately the same period belongs an *Égloga nueva,* attributed to Diego Durán, which represents with certain variations the conventional *recuesta de amores* theme. A shepherdess, seeking her flock, meets a mendicant friar who compliments her on her beauty and offers her his love. She reminds him of his holy calling, and he answers that those who carry on God's work are more often wounded by Cupid's arrows than anyone else. He becomes insistent, the maiden indignantly repels him, and a taffy vendor opportunely intervenes. The latter offers his protection to the shepherdess, but consents to play a game of cards with the mendicant and retires, stripped of all his possessions.

Once more the mendicant prepares to assure himself of his victim when a friar intervenes who roundly abuses him for his wicked intentions. In an unedifying scene, these two ministers of the Church accuse one another of gross misconduct, and finally the friar goes off to report the offense to his superiors. Once again the maiden is in danger, but her lover arrives, accompanied by another shepherd, and they threaten to give him a beating which he so richly deserves. They decide to play a game, *¿Dó posa la mariposa?,* which ends with the complete discomfiture of the mendicant. The concluding song shows that it was performed on Shrove Tuesday. The original edition is undated, but its primitive character allows us to conjecture that it was probably composed about the year 1520. The most striking feature of the play is the virulent satire of the morals of certain members of the clergy, which is found in other comedies in the first half of the century. It also shows originality in the versification, by its use of a combination mainly of *redondillas* and *quintillas* for each strophe, and employing a curious popular meter when describing the playing the game of *mariposa.*

An *Égloga* by Juan de París of which the earliest known edition bears the date 1536 combines the conventional *recuesta de amores* theme with Encina's *Plácida y Vitoriano* and the *Cristino y Febea*. Estacio, heartbroken over the disappearance of his sweetheart Numida whom he seeks in vain, determines to put an end to his life, but is persuaded by a hermit to banish love from his thoughts and to devote himself to the service of God. The author was well acquainted with Ovid's *Remedies of Love,* and the hermit—virtuous for a change—makes use of those arguments and examples in behalf of Estacio's welfare. In the meantime, Numida is also seeking her lover and is accosted by a shepherd who is unable to understand the cause of her grief, and proposes himself as a substitute for the missing Estacio. However, the shepherd is instrumental in reuniting the lovers, and one glance at Numida suffices to cure Estacio of his desire to lead the monastic life. The burlesque marriage ceremony humorously performed by a shepherd indicates that the play was written to be performed at some wedding.

Diego de Negueruela's *Farsa llamada Ardamisa* begins with a witty *introito* imitated from the Naharresque type of prologue, and the play proper consists of the conventional *recuesta de amores* theme which we have found in Encina and Fernández, but carried to an illogical conclusion. Ardamisa is alone searching for her lover Galirano, and she meets on her way with one man after another who, over promptly, tells her how much he loves her, when the girl is saved from an awkward predicament by the arrival of another suitor. Meanwhile, the missing Galirano has fallen in with a friar who piously preaches a sermon on the advantages of a life of single blessedness, and who later on enters into a conspiracy with most of the other characters to get possession of Ardamisa. The situation is quite knotted and the *dénouement* comes very suddenly and over abruptly, and the play ends with an interesting song and a sword dance. The lovesick Portuguese, the cowardly braggart, and the gipsy fortune teller are stock figures in sixteenth-century comedy, but they are amusing and well done. The shameless friar indicates again the popular attitude toward the unworthy members of the religious Orders.

Nothing is known about the author. The only early edition bears no date, but I should guess that it was written about 1530. From the text the play was almost certainly written to be performed at some wedding. In the matter of verse forms, approximately three-fourths are in *coplas de pie quebrado* and the remainder in *coplas de arte mayor*, with a few songs.

The *Farsa llamada Cornelia* by Andrés Prado, about whom we know nothing save that he was described in the only extant early edition as a "student," was printed at Medina del Campo in 1603. Moratín cites an edition of 1537, and the play belongs undeniably to that period even though he, by mistake, confuses it with the edition printed in 1603 by Juan Godínez de Millis. The lusty shepherd, Benitillo, recites the prologue which draws details, indecent and otherwise, from various plays of Torres Naharro. The author makes fun, in a bungling way, of the *recuesta de amores* situation. After Cornelia goes through many unpleasant experiences in the hope of being reunited with her lover, she refuses to open the door to receive him on the ground that their affairs were common gossip. It ends, not in suicide for the lover, as in Fileno's case, but in a game of blindman's-buff!

All of the ingredients of a *recuesta de amores* theme are found in the anonymous *Coplas de una doncella y un pastor*, but they are treated seriously, and in the end, devoutly. A distraught maiden rejects the advances of a boorish shepherd, but he insists until finally he is frightened away by the appearance of a solitary man (*salvaje*), living in the desert but showing no other sign of a "wild man" except perhaps abysmal melancholy. Of course, he falls discreetly in love with her, and they go to a hermitage where we leave them praying to the Virgin. The play was probably written to be performed at a marriage, but if such be the case, the tone is quite different from the other wedding plays.

The exceedingly rare edition of which we have any record was assigned by Salvá to about 1530; Moratín cited an edition of 1540 Valladolid; Gallardo reprinted the edition of Alcalá de Henares 1604 containing numerous gaps in the text, and finally Salvá mentions an edition of Cuenca 1619 where the author's name is said to be Eugenio Alberto. Cotarelo has reprinted the text of 1604 as an appendix to his facsimile edition of Fernández's plays on the ground that it was probably his. Gallardo first had the idea of attributing the *Coplas* to Fernández because in the *Registrum* of Fernando Colón, the latter mentioned seven plays as forming the volume printed in 1514, and the only copy known has six plays and the brief *Diálogo para cantar*. If one counts it as one of the plays, there is no occasion for attributing the *Coplas* to Fernández. There is undeniably a general resemblance between this and the secular plays of Fernández in the choice of subject which was in a sense conventional, but the two authors were poles apart in dealing with the same situation.

The same note of burlesque of the pains caused by love is found in the *Farsa de la Hechicera* by Diego Sánchez. Imitating closely Encina's Fileno, a lovesick gallant calls upon death to free him from his suffering. He is about to strike himself to the heart when courage and strength fail him, and he falls in a faint. He is found by a shepherd who places garlic in his mouth as first-aid treatment, and hurries off in search of a witch who is expert in the treatment of cramps. Finding that she has to deal with a more serious malady, she draws a circle on the ground, scatters grain in the form of a cross and begins a magic spell that will kindle love in the heart of the lady whom the gallant adores. A devil appears and is sent off to reunite the lovers while the shepherd, very much frightened, takes refuge with the old woman inside the magic circle. He is finally carried off to prison by the magistrate on a false charge brought by the witch, and the spectator, or reader, is left in doubt as to the fate of the unhappy lover. This is a little master-

piece of keen satire and rollicking horseplay. It is probable that it was written for performance at a wedding.

Another type of wedding play was derived from songs
that were sung on the occasion of the betrothal or marriage,
and we have precious evidence in the *Libro de buen amor*
of what these contained: a list of presents demanded by
the girl for her dower, and a similar list of things in which
the prospective groom was proficient (*coplas* 999–1005 and
1035–38). We find in the *Cancionero Musical*,[10] for example, No. 383, a composition by Encina beginning with
the *villancico, Ya soy desposado,* telling the many gifts that
he will make to the bride, and the same thing was done by
him in the *Égloga en reqüesta de unos amores.*

The next step was to write a play including a pedigree
of the bride and groom and the presents to both, and this
was done by Lucas Fernández, as we have seen, in the
Comedia de Bras-Gil y Beringuella, which was written from
about 1498 to 1500 and was printed in 1514. Another
advance was made by Diego de Ávila's *Égloga Interlocutoria* which was printed in 1511 or earlier. Here is described the betrothal and marriage of a peasant youth,
Tenorio, to Teresa Turpina, a country girl, through the
mediation of Alonso Benito, a professional matchmaker.
The latter recites a comic pedigree and a long list of articles
that make up her dowry. Tenorio's father is not outdone
in generosity and promises in his son's behalf an equally
long list of presents. Both parties are satisfied and a
priest, accompanied by a sacristan, performs a burlesque
marriage ceremony. After a contest in *pullas* [11] in which
all except the bride take part, the play concludes with a
wedding song.

Kohler [12] in the introduction to his edition says that this
play has no model in Spanish literature, and ascribes it to
the influence of Italian plays. Whether the author ever
lived in Italy or not—it is by no means certain that he did
—he got his material nearer home. The comic pedigree,
the gifts, and the matchmaker were found in Fernández's

Comedia de Bras-Gil y Beringuella. What was easier than to have Diego de Ávila add in his wedding play the priest, the sacristan, and the burlesque service? It is true that so far as is known Fernández's play was printed later, but Ávila may have seen the *Comedia de Bras-Gil* performed or have heard of its performance. If such was not the case, he used some other native material, written or oral, for the plot and situations. The *pullas*—a versified contest in abuse—were popular in many wedding plays.

It is dedicated to Gonzalo Fernández de Córdoba, and the play is abruptly interrupted to give an opportunity to Hontoya and Benito to speak of the glorious achievements of the Great Captain. Benito refers to him as *nuestro amo,* meaning that the author belonged to his personal retinue. It was probably written for performance in 1509 at the betrothal festivities of Elvira, his only daughter, to his old friend Bernardino de Velasco, Constable of Castile. The plans, however, went awry owing to the growing resentment against the Great Captain by the queen Germaine, and Elvira married, after her father's death, Don Luis Fernández de Córdoba, fourth Count of Cabra.

The original manuscript of the *Farsa de la Constanza* by Cristóbal de Castillejo, preserved in the Escorial Library, was borrowed by Gallardo and lost in Seville in 1823, but Moratín had seen it fortunately before its disappearance, and had summarized it and had copied 198 lines. Foulché-Delbosc printed Moratín's complete summary, which could not be published in full in his *Orígenes* because of the censor, as well as the verses. It consists of seven acts, preceded by a prologue in Latin and *coplas de pie quebrado* recited by the god Hymen. Two married couples air their domestic grievances in exceedingly coarse language, and finally the husbands agree to exchange wives. A priest announces to his congregation that a learned friar, a foreigner, will preach to them. After a little hesitation, the friar mounts the pulpit, and talks about love and of the woes it causes to animals and mankind. In the last act the priest pronounces the former marriages void, and re-weds the two couples according to the terms of the exchange.

It is difficult to say anything definite about a play for which we have only a brief statement of the plot and 198 verses of text. With respect to the third and fourth acts where we have the witty conversation between the priest and the learned friar, and the latter's *sermón de amores,* it is quite probable that Castillejo later on amplified greatly this material with the title *Sermón de amores* which was first printed in 1542.[13] So far as the *Farsa de la Constanza* is concerned, it was probably writen to be performed at some wedding.

The *Farsa del Matrimonio* of Diego Sánchez bears specifically the rubric *para representar en bodas.* The shepherd who recites the prologue makes a burlesque defense of marriage, explaining how unhappy Adam was until Eve was created. This is followed by a bitter dispute between husband and wife regarding the relative superiority of man and woman, which mentions some of the arguments in defense of women made by Rodríguez del Padrón's *Triunfo de las Donas.* The friar who interrupts this quarrel talks quite seriously of the part which husband and wife must share in marriage, but the lewd hypocrite conceives the idea of marrying his servant to Menga, daughter of the disputants, in the belief that he alone will profit by the arrangement. After the ceremony is performed and the intentions of the friar are discovered, his summary punishment is described with brutal realism and ribald mirth. In this play pious preaching on marriage is allied with cynical frankness of lust. If Diego Sánchez had been better known, doubtless the *Farsa del Matrimonio* would have fallen into the hands of the Inquisition, but it is incredible that a printer could have obtained permission to reprint the play in 1603, albeit with minor corrections.

The *Comedia Florisea* of Francisco de Avendaño, first printed in 1551 and also in 1553, follows Encina's *Égloga de tres Pastores* and *Plácida y Vitoriano* in the subject matter, but he must have been well acquainted with the plays of Torres Naharro. In the *Florisea* he reduced the number of acts from five to three, an innovation at that time. After a comic prologue which resembles parts of the prologue of the *Trofea, Jacinta,* and the *Calamita,* two unfortunates, Muerto and Floriseo, the one a victim of the cruel blows of fortune and the other of unrequited love, determine to put an end to their lives, but this double suicide is averted by the arrival of a shepherd who makes sport of their laments. After the usual experiences that fall to the lot of young women traveling alone according to the conventions of pastoral plays, Blancaflor finds her missing Floriseo, and a comic wedding ceremony, performed by the shepherd, unites the lovers. Fortuna appears opportunely to present the couple with a wedding gift of a thousand ducats and with a promise to provide abundantly for Muerto.

It is a well-written and interesting play. It was dedicated to the *muy noble y valentíssimo señor don Juan Pacheco, Capitán General de la gente del illustríssimo señor Marqués de Villena, mi señor,* and Don Juan Pacheco is mentioned in laudatory terms in the text (924–938). Avendaño was then in the service of the Marquis of Villena, probably Don Diego López Pacheco who succeeded his father in 1529 and who died in 1556. The play was probably written to celebrate the marriage of Don Juan Pacheco, a relative of the Marquis.

Finally, there is a *Farsa* written by Alonso de Salaya which Gillet has recently edited from a manuscript copy preserved in the Biblioteca Menéndez y Pelayo at Santander. Cañete read the play and quotes the first twenty-five lines in the preface to his edition of Carvajal's *Tragedia Josephina,* but the original edition has been lost.

The *Farsa* consists of 1400 lines, for the most part written in ten-line *coplas de pie quebrado.* Salaya had read the plays of Torres Naharro, particularly the *Aquilana,* and also now and then, the *Himenea* and the *Jacinta,* and he was also familiar with Encina and with the *Celestina*. The young gallant Laurelo, after longing for death because of the indifference of Florimena, through the efforts of his servant Ciarino, is granted an interview by his lady. She abuses him unmercifully, but Laurelo is patient, and gets his reward with a promise of marriage.

Even the approximate date of this play is uncertain. We might agree with Cañete who placed it during the early years of the sixteenth century, but Salaya apparently belonged to the middle of the century, and " if, however, the Portuguese's reference to *el rey prudente* (l. 1155) is an allusion to Philip the Second, as it well be, the play may have been composed some time after that monarch's accession in 1556, although hardly as late as the annexation of Portugal in 1581," as Gillet states.

ROMANTIC COMEDY AND THE COMEDY OF MANNERS BEFORE LOPE DE RUEDA

ROMANTIC comedy received its first impulse and its general direction for half a century from Bartolomé de Torres Naharro. As to his biography, archives in Spain and in Italy have contributed nothing as yet, and we are obliged to depend mainly upon a letter included in the prefatory matter for Naharro's works. This was written in Latin by a Frenchman, called Mesinierus I. Barberius who was in the service of Belisario Acquaviva, named the Duke of Nardò or Nérito by Ferdinand the Catholic, and was addressed to a Belgian humanist and printer, Jodocus Badius Ascensius, more commonly known as Josse Bade, the friend of Erasmus. In it the writer tells something of his friend, Torres Naharro. His family name was Naharro and he was born at the town of Torre de Miguel Sesmero near Badajoz; presumably in Italy he adopted the form Torres.

We know nothing of his education except that he shows an acquaintanceship with Latin comedy and, according to his friend, he knew Latin sufficiently well to have written his plays in that language. On one occasion he suffered shipwreck, and to add to his misfortunes, he was captured by pirates and was taken to Africa. He obtained his ransom and arrived at Rome, probably about 1513. In a decree of Leo X granting to the author sole rights to the publication and sale of the *Propalladia,* Naharro is spoken of as a cleric of the diocese of Badajoz, but we do not know whether he entered the Church before or after his arrival in Rome. We have a direct reference that he was a soldier, in the last line of the Latin composition of Joannis Murconius, " so Mars and Minerva sparkle." In the *Comedia*

Soldadesca he gave evidence of being well acquainted with the Spanish soldiery in Italy, and it is thought that he refers to himself in the same play as an Andalusian soldier in the service of the Cardinal of Santa Cruz, Bernardino Carvajal. It is quite possible that he served in the army under the Duke of Nájera, Pedro Manrique de Lara, for he penned some really eloquent verses in the *Retrato* when the great soldier died in 1515.

His residence in Rome brought with it bitter disappointments. Driven by poverty to seek patronage, he found that merit was not rewarded, and that rascals were successful while honest men starved. He obtained some sort of post in the household of the turbulent Bernardino Carvajal, Cardinal of Santa Cruz, who belonged to a noble family of Plasencia and who had had the temerity to defy openly Julius II with the other schismatic cardinals and was excommunicated by him in 1510. After Leo X was chosen pope in February 1513, the rebellious Carvajal abjured his errors in June of that year, and was allowed again to sit with the Sacred College. It is impossible to say whether or not Torres Naharro entered the service of Carvajal during the three years that the Cardinal was absent from Rome, but doubtless he was well known there later as a poet and entertainer for an aristocratic gathering, and he was chosen to write a play, as we have seen, in honor of the Portuguese mission led by Tristão da Cunha (1514). Under the patronage of Carvajal, he wrote the *Comedia Tinellaria* to whom the *suelta* edition was dedicated, before the play was published in the *Propalladia*. A distinguished audience witnessed its performance, including the Pope and his cousin Giulio de' Medici who became Pope in 1523 under the title of Clement VII. From internal evidence the play was probably performed in 1516.

The mysterious Barberius, whose letter gives us valuable information about Torres Naharro, is more mysterious than ever when he says, "Unexpectedly he left Rome and went to Naples." The Pope's letter granting permission to publish the *Propalladia* was signed on April 15, 1517, the volume was printed at Naples and was dedicated to Ferrante Francesco D'Avalos, Marquis of Pescara, who belonged to a family long distinguished in the annals of Spanish and Italian history. As the husband of Vittoria Colonna, and the object of some of her best verse, a sentimental interest attaches itself to D'Avalos' name in spite of his infamous treason after the battle of Pavia. In this dedicatory letter Naharro refers to a post which he held at that time with Fabrizio Colonna, Grand Constable of Naples and father-in-law of the Marquis of Pescara.

The *Propalladia* was reprinted with an additional comedy, the *Calamita,* at Seville, 1520, and again at Naples 1524 with an added play, the *Aquilana.* Gillet [1] has pointed out that an undated *suelta* of the same play, and earlier than the *Propalladia* 1524 version, contains a reference to Naharro's death. It would appear, then, that his stay at Naples was brief, because there are traces of Ariosto's *I Suppositi* in the *Aquilana,* and Torres Naharro may have been in Rome to see the performance of the play in 1519.

As for the Greek name *Propalladia,* he explains that it means "the first things of Pallas," as distinguished from the later things which he might write with more maturity. It is clear that the term "maturity" refers only to his publications, and not to his years. Those compositions that can be dated in the *Propalladia* were written between 1513 and 1517. As the appetizer and dessert, as he says, he serves forty-two short lyrical pieces. By far the most significant of these are the *sátira* and the third *capítulo* in which, with rapier-like thrusts, he lays bare the seething corruption of Rome. Here he appears in the rôle of a stern moralist, which ill accords with the easy-going tolerance exhibited in plays like the *Serafina.* "Rome is a school for sin," he says, "where no evil is left undone." "Reason and kindliness are out of fashion; faith and love are dead." As a master of invective and of an epigrammatic style Naharro has scarcely an equal in Spanish literature.

Next in order of merit is the composition to Pedro Manrique de Lara, already referred to, in which he gives expression to his ardent patriotism, and also a poem in honor of the Great Captain. His love poems are attractive, but are lacking in warmth. In all of his verses, with the exception of three sonnets in Italian, he employs the traditional Spanish measures. In view of his acquaintance with Italian literature, it is perhaps surprising that he did not make the experiment of introducing or reintroducing the hendecasyllable into Castilian which was realized a decade later by Boscán.

In the *Prohemio* or prologue to the *Propalladia,* Torres Naharro initiates dramatic criticism in Spanish literature. After modestly stating his desire to print in correct form his plays which were circulating in unauthorized versions, he refers briefly to his lyrical verses and then quotes a few opinions of the ancients, chiefly from Donatus, concerning drama. He distinguishes between comedy as the representation of civil and private fortune, without peril of life, as distinguished from tragedy which occupies itself with heroic fortune in adversity, and cites Cicero's definition that comedy is " a copy of life, a mirror of custom and a reflection of truth." The poet Acron, to whom certain *scholia* on Horace were incorrectly ascribed, is mentioned as authority for a sixfold classification of comedies, and also for the four parts in which a comedy is divided. He agrees with Horace that the five-act division is necessary, and that decorum should be preserved.

Having thus paid his respects to classical authority, he proceeds to discuss comedy from his own experience and judgment. " Comedy," he writes, " is an ingenious arrangement of notable incidents, ending happily, and in dialogue." " The division into five acts not only seems to me good, but also very necessary, although I call them *jornadas,* because they seem to me more like resting-places than any-

thing else." Naharro was the first to use the word *jornada*
as a substitute for act. Whether he invented the special
meaning of the term or merely translated the Italian
giornata, which was occasionally employed in this sense in
the Italian *sacre rappresentazioni,* we cannot say. At all
events, the claim made by Juan de la Cueva in his *Exemplar
poético* that he first used the word is obviously incorrect.

A play should contain from six to twelve characters,
Naharro tells us, and propriety must be observed by as-
signing to each his proper place. He proposes an interesting classification of comedies, namely, *comedia a noticia,*
based upon something actually seen and akin to our comedy
of manners, and *comedia a fantasía* based upon fictitious
material, with an appearance of truth, and may be translated as romantic comedy.

Seven plays, namely the *Soldadesca, Tinellaria, Trofea,
Serafina, Himenea, Jacinta* and the *Diálogo del Nascimiento,* including the *Adición del Diálogo,* are contained in
the volume entitled *Propalladia.* The form of the titles
is derived from Plautus. In the *introito* to the *Tinellaria*
we are told that the title comes from *tinello,* as the *Asinaria*
of Plautus from *asinus.*

Each of these plays, except the *Diálogo,* is preceded by
a prologue or *introito,* which concludes in every case with
a fairly detailed summary of the plot. The latter was
necessary because dramatic art had not advanced far enough
to present a series of scenes that would be intelligible to
an audience without explanation. The prologue is recited
by an uncouth shepherd, using the conventional so-called
sayagués dialect, who sometimes playfully greets his audience or expresses surprise on finding himself in such a
distinguished gathering. His function is to entertain, and
for this he resorts to broad farce. In some he relates with
relish a lewd escapade, while in others he contents himself
with narrating his accomplishments, after which he withdraws from the stage after reciting his lines.

With respect to the origin of the Naharresque prologue, it only borrowed from Latin comedy the name *argumento* and a brief outline of the plot. The term *introito* which Naharro used in that part of the prologue which preceded the argument seems to have a liturgical connotation. It has been pointed out that Alione, an obscure writer of carnival plays from Asti, in northern Italy, used the same word for prologue as Naharro, and that the two prologuists resemble one another in making facetious remarks to the audience. Alione's plays were first published in 1521, and one can safely assume that Torres Naharro and Alione had never heard of one another in writing their plays. The use of the term *introit* must have been a coincidence in the two playwrights when they gave a liturgical word which was the direct opposite of what one might expect.

The prologue as conceived by Naharro was a Spanish product and to him alone is due the amalgamation of various elements which were found in the dramatic and lyrical poetry of his day. As Meredith [2] has said, the closest approximation to the *introito* before Naharro is to be found in the *Égloga o Farsa del nascimiento* of Lucas Fernández, although certain elements were contributed by Encina and possibly by Vicente.

Of the seven plays printed in the first edition of the *Propalladia* and the two plays which were published a little later, we have definite information regarding the performance of only two plays, the *Tinellaria* and the *Trofea*. However, we may assume that these other plays were represented in Rome, and possibly in Naples, with the support of some patron such as the Cardinal of Santa Cruz or some wealthy and influential layman. The audiences must have been similar to those which witnessed the plays of Ariosto, the *Calandria* of Bibbiena, and Machiavelli's *La Mandragola* at Rome at about the same time.

Torres Naharro may have imitated Gil Vicente's practice, when it suited him, of introducing a person or persons speaking a different language from the rest of the characters in the play. What must one think of the language capacity of an audience that witnessed the *Tinellaria,* for example, in which people speak, besides Spanish and Italian, Portuguese, so-called French, Valencian, macaronic Latin, a Basque who talks something which is meant for Castilian, and a German who speaks Latin and an approximation to German words? These are undeniably funny scenes, provoking hilarity on the part of the audience, and foreign languages are used for comic effect in the *Serafina* and in the *Soldadesca.*

Taking up first the *comedias a noticia,* the *Comedia Soldadesca* presents a Spanish captain who is recruiting soldiers for the Pope's service. Some of those he enlists are veterans who have taken part, under Gonsalvo de Córdoba, in the famous victories at Cerignola and Garigliano (1503) and who also have fought at Bugia and Tripoli (1510). Peace is irksome to them and they long for war " as do the poor for summer." They are joined by a poverty-stricken friar and others, who swagger about with lofty bearing as soon as they carry arms, and treat in a high-handed fashion an Italian tavern-keeper who is unable to understand their language. Many Italian plays contain the figure of the Spanish braggart soldier which, after making due allowance for national prejudice, serve to complement this picture given to us by Naharro. Allusions to the new break between the Spanish king and the French, and the preparations of the Pope for war refer to the invasion of northern Italy by Francis I in the summer of 1515. As a picture of a Spanish officer under Leo X, lamenting the good old times of Pope Alexander, with his veterans and new recruits, it is highly attractive and seems to be true to life.

As has already been stated, the *suelta* edition of the *Comedia Tinellaria,* printed before its inclusion in the *Propalladia,* is dedicated to Cardinal Bernardino Carvajal. In the preface to that edition, Naharro states that it had been performed before the Pope and Monseñor de Medicis, his patron, and that Carvajal had asked the author why he did not publish it. The statement is interesting since it shows that Giulio de' Medici had shown some favor to the poet.

After a humorous prologue which may have been recited by Naharro himself, we are introduced into the servants' dining room (*tinello*) of the Cardinal of San Iano. From the first scene, in which the well-named Barrabás, the chief butler, is quarreling with his mistress, and shows cynical disregard for his master's property and a desire to exploit him to the utmost for his own advantage, until the drunken orgy of the last act, we have an amazing picture of petty greed and maladministration. Not only does the good name of the cardinal suffer from the rapacity of his trusted officers. The true victims are the underlings, who are dependent for their sustenance upon the cardinal's bounty, and who are nearly starved by the wretched fare that is served to them. The third act is a masterpiece of humor of its kind which describes a noisy, brawling meal in the *tinello* which begins with the blessing for food, such as it is, and ends with the benediction, but Naharro's criticism is eloquent concerning such conditions of life. When not complaining about food and drink, these petty servants quarrel over questions of national honor in language that is far from parliamentary.

We can readily appreciate the virulence of this satire which was designed, so we are told in the preface, to show the cardinals what actually went on in their kitchens. The chief figures must have been recognized by the audience, but unfortunately we have not sufficient evidence to identify them. We do not know who was the prototype of Barrabás, who rose in three years from the post of scullion to that of administrator of an important household. The identity of Cardinal of San Iano is not quite certain, but it is probable that he was Giulio de' Medici, since people were saying in 1516 that he would be the next pope, and Naharro makes several similar allusions to the Cardinal of San Iano. The references to Bramante's work on St. Peter's and Maestro Pasquin are interesting, and the mention of Orlando in the second act—*perch' hanno più fantasia / che non hebe mai Orlando*—may be another argument for dating the play in 1516.

Among the *comedias a fantasía* the earliest is undeniably the *Comedia Jacinta,* which because of its lack of a plot merits the name of entertainment rather than a play. After a humorous but restrained prologue, we meet in turn Jacinto, Precioso, and Fenicio, disillusioned with life, who have traveled from Germany, Italy, and Spain. They are stopped in turn by Pagano, a servant of a lady of great virtue and nobility named Divina, who persuades them to present themselves before his mistress. As they proceed to the lady's castle, they express their high admiration for women, attributing to them everything good in life. Divina receives the travelers courteously and offers to accept one of them as a husband, and the other two as brothers.

The closing *villancico* of this pleasing but uninspired entertainment, beginning with the words

> Una tierra sola, Roma,
> Y un señor y solo Dios,
> Y una dama sola, vos,

and ending

> Hizo os Dios tan gran señora
> Y en las damas tan sin par
> Que no debrian culpar
> A quien por tal os adora;
> Y asi los tiempos d'agora
> No se hallan tales dos:
> Ni otra Roma, ni otra vos,

may give us a clue in regard to a lady in whose honor it was written and probably performed. During the winter of 1514–1515 the celebrated Isabella d'Este, Marchioness of Mantua, with her maids of honor, paid a visit to Rome

as the guest of Pope Leo and the princes of the Church, and
her wit and beauty won all hearts. Bibbiena and Giuliano
de' Medici accompanied her from the Papal frontier to the
Vatican, and for four months the Marchioness and her
ladies were entertained with festivities of every description.[3]
The performance of Cardinal Bibbiena's *Calandria* was
only one of the plays which the Marchioness graced. It
is highly probable that Torres Naharro wrote the *Comedia
Jacinta* to celebrate under the name of Divina this distinguished lady, the reigning beauty: [4]

> Y asi los tiempos d'agora
> No se hallan tales dos:
> Ni otra Roma, ni otra vos.

In the *Comedia Himenea* we have a comic prologue
treating in part a burlesque *recuesta de amores* theme. In
the play proper, situations that have become the common-
places of romantic comedy, made their first appearance on
any stage. The infatuation of a gallant for a young lady;
a first interview with musical accompaniment; the jealous
watchfulness of the lady's brother who swears to avenge
himself upon the betrayer of his honor; the rendezvous
with the exchange of vows of undying love, brusquely interrupted by the brother, who after the momentary flight
of the lover, demands his sister's life as a price of her
dishonor; the lover's return and the offer of marriage which
is accepted: these are the scenes that must have charmed
by their novelty that first audience, and which even now
delight us.

In presenting his characters, he makes effective use of
contrast. The sentimental Himeneo, who melts to tears
at the mere thought of Febea, has two servants, Eliso and
Boreás, who are cynical regarding women and think their
master's passion a form of lunacy that permits them to
extort additional pay. Himeneo fears nothing but a re-
buff from his lady, while his servants boast mightily of their
valor, and leave their master in the lurch at the first sign

of danger. Contrast is again the motive in the love-making scene between Boreás and Febea's maid Doresta which playfully and in a lower key reproduces the incidents of the first interview of Himeneo and Febea, a situation that recurs in countless plays of the seventeenth century in Spain and elsewhere.

The argument of the *Comedia Himenea* is derived from the twelfth, fourteenth, and fifteenth acts of the *Comedia de Calisto y Melibea*.[5] In both versions the action is limited to twenty-four hours, and except for the difference in the *dénouement*, the incidents agree in general outlines. Himeneo, like Calisto, is a sentimental, somewhat ingenuous lover; Febea and Melibea have the same charming simplicity of character that is capable of heroism when the occasion demands it; Eliso and Boreás correspond closely to Pármeno and Sempronio. With all these similarities, however, the play should not be regarded as merely a dramatization of a part of the *Comedia de Calisto y Melibea*. Naharro saw the dramatic possibilities of the central situation, added the character of Febea's brother, and portrayed in his own language that supremely interesting conflict of love and honor which anticipated by nearly a hundred years a situation frequently found in the *comedia de capa y espada*.

Probably the last play written by Naharro before the first edition of the *Propalladia* was printed is the *Comedia Serafina* which describes the predicament of the young Floristán on finding himself with two wives, a Valencian *demi-mondaine* named Serafina, and Orfea, an Italian lady whom he had married at his father's orders. Serafina, accompanied by her maid Dorosía, follows her erring lover to Rome and upbraids him, in impassioned Valencian, for his infidelity. Floristán generously assumes all the blame, which is self-evident, renews to her his pledge of undying love and declares that either Orfea or he must die. After due consideration, he finally settles upon the former alternative. He confides his purpose to the friar Teodoro, who cynically promises his aid, but insists that the lady must have an opportunity to confess her faults. Floristán explains tenderly to Orfea why her death is necessary to him, and she, like a dutiful wife, pardons him for his offense and prays to God for mercy! The *dénouement* is brought about by Teodoro's suggestion that since Orfea's marriage to Floristán had not been consummated, she should marry Policiano, Floristán's brother, who had returned quite opportunely to Rome, and who had been long in love with her.

Critics have found the play puzzling and some have called it a *bufonada,* accepting the opinion of Menéndez y Pelayo. In my opinion, Naharro did not write the play as a *bufonada,* but it undoubtedly deserves that name today owing to the poet's awkwardness in handling his source materials. I think that in reading Terence's *Andria* Naharro became interested in the dilemma of Pamphilus who was ordered by his father to marry Philumena on the very day that Glycerium, who is, to all intents and purposes, his devoted wife, awaits the arrival of their first-born child. He took over merely the setting of the Latin comedy—not the dialogue—and replaced the original triangle by Floristán, Serafina, and Orfea. Changes were made in the first two characters only because the counterpart of Orfea does not appear in *Andria,* but the modifications are helpful in the appraisal of Naharro's conceptions of art. Floristán, compared with Pamphilus, is vague and uncertain, and is apparently driven into marriage with Serafina because of her unexpected arrival. The latter is the typical *demimondaine* of comedy who is far removed from the essential purity and delicacy of feelings of Terence's girl from Andros. In both plays the knot was untied with the same unexpectedness: Glycerium turns out to be the daughter of Chremes, and as for Philumena, she has long been loved by Charinus, while in the *Serafina,* as we know, Floristán's brother Policiano, who had long loved Orfea, returns after a three years' absence.[6]

The friar Teodoro, speaking macaronic Latin, is the character who is responsible for untying the knot. He is a crafty hypocrite, thoroughly at home with love's stratagems, a figure who may have been suggested by Fra Timoteo in Machiavelli's *La Mandragola*. This may be true, but it is also a fact that while Naharro may have seen a performance at Florence or have read a manuscript copy, he took only the external features and as a result Teodoro is nothing more than a pale reflection of Machiavelli's great conception. The *Commedia in versi*, formerly thought to be by Machiavelli, and now attributed perhaps to Luigi Strozzi, has been mentioned as a source of the *Serafina*,[7] but I think that Naharro got very little from the Italian play if he read it at all.

If the construction leaves much to be desired, it is redeemed by the epigrammatic sayings of Lenicio, Floristán's servant, who adds to the rôle of slave bequeathed by Terence, the class consciousness vaguely felt by some dramatists in the sixteenth century and of which Naharro serves as a mouthpiece. When his master accuses him of lukewarm attachment to his interests, Lenicio replies with uncommon frankness which would not be tolerated in any ancient comedy, " You masters still think that your servants are slaves. I never go to market without stopping at a brothel to leave what I have pilfered from you." Floristán asks helplessly whether he realizes the enormity of his sin, and the servant answers, " A servant is a fool who waits for his master to pay when he himself can collect his due." Lenicio's comments on life are brutally cynical and more delicately etched than even those by Sempronio and Pármeno in the *Celestina*.

The *Comedia Calamita*, first printed so far as we know at Seville in 1520, more nearly approaches classical comedy than any of Naharro's plays, and also contains the best constructed plot. Young Floribundo falls madly in love with Calamita, a girl of apparently humble condition, thereby incurring the displeasure of Euticio, his father

Through the aid of his servant Jusquino, Floribundo succeeds in entering the house of Calamita, declares to her his love, and readily agrees to the condition of marriage which she imposes. Euticio is very angry when he hears of what he considers his son's crowning act of folly, but a solution is brought about by the discovery that Calamita is the long-lost daughter of a Sicilian gentleman and an old friend of Euticio. The sub-plot is made up of the marital difficulties of Torcazo, who is supposed to be Calamita's brother, and his wife Libina. Torcazo is a simpleton, incapable of detecting Libina's infidelities, but who is able effectively to enforce his arguments with her with a club. These two elements are well knit together, and the play gives an impression of dramatic unity.

In reading Terence's *Heautontimorumenos,* he took for a new play the characters of Menedemus, an old man, with a son Clinia who was in love with a girl supposed to be a courtesan named Antiphila, but actually the daughter of Chremes, an old friend of Clinia's father. He suppressed the rest of the plot and sub-plots, rewrote the dialogue and modernized the situations in accordance with sixteenth-century life, and the characters reappear in the Spanish play as Euticio, Floribundo, and Calamita. To make up the sub-plot, Naharro used certain scenes from Cardinal Bibbiena's *La Calandria* which he doubtless saw at Rome in the autumn of 1514 when it was performed before Isabella d'Este, or in Naples in 1518. From that source he took Torcazo, a type of complacent husband, which goes back to Boccaccio's Calandrino, and it has been pointed out that Jusquino's instructions to Torcazo how to feign death in the fifth act of *Calamita* are derived from the ninth scene of the second act of *La Calandria.* Two other scenes in the *Calamita* seem to prove the author's acquaintance with Bibbiena's celebrated play.

In the *Comedia Aquilana,* first printed so far as we know at Naples in 1524, we are introduced into the land of romance. Aquilano, Prince of Hungary, woos Felicina, a princess of the kingdom of Leon, but indignantly rejects his servant's suggestion that he make known his identity, because by his romantic code the prize must be won by the ardor of his love, or not at all.   One evening the princess grants him an interview in the garden, but as he unburdens his tortured soul of its secret, the princess hears a noise and brusquely dismisses him.   The oversensitive Aquilano faints and is found almost lifeless by two gardeners.   He tells them that he is mortally ill, for Cupid has made a wound that will never heal, but they make fun of his rhetoric.

King Bermudo, Felicina's father, is alarmed over his serious condition, but the most celebrated doctors fail to diagnose the cause of his malady until one of them adopts the expedient used in the well-known case of Antiochus as told by Plutarch's *Life of Demetrius,* which Naharro probably read in the edition of the Latin translation of the *Vitae* printed about 1470 by Leonardo Bruni Aretino and others, or perhaps in Leonardo Bruni's *novella* on the same subject printed in 1511.   When the physician discovers that Aquilano's pulse quickens at the sight of Felicina, he tells the king of the young man's symptoms and declares that he is in love with the physician's wife, but after the king pleads with him to allow them to marry, the doctor then tells him that the young man is enamored of Felicina.   On learning this, the king determines to put Aquilano to death and Felicina contemplates suicide, but the prince's identity is established by his servant, and Bermudo consents gladly to the marriage of the young lovers.

No definite source of the main story has been found, although resemblances have been noted between the *Aquilana* and Gil Vicente's *Comedia del Viudo* and his tragicomedy *Don Duardos,* the romance of chivalry *Primaleón* (1512), and the *Pietà d'Amore,* a Sienese comedy, printed in 1518 or before, by Mariano Maniscalco.[8]   It is possible that the story is connected with a popular motif in ballad literature.   It is probable that the scene in which Dileta, Felicina's maid, teases her mistress, insisting on exchanging rôles with her before telling her the glad news of Aquilano's safety, is derived from a somewhat similar scene in the third act of the *Asinaria* of Plautus, to which in another connection Naharro makes reference. The two gardeners who contribute the farcical element closely resemble the shepherds of the early pastoral plays.

While Encina was the founder of the Spanish drama, Torres Naharro was Spain's first real dramatist. In place of the dainty triviality of Encina's pastoral eclogues and the rhetorical versified monologues of the *Égloga de tres pastores* and the *Égloga de Plácida y Vitoriano*, in which the protagonists studiously avoid one another through fear of terminating the play too soon, Naharro offers us a real human interest, a conflict of wills and, at times, a psychological development of character. Family honor, which was destined to furnish so many dramatic situations later on, made its first appearance on any stage in the *Himenea*. He did not disdain the use of farcical material, but his conception of comedy was more reflective and subtle than his predecessors. His lackeys are the very antithesis of the blockhead as he is found in Encina and Fernández; keen-witted, sophisticated opportunists, they anticipate both the *pícaro* Lazarillo de Tormes and the *gracioso* of Lope de Vega. His dramatic work is uneven, but in the *Himenea*, *Calamita*, and the *Aquilana*, Spain had its first *comedia de capa y espada*, its first comedy of intrigue and its first romantic play.

In respect to strophes of his verse, the eight secular plays are written in three types of meter: the twelve-line octosyllabic *coplas de pie quebrado*, used in the *Himenea*, probably imitated from the Italians; the twelve-line octosyllabic strophe in the *Jacinta*, an innovation which was never tried later; and the rest of the plays were written in native *coplas*, either *coplas de pie quebrado* or *redondillas dobles*. Most of Naharro's imitators followed him in the metrical forms employed; the division into five *jornadas*, the use of a comic prologue. and the subject matter derived directly or indirectly from the *Himenea, Aquilana,* or the *Celestina.*

While it is unlikely that any of his plays was performed in Spain, the *Propalladia* had a well-merited vogue.[9] Besides *sueltas* of separate plays, the *Propalladia* was reprinted eight times, and the appearance of an expurgated edition in 1573 proves that it was still a popular book. References by Juan de Valdés and Francisco Delicado, the author of the *Lozana Andaluza,* show that in Italy Naharro could find favor in two unlike points of view, and in Spain, besides the imitations, he was remembered for a hundred years as a dramatist and as a lyric poet who had used only native measures in his Spanish verses.

A very early imitation of the *Celestina* is the anonymous *Comedia Ypólita.* It is written in five *cenas* (*escenas*) or acts in *coplas de pie quebrado,* but without a prologue. Probably printed at Valencia about 1521, the subject matter is not only derived from the *Celestina,* but also has many points of contact with two dialogued novels, the *Comedia Serafina* (not to be confused with Naharro's play) and more especially the *Comedia Thebayda.* It is believed that if the author of the *Ypólita* did not also write the *Thebayda,* he drew on it for some of his material, and that he was also acquainted with the novel *Serafina.* Gross and lewd in its theme, it is unintelligent in its plan, and graceless and careless in its execution.

The *Celestina,* and to a lesser degree the *Himenea,* influenced a number of plays written between 1520 and the middle of the century. One of the earliest was the anonymous *Comedia Clariana,* printed at Valencia in 1522, which was mentioned by the Spanish translators of Ticknor and was presumably based upon material taken from the *Celestina,* but no copy is known to exist. We have two plays of the same type by Jayme de Güete, the *Comedia Tesorina* of which we have only an undated *suelta* and an edition of 1551, and the *Comedia Vidriana* which is preserved in only one *suelta* without date. They were probably printed in 1535 or earlier. Nothing is known of the author save that he was an Aragonese. Both are written in five acts, in *coplas de pie quebrado*, and are preceded by a comic prologue in Naharro's manner.

The *Tesorina* presents the wooing of Lucina by Tesorino, who by a clever ruse gains access to her house and then secures the services of Fray Vegecio to unite them in marriage. The friar's lisping speech adds a touch of humor to the ceremony, which ends in a witty *sermón de amores*. The anxiety of Timbreo over his daughter's disappearance is somewhat relieved by the friar's explanation, and he is finally reconciled to the marriage. It is unfortunate to have to compare Tesorino, Lucina, and Pinedo with their illustrious prototypes Himeneo, Febea, and Boreás, because by so doing we realize only too well the difference between an original and an imitation. Vegecio recalls the friar of Naharro's *Serafina*. A negress also appears in the fifth act to create dramatic suspense by her incoherent account to Timbreo of his daughter's elopement, a figure employed in a similar way by Lope de Rueda.

The *Comedia Vidriana* has few redeeming qualities. The author adopts the chief incidents of the *Celestina*, omitting the figures of the bawd and her infamous associates, but he is plainly embarrassed in giving to these scenes dramatic unity. New characters are introduced at random, and farcical scenes are added without organic relationship to the main plot. The consuming passion of Calisto becomes commonplace in Vidriano's love-making, and the keen wit of Calisto's servants degenerates into buffoonery. As a substitute for the tragic *dénouement* of the *Celestina*, we have Vidriano's attempt to abduct Leriana, which is frustrated by the lady's father. Vidriano makes a lame excuse for his rash act and makes an offer of marriage to Leriana, which is acceptable to her parents. Güete was a dull, unimaginative writer who made up in horseplay for the wit which he lacked.

The *Comedia Radiana* of Agustín Ortiz, also composed in five acts of *coplas de pie quebrado*, again shows the

influence of Naharro. Through the aid of his servant
Turpino, Cleriano secures an audience with Radiana, who
accepts his love with incredible facility. The escape of
the lovers is prevented by Lireo, Radiana's father, who
swears to avenge the injury to his honor by taking their
lives. A priest arrives from nowhere and obtains his con-
sent to the marriage ceremony, which is straightway performed. The chief merit of the play is its brevity. The
first act consists almost entirely of Lireo's grief over the
death of his wife, possibly suggested by the opening scene
of Vicente's *Comedia del Viudo,* and apparently was introduced for the sole purpose of explaining the absence of
Radiana's mother. The heroine does not appear until the
fifth act, and there are many farcical scenes without the
remotest connection with the rest of the play. In several
scenes the author imitated the *Himenea.* From internal
evidence the play was written between 1533 and 1535.

The influence of Encina, as well as that of the *Celestina*
and of Naharro, is evident in the *Comedia Tidea* of Francisco de las Natas, a cleric of the diocese of Burgos. The
only edition known is of the year 1550, but the date of its
composition is much earlier since its author published a
translation of the second book of the *Aeneid* in 1528, and
an unextant *Comedia Claudiana* in 1536. The love-affairs
of Tideo and Faustina follow closely those of Calisto and
Melibea, and Celestina herself plays a prominent rôle in
the person of Beroe. Tideo uses the same rhetorical language as Vitoriano in Encina's eclogue, and an interlude in
the second act recalls the *Auto del Repelón.* The *dénouement,* brought about by the discovery that Tideo is a prince
in disguise, may indicate an acquaintance with the *Aquilana.*
The play contains a considerable amount of coarseness and
irreverence which ill accords with the author's calling, and
which probably was responsible for its appearance on the
Index of 1559 and 1583. By virtue of its harmonious
arrangement of scenes, natural development of the action,

and lively dialogue, we may regard it as the best imitation in dramatic form of the *Celestina* and the *Himenea.*

In the anonymous *Farça a manera de tragedia,* printed at Valencia in 1537, the tragical consequences of love are presented, and we are told in the prologue that the play is based upon an actual occurrence. The shepherd Torcato and the shepherdess Liria, who talk like gentlefolk, are happy in their new-found love, but Carlino, Liria's half-brother and a priest, spies upon her and convinces himself of her infidelity. Her husband, the peasant Gazardo, refuses complacently to give credence to Carlino's accusations, but finally consents to set a trap for her by a forged letter. When Torcato receives this, apparently signed by Liria, in which she tells him of the discovery of their secret and that she no longer loves him, he writes a letter in his own blood and stabs himself. When Liria finds her lover's body, she commits suicide.

The prologue and the division into five acts remind one of Torres Naharro, and two or three incidents recall the *Himenea,* but the rest of the play with its double suicide and its impassioned rhetorical language goes back to Encina's *Tres Pastores* and to *Plácida y Vitoriano.* It is still primitive and undeveloped, of course, but it shows considerable progress in tying up the emotions which lead to the inevitable catastrophe. The stupid husband recalls Torcazo in *Calamita* and is a worthy forerunner of Cornalla in Timoneda's *Carmelia,* and other types of contented dupes. The play is written in *quintillas.*

The *Auto de Clarindo* deserves only casual mention. The rubric bears the statement, *sacado de las obras del Captivo por Antonio Díez, librero sordo, y en partes añadido y enmendado.* We have no means of guessing the identity of " the Captive " nor of determining the additions made by the " deaf bookseller." It does not matter much, however, because the play is devoid of any merit. Based upon the *Celestina,* we have not one gallant, but two, who are in love with stepsisters. After incidents without interest and silly shepherds' scenes and incantations, the lovers succeed in abducting the young women from a convent. It is written in five-line *coplas,* and in the opening lines of the prologue it has eight verses of the Valdovinos ballad. The play is written in three acts, and if the statement made by the Spanish translators of Ticknor is correct that it was printed in 1535, the *Clarindo* has the honor, but only that, of being the earliest Spanish play divided into three acts.

The *Comedia Grassandora* by Juan Uceda de Sepúlveda, printed in 1539 or before, is written in four *jornadas* in *coplas de pie quebrado,* with a Naharresque prologue. The plot, if it can be called such, is a close imitation during the first two acts of the *Celestina* with Grassandor's unmotivated infatuation for Florisenda, and his two servants, a pair of rascally cowards, who meet their unmotivated death off-scene.

In the last two acts, following Encina, we find Grassandor driven to the point of suicide by the lady's curt reply to his letter, but Cupid takes charge and finally unites Florisenda and the lover in the presence of a hermit. It was probably written to be performed for a wedding at Toledo, and its dedication to Don Íñigo de Arellano, probably related to the Count of Aguilar, may furnish a clue to the date.

After such drab and dull compositions as the two last mentioned, we look with real delight at Gil Vicente's *Comedia del Viudo,* written entirely in Castilian, and presented in 1514 and reworked after 1521. A widower mourns the death of his wife, and neither finds comfort in the sympathetic words of a friar nor in the jests of a friend who is unable to rid himself of a shrewish mate. A young nobleman named Rosvel falls in love with the widower's two daughters, Paula and Melicia, and obtains from him employment as a workman. From this point of vantage he courts the young women. He wishes to marry one of them, but both are so charming that he is unable to express a preference. This embarrassing question is submitted to the young Prince John, who was a spectator, and who decides that Rosvel shall marry Paula. Gilberto, Rosvel's brother, arrives opportunely and wins the hand of Melicia. The father consents with reluctance to his daughters' betrothal, and a priest, who performs the marriage ceremony, preaches a brief sermon in which he reminds the newly married couples of the Scriptural injunction to " be fruitful and multiply." It is a work of real beauty, with its lovely songs, and is not surpassed in charm by any Spanish play of the first half of the century.

Written as a wedding play, Vicente took from *Primaleón* (1512) the lover Prince Duardos who adopts a disguise of a gardener to be near the lady of his heart's desire, and who further complicated matters by making both girls fall in love with Rosvel. It is believed by many critics that the play has a personal significance because of the fact that the names of the two daughters are Paula and Melicia, the first being the name of Vicente's eldest daughter and the second being that of his second wife.

Vicente realized, as did no Castilian writer of his time, the dramatic value of the material presented in the romances of chivalry. The idealization of love and personal courage with its romantic setting was peculiarly appropriate for a court whose social code had been molded by traditions of chivalry, and in this world of fancy Vicente's poetic imagination found free expression. In *Don Duardos,* written entirely in Castilian, he dramatized the episode of his love for Flérida, daughter of Emperor Palmerin, as it is told in the *Primaleón* (1512).

Don Duardos, Prince of England, becomes enamored of Flérida while engaged in combat at her father's court, but he does not disclose his identity. After many adventures he returns and secures employment as a gardener so that he may see and talk with the Princess. His ardent love awakens in Flérida's heart an uncommon interest which turns into real affection after she drinks from an enchanted cup presented to her by him. She calls upon him to declare his identity, but he romantically prefers to gain her favor with the sacrifice that his humble station seems to involve. The play ends with a ballad, incomparable in its beauty, and they embark together into the great unknown. A sort of comic interlude which treats of the appearance of Camilote and Maimonda at the Emperor's court shows Vicente's critical spirit with a tendency to burlesque in handling his material, but in the main he deals with it sympathetically and surrounds his chief characters with a poetic atmosphere.

We have two versions of the play: [10] the first included in the *editio princeps* (1562) of the *Copilaçam,* and the second in the 1586 edition of his collected works with a dedicatory letter to King John III, which must go back to the original first edition of the play (1525). It seems that Vicente, contrary to his usual practice, wrote and had printed *Don Duardos* without having it performed, although it is quite possible that the play was presented, after its publication, to celebrate the marriage of the Infanta Isabel, John's sister, to the Emperor Charles on November 1, 1525.

In *Amadis de Gaula,* performed at Evora before King John in 1533, Vicente shows signs of weariness; perhaps he had become tired of writing, or possibly he was unable to find suitable material for a play in the novel. He chose the episode from the second book of *Amadis of Gaul* which deals with Oriana's cruel letter to Amadis, charging him with insincerity, his change of name to Beltenebros; and his retirement to a life of penance on the Peña Pobre until Oriana forgave him for the fancied wrong. This is a story which excited Don Quijote's overwrought mind and which he imitated partially (First Part, chapter xxv), but as material for a play, it wholly lacks dramatic possibilities. The grief of Amadis is too extravagant to awaken our sympathy, and we are not quite sure whether this picture of the hermit-knight was drawn in a serious or in a mocking mood.

Vicente's last play, the *Floresta de enganos,* performed at Evora in 1536 and written in Portuguese and Castilian,

is a bizarre composition. Preceded by an ingenious prologue in dialogue form, it presents a series of deceptions
and tricks with little relationship to one another. Two of
these, the trick played by a youth upon a merchant who
tried to deceive him, and the discomfiture of an unscrupulous
officer of justice, are conceived in the same spirit as Lope
de Rueda's *pasos.*

Among the farces of Gil Vicente we are here concerned
only with the *Farsa de los Gitanos* (probably performed at
Easter 1525), written entirely in Spanish, and the *Farça dos
Fisicos* (probably written at the end of 1524 or at the beginning of 1525), which contains a considerable amount of
Castilian. The former is a brief composition, without
much dramatic interest, presenting eight lisping gipsy characters, the girls who announce to imaginary clients their
skill in fortune telling, and the men who offer their services
as horse traders. The latter is an exceedingly witty satire
of the medical profession and of the lax morals of certain
members of the clergy. Four doctors, prominent figures
at Court, are called in to attend a priest, and make as many
diagnoses concerning the cause of his illness, without realiz-
ing that he has been brought to death's door by the curt
refusal of a woman to accept his love. He confesses the
truth to a friar, who reproaches him only for lack of patience, and comforts him by declaring that he is merely
obeying the Divine command to Adam that man shall for-
sake all for woman. This little play is a masterpiece of
cynical humor, and was written in the same anti-clerical
spirit as the *Jubileu de Amor,* with which it probably belongs in point of time.[11]

The *Farsa Salamantina* of Bartolomé Palau presents
once more the familiar incidents of the *Himenea,* and the
structure of the play in five *jornadas,* comic prologue, and
coplas de pie quebrado, reveals imitation of Naharro and
his followers. Palau shows unmistakable acquaintance with
Güete's *Tesorina,* for although the dates of both plays
are unknown, it is absolutely certain that, in view of the

similarities between them, the conventional type as represented by the *Tesorina* has been used by the author of the *Salamantina* who introduced certain original elements. Here the sentimental lover appears as a *pícaro*—an early mention of the word as *pícaro matriculado* is used in reference to the Estudiante's servant—and the romantic passion of Himeneo degenerates into a sordid abduction with robbery as a motive. There is no contrast between sentimentality and common sense, since both master and servant are anti-heroes and have the same ethical code, or lack of one. Most of the incidents might readily form a chapter of a picaresque novel.

The background of student life at Salamanca, with its discomforts, is vividly portrayed, and there is biting criticism of the contemporaneous standards of justice in the lackey's description of the harsh treatment accorded to servants. The only old edition known belongs to the year 1552, but since Palau refers to himself in the rubric as a " student of Burbáguena," a town in the province of Teruel, it is likely that it was written at approximately the same time as his first play, *Farsa llamada Custodia del hombre,* which was composed between 1540 and 1547. Five episodes in the play, which have little connection with the main plot, recall Lope de Rueda's use of the *paso,* and seem to indicate that he knew the plays of his illustrious contemporary. It has been conjectured that Rueda referred to Palau in describing the licentiate Jáquima in his *paso* entitled *El Convidado.*

The *Comedia Pródiga* of Luis de Miranda of Plasencia, printed at Seville in 1554 and possibly written shortly after 1532, presents in seven acts in *redondillas dobles* the Parable of the Prodigal Son, a favorite subject for school dramas throughout Western Europe. The author, soldier and cleric, expressly states his desire to show young men the consequences of dissolute conduct, and while we should not question his sincerity, it must be admitted that he describes with relish Pródigo's downfall. A victim of thievish parasites and unscrupulous harlots, the youth is speedily reduced to poverty and repentance, and returns to his father, richer only in experience. The author is skilful in presenting these picaresque characters, who were undoubtedly imitated from the *Celestina,* and the play has considerable human interest. It was probably performed at Plasencia, an important center for dramatic activity in the sixteenth century.

The first printed *Index librorum prohibitorum* was issued at Valladolid in 1559, which marks a convenient date to divide the sixteenth century into two parts. What Spanish plays were prohibited on that first list? Encina's *Plácida y Vitoriano,* including the *Vigilia de la enamorada muerta,* all of works of Torres Naharro included in the *Propalladia* with special condemnation of the *Aquilana* and *Jacinta,* Güete's *Tesorina, Tidea* of Francisco de las Natas, very likely Carvajal's *Josephina* and a number of other plays— at most a dozen—of which we know only the title. These unidentified plays whose titles appear on the 1559 *Index* may have been masterpieces, but I doubt it. When the *Index* was first issued, judging from contemporaneous criticism, the only protest was on behalf of the plays of Torres Naharro, which were printed in an expurgated version in 1573. It is probable also that Carvajal's *Josephina* was remembered forty-odd years after its name appeared on the first *Index* and attempts were made—unsuccessfully—to have the name removed.[12] With the exception of the two writers, the banning of the printed versions provoked apparently no interest whatever. In the case of Gil Vicente and of Lope de Rueda, however, whose works had not been printed before the appearance of the *Index,* permission to print after 1559 could only be granted if they met the dictates of the censorship in respect to theology and to moral standards.

VI

LOPE DE RUEDA. PASOS AND ITALIANATE COMEDY

WE have already noted that in the Nativity scene of Íñigo López de Mendoza's *Vita Christi,* and in the Christmas plays of Encina, Vicente, Fernández and their successors, shepherds appear whose quarrels and games enliven the presentation of incidents of sacred story, and whose ignorance served as a pretext for the explanation of theological doctrines. Singing and dancing were prominent features of these compositions, but only in Encina's second *Égloga en reqüesta de amores* are a song and dance used to separate two scenes. In a similar manner, the *Égloga de Plácida y Vitoriano* is divided into two parts by a song, and two shepherd's scenes are introduced for the sake of comic relief.[1]

In the course of time, the incidental comic scenes were developed with more detail and completeness until they possessed unity of action, without reference to the play of which they formed a part. Such, for example, is the trick played upon Gomecio by Lenicio at the opening of the fourth act of the *Serafina* of Naharro. An incident of the first act of the *Calamita* in which Jusquino convinces Torcazo of his supposed relationship to him, and the description of the trick by which Fileo relieves Torcazo of certain provisions, have dramatic unity, and above all, the ruse in the fifth act by which Jusquino persuades Torcazo to feign death, all resemble in content and in spirit the *pasos* of Rueda. A similar use of comic scenes, without organic connection with the main plot, is also found in the *Radiana* and *Tesorina.* The characters of these comic scenes, which later were to develop independently, are invariably taken from the lower classes of society.

Several plays of Diego Sánchez contain excellent examples of a brief action completely developed and with little relationship to the chief plot. In the *Farsa Teologal* a shepherd frightens a braggart soldier almost to death with a jack-o'-lantern, and the soldier finally explains that severe toothache had caused him to faint; whereupon an obliging dentist extracts two of his teeth before his hapless victim confesses the truth. The episode has dramatic unity, and the same is true of the scenes of the *Farsa Militar* that recall Timoneda's *Paso de dos ciegos y un moço.*

At least two of the later plays of Vicente show the development of a comic incident into a separate entity. The diverting episode of Ninguem and Todo o Mundo has no definite relationship with the *Auto da Lusitania* (1532), and the religious element in *Os mysterios da Virgem* (1534) is so completely overshadowed by the delightful interlude of *Mofina Mendes* that the latter gives to the play a new title.

It is evident that by the second or third decade of the sixteenth century a farcical scene with dramatic unity and with characters drawn from the lower classes was occasionally used for comic relief. We do not know how long before the middle of the century the term *paso* was applied to these independent scenes, nor at what period they were first regarded as a separate dramatic form. The same uncertainty exists with respect to the term *entremés,* which seems to have been first used in Valencian and Catalan territory, and which after being employed with the meaning of " entertainment " in its broadest sense, and later " show " or " pageant," finally became synonymous with *paso.*

The earliest recorded use of the name *entremés* with the meaning that was to prevail later, occurs in the prologue to the unnamed *comedia* by Sepúlveda (1547). The word is also used to designate an amusing scene in Horozco's *Representación de la historia evangélica del capítulo nono de Sanct Joan,* in which a lawyer completely fleeces a client before undertaking his case, and which belongs to approximately the same period. The last-named also wrote an *entremés* without title, performed at Toledo on St. John the Evangelist's day. This vivid picture of picaresque types, with its pronounced clerical satire, must have produced a strange impression upon the audience of nuns for which the author states that it was written!

While it is true that Lope de Rueda was not the creator of the *paso*, it cannot be doubted that he perfected this new literary form in Spain; not only that, he was the outstanding dramatist in Spain at the middle of the century, and was the first actor-manager of whom we have any record in the Spanish drama.

In the preface to his volume entitled *Ocho Comedias* (1615), Cervantes writes with enthusiasm of his youthful recollections of the plays of Lope de Rueda. "He was a native of Seville," says Cervantes, "and a gold-beater by trade. He was a marvel in pastoral poetry, and in that style he has not been surpassed by any one, either in his own day or since. I was only a boy then, and could not form a reliable judgment of the merits of his verse, but now at a mature age I have read some of the lines which have remained in my memory, and I find that what I have said is true. If it were not out of place to do so in this preface, I should quote here some lines which confirm my statement." After giving us valuable information concerning the staging of his plays, he continues: "Lope de Rueda died at Cordova, and because he was an excellent and famous man, they buried him in the cathedral of that city between the two choirs."

Recent investigations have contributed a few additional facts to his biography. We do not know when Rueda adopted the profession of actor, but by 1551 he had become a professional actor-manager, and he took part with his company in celebrating the return from Flanders of Prince Philip at Valladolid in July of that year. On that occasion he was entrusted with *el carro y danzas*. From that time until 1559 Rueda lived at Valladolid, acting there with his

company and occasionally traveling with it to some neighboring place, as he did in 1554 when he was called to perform a religious play at Benavente as part of the festivities
sponsored by the Count of Benavente in honor of Philip II,
who was en route to England to marry Queen Mary. From
1554 to 1557 Rueda was at Valladolid with his wife
Mariana, a strolling singer and dancer, as appears from
the curious court records of a suit brought by him against
Don Juan, heir to Don Gastón de la Cerda, Duke of
Medinaceli, for services rendered by Mariana from 1546
to 1552. In 1558 we find him performing *una gustosa
comedia* at the dedication of the new cathedral of Segovia,
and the following year his company presented two *autos*
entitled *El hijo pródigo* and *Navalcarmelo* at the Corpus
festival at Seville.[2]

He is said to have performed Corpus plays at Toledo
in 1561, and we find him in that year living at Madrid where
he received payments from the royal treasury for two plays
presented at the instance of the Queen. It was probably
in this year that Cervantes witnessed one or more of Rueda's
performances. The sojourn in Madrid was not financially
profitable, and in the latter part of 1561, the actor-manager
with his second wife, Rafaela Ángela Trilles, went to
Valencia, her birthplace. We do not know how long he
remained there, nor in what year he went to Cordova,
where he died in 1565.

The rise of traveling theatrical companies in Spain about
the middle of the century is a fact of great importance in
the development of the drama. There had been actors in
Spain before that time, but they were on a non-professional
basis, whether they were presenting secular or religious
plays. The earliest reference to professional actors occurs
in an edict promulgated by Charles V in 1534 against extravagance in dress, in which it is stated that the same
restrictions apply to *los comediantes hombres y mugeres,
músicos y las demás personas que asisten en las comedias* as
to other persons. This ill accords with the statement of

Cervantes concerning the meager stage properties used by
Rueda, and we may assume that the decree had in view
court entertainments rather than popular performances.
Theatres were, of course, unknown, and Rueda was willing
to play whenever an audience could be gathered in some
square or yard.

We shall first take up a collection of seven *pasos* of
Rueda *para poner en principios y entremedias de colloquios
y comedias*, which was printed at Valencia by Timoneda
with the title *El Deleitoso*. In a prefatory sonnet, the
editor uses *paso* and *entremés* as synonyms, but as a dramatic form *paso* is undeniably earlier. For example, in
the *Tres pasos de la Pasion*, printed in 1520, *paso* means
"incident" or "scene," while the first dramatic use of
entremés is found, as already stated, in 1547, but after the
middle of the sixteenth century *entremés* was gaining in
popularity when referring to a short play. In Rueda's
time, the *paso* or *entremés* might be used as an interlude or
as a prologue which replaced the old *introito*. Two *pasos*
included in *El Deleitoso*, the fifth and seventh, were suited
to serve as opening scenes, and the others for interludes.

The first in *El Deleitoso* deals with the inability of the
lackey Luquitas and the simpleton Alameda to explain to
Salcedo's satisfaction their long absence from home, and
ends in the conventional drubbing. The booby and the
master appear in the second *paso,* either because these
scenes originally formed part of the same play, or these
names were in a sense frequently used in Rueda's company
for the said parts. Here Salcedo plays upon the credulity
of Alameda, who proves in a moment of inspiration that
he is not so great a fool as his master believed. The third,
often called *Cornudo y contento*, describes the sacrifices
made by the credulous Martín to cure his wife of her illness, while she diverts herself with a young student. The
fourth, called by Moratín *El Convidado,* describes the em-
barrassment of an impecunious student who, after invit-
ing a fellow townsman to dinner, is obliged for financial

reasons to feign illness in order to cancel the engagement
gracefully, and is betrayed by another student in whom he
had confided. The scene was probably based upon an
actual occurrence, and is related as such in both *El Crotalón*
and *El Escolástico* of Cristóbal de Villalón. The fifth
shows how easily the gullible Mendrugo is robbed of his
provisions while he listens to a glowing account of the delights of the land of Cockayne. The seventh, commonly
called *Las Aceitunas*, describes a quarrel between man and
wife over the price they will ask for olives that are not yet
planted. The characters and situations are vividly real
and lifelike. It is the best *paso* or *entremés* written in
Spain in the sixteenth century, and the inclusion of *El olivar
de Lope de Rueda* in Correas' *Vocabulario* of proverbial
phrases gives an index of its popularity.

The six *pasos, así de lacayos como de simples y otras
diversas,* of Rueda *y otros diversos autores,* published by
Timoneda in 1570 in a volume entitled *Registro de representantes,* have less literary and dramatic merit but show
that the form has become fixed, with characters and situations which in the course of time became conventional.
The fourth, fifth, and sixth *pasos* are attributed to Rueda
by Timoneda, and the first three *pasos* are printed without
any indication of authorship.

The fourth in the *Registro* tells wittily of a cutpurse who
is unable to avoid prison in spite of a glib tongue. A reference to the battle of St. Quentin shows that it was written
after 1557. The fifth is a *paso de rufián cobarde,* which
closely resembles the second scene of the *Eufemia* of Rueda,
but the figure of Sebastiana, Sigüenza's mistress, who takes
advantage of his cowardice to make off with Estepa, lends
a note of added merriment. The theme of the sixth is the
unsuccessful attempt of the simpleton Pancorbo to shift
upon another the responsibility for having eaten a pound
of sweets.

The first three *pasos* in the *Registro* were presumably
not written by Rueda, and are dull, witless compositions

when compared with his work. The first presents a scene frequently found in later *entremeses* in which a roguish servant, aided by a blockhead, attempts to prescribe for their master's patients during his absence, with lamentable consequences. The second describes the success of two students in a school for thieves in relieving a dolt of his provisions by a clever trick. In the third, the blockhead Rodrigo de Toro uses the argument of a club to escape from a trap that has been set for him.

In these compositions, no attempt is made to create a background nor to study character. The length of the action is the same as the time required to present it, and no more. There is no exposition of a plot, for the action is too rapid, and besides, the situation is never complex. A couple of hungry fellows may meet a peasant carrying provisions. The audience knows at once without explanation that there will be a contest of wits, with the food as a prize. The basis of these scenes is usually a time-worn deception or practical joke, which was susceptible of countless new settings and variations.

The *Entremés del mundo y no nadie,* attributed to Lope de Rueda in the manuscript in which it is preserved, apparently was written to introduce a religious play. Here the thesis that to him that hath shall be given is illustrated by a brief scene between Mundo and No Nadie, which even in its crude form resembles versions of the Somebody and Nobody conceit found in other literatures. It shows none of the characteristics of Rueda's *pasos,* and its verse form —in *quintillas* with some prose portions—is also an argument against his authorship. The fact that his name occurs as one of the characters merely shows his popularity as an actor and playwright.

It is unfortunate that we do not possess the original text of Rueda's comedies. These were published in 1567 by Timoneda who states in the preface to the *Eufemia* and *Armelina* that he had changed certain portions of the original manuscript before soliciting permission to print, omitting *algunas cosas no lícitas y mal sonantes, que algunos en vida de Lope habrán oído.* In the preface to the *Comedia de los engañados* and the *Medora,* the same editor complains of the labor involved in making many corrections in the original. We are unable to determine whether Timoneda limited himself to changes of minor importance or whether he actually attempted to rewrite the plays.

We have not sufficient evidence to assign dates to the composition of these four comedies, nor even to determine their chronological order, but it is likely that the *Medora* was first, because of its faulty construction and lack of originality. Here Rueda made free use of *La Zingana* by the Italian poet-painter Gigio Arthemio Giancarli, which was performed at Ferrara and Mantua, and was first printed in 1545 or 1546. This play, in five acts and in prose, is one of the most curious dialectal comedies of the Cinquecento; one character speaks a medley of Greek and Italian, another Venetian, others speak Bergamask, Paduan, and a gipsy dialect, while the rest talk Italian. The plot turns on the resemblance of twins, a boy and a girl, and the identification finally effected by a gipsy woman who had stolen the boy from his cradle, and the chief sources are the *Menaechmi* and *La Calandria.* It seems to have enjoyed unusual popularity in Italy, and its influence upon a number of later compositions has been noted. Rueda retained the main incidents, but omitted many scenes of minor importance, and added four new characters, the *rufianes* Peñalva and Logroño, the blockhead Ortega and the page Perico. He also gave increased importance to the braggart Gargullo, a part in which he excelled, and he invented a few comic scenes which may be classified as *pasos.*

Two cases of mistaken identity, which recall the plots of two Italian plays, *Il Servigiale* of Giovan Maria Cecchi and *Altilia* of Anton Francesco Raineri, form the basis of the *Comedia Armelina.* The anagnorisis is brought about by Neptune who, after saving Armelina from a misalliance with a shoemaker, restores to one father a long-lost daugh-

ter and to another a long-lost son.   Whatever may be the
debt of Rueda to the above-mentioned Italian dramatists,
the play is redeemed from utter absurdity by a few comic
scenes of his own invention.   Lope de Vega had this play
in mind when he wrote in *El arte nuevo de hacer comedias*
about Rueda's prose comedies which introduced tradespeople and the love-affair of a smith's daughter.

In writing *Los Engañados*, Rueda made a free version
of the anonymous *Gl' Ingannati*, one of the best Italian
comedies of the Cinquecento, and first performed by the
Intronati of Siena in 1531.   *Gl' Ingannati* was first printed
in 1537, and its success is attested by many editions; by its
translation into Latin by Juan Pérez with the title *Decepti*
(1574), by an anonymous Latin version made in England
about twenty years later with the title *Laelia*, and by the
fact that it was the direct or indirect source of *Twelfth
Night* and other plays.

For the five acts of *Gl' Ingannati*, he substituted a division into ten scenes.   Finding his Italian original too long
for his purpose, he suppressed many relatively unimportant
incidents and concentrated the interest upon the love of the
girl-page Lelia for Lauro, and the complications arising
from the resemblance between Lelia and her brother
Fabricio.   Certain scenes were omitted in the interest of
decency, while the comic elements, with the *bobos* Pajares
and Salamanca and the negress Guiomar as the chief characters, are almost entirely original.   In his adaptation,
Rueda showed himself a good judge of dramatic values,
but the play does not rise above the level of an ingenious
comedy of intrigue.   It is obviously unfair to compare
Rueda with Shakespeare, but it is nevertheless true that *Los
Engañados* would give us more enjoyment if *Twelfth Night*
had not been written.   The incidents are sufficiently similar
for us to expect Viola and the Duke when it is only Lelia
and Lauro, and Rueda's clowns are poor substitutes for Sir
Toby and Sir Andrew.   *Los Engañados* presents a few

romantic situations, but is devoid of the saving grace of charm and poetic fancy.

It is likely that Montemayor saw a performance of *Los Engañados* by Rueda's company at Valladolid. Finding it interesting, he retold it in a simpler form, and included it as the story of Felix and Felismena as a part of *La Diana* on which he was engaged at that time. Rueda's play had, of course, ended as a comedy, but Montemayor made it end unhappily as being more in harmony with the tone in a pastoral novel. And Shakespeare, as is well known, was so fond of *La Diana* that the story of Felix and Felismena was used in writing the *Two Gentlemen of Verona*.

Greater originality is shown in the composition of *Eufemia* which, like *Cymbeline*, is a free version of the ninth story of the second Day of the *Decameron;* as a matter of fact, Rueda simplified and altered Boccaccio's *novella* so that it is well-nigh unrecognizable. In the latter version, the testing of a woman's virtue and the false charge brought against her are the result of a wager, while in Rueda's play jealousy is the motive for the attempt to discredit the heroine. In *Eufemia,* the protagonists are a brother and sister, and in the *Decameron* a husband and wife. The wanderings of the outraged wife, which occupy so important a place in Boccaccio's version, are not found in Rueda's play, and the *dénouement* is entirely different. There are few scenes in the early Spanish drama more compelling than when Eufemia confronts her traducer and ingeniously extorts from him an acknowledgment of her innocence. Aside from the parallel situations of the husband and wife in Boccaccio's story and the brother and sister in Rueda's play, the chief point of contact lies in the manner in which the false evidence is obtained, and other scenes, whether they be grave or comic, must be regarded as Rueda's own invention. The fifteenth tale of Timoneda's *Patrañuelo* (1567) contains another version of the story which shows that the author followed Boccaccio's story far more closely than was done by Rueda.

It will be recalled that Cervantes praised inordinately
Rueda's pastoral verse, but his few extant pastoral compositions in no way deserve so high a praise, and furthermore we have few examples of his use of verse. We have
two long pastoral colloquies in prose, with occasional
snatches of verse, published together with the four comedies
by Timoneda in 1567, which have only a superficial relationship with the conventions of the earlier Spanish pastoral drama. The first scenes of the *Coloquio de Camila*
attempt to reproduce the artificial pastoral setting of
Sannazzaro's *Arcadia* or of Montemayor's *Diana*, but the
plot repeats, with few changes, the tiresome incidents of
the *Comedia Armelina*. A reference in the play to the
carretón del Hijo pródigo probably alludes to the play that
was given by Rueda's company on the Corpus Christi festival in Seville in 1559. In the *Coloquio de Tymbria*, dis-
enchantments alter so frequently the identity and sex of the
principal characters that the patient reader reaches the
finale with patience exhausted.

An appendix to Timoneda's edition of Rueda's comedies
and colloquies contains a list of the *pasos* included which
might be transferred to other compositions. This clearly
indicates that these farcical scenes were regarded as independent entities, which might be used in any play without
reference to the original context. The *Armelina* contains
one episode of this sort, in which Mencieta attempts to cure
the simpleton Guadalupe of chronic drowsiness, and the
Comedia de los Engañados has another in which the stupidity of Pajares furnishes the chief comic element. In
the *Eufemia*, there is the amusing *paso* of the *rufián cobarde*
Vallejo in the second scene, and the one between the lackey
Polo and the Negress Eulalla in the same play serves the
purpose of allowing the audience to feel that a sufficient
time has elapsed to allow characters to travel a considerable
distance. *Medora* opens with a highly diverting *paso* of
the discomfiture of the *rufián cobarde* Gargullo, and the
second and fourth scenes of the same play present bits of

roguery which are so frequently found in these detachable actions. The *Coloquio de Camila* includes two *pasos*, and whatever interest the *Coloquio de Tymbria* may possess is due to its *pasos*. In time, the use of certain characters in these brief episodes became conventional, and in the preface to his *Ocho Comedias*, Cervantes speaks of the skill of Rueda in acting *entremeses de negra, de rufián, de bobo y de vizcaíno*.

Rueda's *Coloquio llamado Prendas de amor* was included in the volume entitled *Registro de representantes* (1570), and is written in *quintillas*. Two shepherds, Menandro and Simón, have received gifts from the shepherdess Cilena, and fall into a dispute as to which has obtained the greater mark of her affection. When they refer the question for decision to her, the maiden answers by giving to each another present. This *questione d'amore*, as it was termed in Italy, is somewhat similar to the first question of Boccaccio's *Filocolo*, as we shall see later in discussing the prologue to Timoneda's *Amphitrión*. Rueda was lacking in poetic fancy which was required to redeem from banality these trivial scenes. His power lay rather in portraying characters drawn from everyday life, and in reproducing in inimitable dialogue the popular speech of his day.

A brief *Diálogo sobre las calzas*, written in *quintillas*, printed in the volume of comedies and colloquies, and a fragment of thirty-five lines in *quintillas* which Cervantes inserted in his *Los baños de Argel*, are the only other certain examples of Rueda's verse. It is very probable, as mentioned by Schevill and Bonilla in their edition of the plays of Cervantes,[3] that they belong to a colloquy called *Gila* of which Lope de Vega cites two *quintillas* in the introduction to the *Justa poética* to honor St. Isidro (1621).

Another pastoral play, *Comedia llamada Discordia y qüestión de amor*, also in *quintillas*, is known only in an edition of 1617 where it is ascribed to Lope de Rueda, "representante." We have no reason to doubt his authorship, for the play undoubtedly belongs to the period when

he was writing, but someone, on printing it later, divided
it into three *jornadas* to accord better with the practice of
the time.   The play presents the same circle of unhappy
lovers [4] that we find in the sixth *Idyl* of Moschus, in the
story of Selvagia of Montemayor's *Diana,* in Vicente's
Auto pastoril portuguez, and in several Italian plays, and
which is familiar to all from its use in *As You Like It.*
With this motive is combined the triumph of Chastity over
Cupid.

To understand properly his dramatic work, we must
realize that he looked upon plays, not solely from the
author's standpoint, but from the actor's and manager's as
well, and that he regarded as of prime importance the entertainment of an audience that would gather on the town
or village square.   Earlier secular plays were written to
be performed before gentlefolk on the occasion of some
wedding or other festivity, but Rueda, after writing a play,
rehearsed it, took a part himself, paid his company and, no
doubt, eagerly looked forward to have a few reales for
himself after the play was ended.

Rueda knew that comedy of intrigue with romantic incidents, interspersed with farcical scenes and horseplay, would
please, and he found some of these elements in the Italian
comedy of his time.   We know that a certain Muzio, with
a company of Italian players, took part in the Corpus festival at Seville in 1538, and that one of Ariosto's comedies
was performed at Valladolid in 1548, presumably by an
Italian company, at the marriage of the Infanta Maria,
daughter of Charles V, to Maximilian, Prince of Hungary.
Also, sometime between 1556 and 1559, Antonio Vignali,
a member of the Accademia degli Intronati of Siena, presented plays at the court of Philip II.   It is reasonable to
suppose that Rueda became acquainted with Italian plays
through the repertory of some itinerant Italian troupe.
At all events, he wrote as a professional playwright, with
more consideration for the requirements of his audience
than care in interpreting faithfully his original if it were

composed in Italian. He realized, too, that humor is essentially local in its appeal, and he usually replaced comic scenes in the Italian that he recast by others of his own invention. It is particularly in these scenes that he shows a mastery of dialogue and a knowledge of the resources of popular speech unsurpassed in Spain of the sixteenth century.

As Torres Naharro occupies first place in the drama of the first half of the century, Lope de Rueda is the dominant figure among the playwrights about the middle of the century. His use of prose constituted an innovation that was followed by Timoneda, Sepúlveda, and Alonso de la Vega, and which, fortunately, was abandoned by later dramatists. For the division into five acts used by some of his predecessors, he substituted a varying number of scenes. His conception of humor was far more primitive than Naharro's. His aim was to provoke loud laughter, and to gain this end, he used the most obvious means, the stupidity and impertinence of a booby, the cowardice of a braggart, and the unintelligible jargon of a Negress, a Moor, or a Biscayan. We do not know to what extent he may be regarded as the creator of these comic types, but there is no doubt that he made them popular. He is important in having enlarged the scope of the comedy of intrigue, but his chief contribution lies in the creation or perfecting of the *entremés*. He was skilful in presenting his characters quarreling, and in these wordy brawls he reflected the popular environment and at the same time shows a delightful sense of humor.

The plays of Rueda were written at a time when the influence of Italian literature was predominant in almost every field of literary activity, and the temporary vogue of Italian comedy in Spain was as inevitable as in France and England where Pierre de Larivey and George Gascoigne likewise laid tribute upon Italian models. The lyric poets, such as Cetina and Acuña, were following the example of Boscán and Garcilaso, and were imitating the Italian poets in form and content. Even the old ballads had difficulty in competing successfully with the translations and imitations of Boiardo and Ariosto, and Italian novels were appearing in Spanish dress.

One of the best comedies of intrigue composed in Spain before the time of Lope de Vega is a *comedia* without title by a certain Sepúlveda, preserved in a manuscript dated at Seville, 1547. It consists of four acts in prose, and is introduced by a prologue in which two friends are represented as discussing the play and its author before witnessing the performance. As in *Los Engañados,* the plot turns on the disguise of page adopted by a young girl in order to be near her indifferent lover, and the discovery by her father of another young woman who had been lost in childhood. Besides, there is the resourceful lackey who is willing to appear to encourage the ridiculous pretensions of an old man in return for generous payment, and who succeeds in effecting the complete discomfiture of a necromancer, his accomplice. The prologue contains a defense of the art of playwriting and an interesting appreciation of the excellence of Italian comedy. The author speaks with some experience, for his own play, including the prologue, is a free version of *Il Viluppo,* by the well-known Italian dramatist and novelist Girolamo Parabosco, first printed at Venice in 1547.

The reduction of the five acts of *Il Viluppo* to four involved changes in arrangement, particularly in the third act, but in general the order of scenes is retained, and most of them are close adaptations of the Italian text. Unlike Rueda in his versions of Italian comedies, Sepúlveda introduces no new comic scenes. It is true, however, that he dealt with his original in a critical spirit, and displayed a real dramatic sense. He showed good judgment in omitting unnecessary monologues and in suppressing the scenes in which the bawd Colombina appears. He also rearranged the scenes of the last act, making a more effective *dénouement* than in Parabosco's play. The prologue contains some original material, including the earliest Spanish reference with which I am acquainted to the dramatic unity of time, and one of the first recorded uses of the term *entremés* as synonymous with *paso*.

It is unfortunate that we have not sufficient evidence to identify the author. His acquaintance with Latin writers and classical mythology is proven by many references, and in one amusing scene he criticizes the superficiality of Greek studies at that time, which implies some knowledge of that language. His own prose is marked by dignity and grace, and gives evidence of a thorough mastery of colloquial speech at its best. The dialogue is natural and in good taste, and his comic scenes never degenerate into the non-sense that mars so many plays of his time. With respect to style and construction, this *comedia* is vastly superior to any play by Timoneda or by Alonso de la Vega, and is not surpassed, in my opinion, by any play of Lope de Rueda.

Juan Timoneda has many points of contact with Spanish literary history about the middle of the sixteenth century. Combining a keen business instinct with a love of letters, he carried on successfully a bookselling and publishing business at Valencia, and printed a number of books of real literary value. As we know, he was the editor and publisher of the plays of Lope de Rueda which appeared in 1567 and in 1570, and to him is due the publication of the three plays of Alonso de la Vega. Furthermore, he himself wrote plays and was possibly an actor and manager as well; he collected and issued short stories gathered from many sources, and was a pioneer in collecting old ballads.

In 1559 he printed a volume that included the *Comedia de Amphitrión, Comedia de los Menemnos* and *Comedia de Cornelia* (or *Carmelia*). He states in the preface that he has attempted to combine the use of prose after the fashion of the *Celestina* with the actable quality of the plays of Torres Naharro.

Amphitrión contains a prologue which presents in dramatic form a subtle question of love. An old shepherd, named Bromio, urges his daughter Pascuala to declare her preference for one of her suitors, Morato or Roseno, both

of whom have served her faithfully. The maiden replies
that she will indicate her choice by a sign, and gives to one
her garland and accepts a wreath from the other. After
her departure, the lovers dispute as to the meaning of her
enigmatical reply, and the audience is asked to decide which
suitor has been favored.

This casuistical discussion is derived from the first question in the fourth part of Boccaccio's *Filocolo*. It will be
recalled that while searching for Biancofiore, Filocolo has
to take refuge from a storm at Naples, where he is cor-
dially welcomed by Fiammetta and her merry companions.
One afternoon, Fiammetta suggests that they amuse themselves by proposing *questioni d'amore* to a king who will
be elected by her comrades. She herself, however, is
chosen as queen, and thirteen subtle questions are offered
of the same type as the troubadours discussed in their *jocs-
partitz*. The first is practically identical with the subject
treated in the prologue of Timoneda's *Amphitrión*. The
dramatic presentation of these *questioni d'amore* was not
uncommon in aristocratic circles in Italy, and we know that
this same problem was the basis of a brief play presented
before Isabella del Balzo, Queen of Naples, sometime prior
to 1497. Timoneda may have known the *Filocolo* in its
original text, or he may have been acquainted with the
Thirteen Questions in the Spanish version by Diego López
de Ayala and Diego de Salazar and printed at Seville in
1546 with the title *Laberinto de Amor,* and again at Toledo
in the same year with the name *Trece qüestiones muy gracio-
sas sacadas del Philoculo del famoso Juan Bocacio.*

Cervantes knew the prologue to Timoneda's *Amphitrión*,[5]
and used it in composing a scene of the third *jornada* of *La
Entretenida* (1606–1608). With characteristic good humor and sanity, Cervantes transformed the courtly *questione
d'amore* of two gallants who are ardently enamored of a
lady, into a pair of faint-hearted bullies who are in love
with a kitchen wench, and as she enters, certain that at least
one of her lovers is dead, she finds that both are amicably

discussing the matter in a wineshop. The whole scene is a take-off on the aristocratic notions of the unsubstantial *caso de amor* when reduced to terms of everyday life. Cervantes apparently thought well of the scene of Cristina and her two lovers, and tried his hand with the same situation in an *entremés*, *La guarda cuydadosa* (1611). Cristina appears as Cristinica who performs the same jobs in the kitchen, but instead of the two lackeys, their places are taken by a young sacristan and an old soldier, both of whom are in love with Cristinica. The lackeys were only sketched in *La Entretenida*, but in *La guarda cuydadosa* their substitutes have acquired life, vigor, variety, and abundant humor.

After so long a digression, let us turn again to the *Comedia de Amphitrión* which bears the rubric, *traduzida por Juan Timoneda, y puesta en estilo que se puede representar*. The second half of the statement is correct, but the first half must be interpreted only in broad terms. Timoneda did not translate the *Amphitruo*, but made an acting version of the translation by Francisco López de Villalobos (1515). This is proved by many cases of verbal similarity, and by the use as his last scene of a spurious addition which is also found in the version of Villalobos.

Timoneda was not a humanist, and was not moved by scholarly zeal to introduce Plautus to a Valencian audience. This witty comedy of adultery, with its equivocal situations, provided him with an interesting plot which he adapted to suit his own needs. The slave Sosia, here baptized Sosia Tardío, has many characteristics of the conventional *bobo* and is more completely Spanish than the other personages. He knows the proverbs of Spain, revels like a true Valencian in olives and rice, and makes many allusions to local customs. By his fidelity to his master and his materialistic philosophy he is a worthy forerunner of the immortal Sancho Panza.

Timoneda's *Amphitrión* and *Los Menemnos* were the first appearance of Plautus on the Spanish stage, as the translation of López de Villalobos was the first rendering

of Plautus in Castilian.   A second free translation of the
Amphitruo was made by Maestro Hernán Pérez de Oliva,
published about 1525, entitled *Muestra de la lengua castellana en el nascimiento de Hércules, o Comedia de Amphitrión.*   It is apparent from the title and dedication that
this youthful effort should be regarded only as an experiment, and does not deserve the harsh criticism that has
been made by Moratín and some other literary historians.
Oliva introduces many changes in his comedy, suppressing
certain scenes with the object of condensing the material
and expanding others, as a consequence of which the dramatic art of Plautus is replaced by Oliva's rhetoric.   Another version by an anonymous writer was printed at Toledo
in 1554 in which the translator says that he had made use
of the versions of Villalobos and Oliva.   Anonymous translations of the *Miles Gloriosus* and *Menæchmi,* printed at
Antwerp in 1555, and Pedro Simón Abril's excellent version
of the six comedies of Terence, first published in 1577,
complete the list of printed Spanish translations of Latin
comedy in the sixteenth century.

The *Comedia de los Menemnos* is preceded by a prologue
in which three shepherds, enamored of the shepherdess
Temisa, present themselves before Cupid and ask him to
decide which the maiden should prefer.   Claudino has
boasted of his physical strength, Climaco has assured her
of his sincerity and generosity, while Ginebro has urged his
suit because of his prudence and wisdom.   Cupid approves
her choice of Ginebro, declaring that neither the strength of
Hercules nor the generosity of Alexander will satisfy a
woman of judgment.   The disappointed suitors, strange
to say, are satisfied with the decision, and recite the argument of the play.   The source of this prologue is the third
questione d'amore of the *Filocolo.*

In the *Comedia de los Menemnos* he shows more independence in dealing with his original.   While the principal
features of the plot of the *Menæchmi* have been retained,
a number of unimportant scenes have been omitted or

abridged, two new scenes have been added, and the play
has been given a Spanish atmosphere.   The doctor of the
Menæchmi is transformed through the influence of Ariosto
into the necromancer Averroyz, and the scenes in which he
takes part are among the best in the play.   Averroyz is
accompanied by a boy named Lazarillo whose relationship
to the famous rogue is vouched for by the doctor himself.
It shows considerable dramatic skill, the situations are
logically constructed, and the action moves along rapidly.
It is hardly reasonable to suppose that Timoneda knew
enough Latin to translate the *Menæchmi,* or at least would
have bothered to translate it when he probably had avail-
able for his purpose the Castilian translation printed at
Antwerp in 1555, or one of the Italian translations.

The *Comedia de Carmelia* (or *Cornelia*) is introduced
by a *caso de amor* that is analogous to the prologues of the
other two.   The play itself is an ingenious comedy of intrigue.   Lupercio is negotiating for the marriage of his
son Fulvio to Carmelia, who is thought to be the daughter
of Polianteo, but the young people have good reasons for
opposing the match.   Carmelia had secretly married
Taucio, son of Polianteo, three years before, and in spite
of his long absence, she still hopes for his return, while
Fulvio has for a mistress Mencía de Logroño, wife of the
doltish Cornalla.   The unexpected appearance of the necromancer Pasquín brings about a solution of all these
difficulties.   Lupercio engages him to cure Fulvio of a
malady that threatens to prevent his marriage; Fulvio
bribes him to keep as a secret that his illness is feigned;
and Taucio enlists his aid to recover his missing Carmelia.
The charlatan succeeds, by rare good fortune, in satisfying
everyone.   He reunites Taucio and Carmelia, and proves
that the latter is the long-lost daughter of Leonardo.   Besides the figures of the necromancer and his attendant, the
Comedia de Carmelia has other points of resemblance with
Ariosto's *Il Negromante.*   In both plays, the expedient of
a sham illness is used to prevent a marriage, and in each

case the young man's father applies to a charlatan to cure his sickness. From a reference to the capture of Bugia by the Moors, its date must be placed after 1555.

In his book on the drama at Valencia,[6] Mérimée calls attention to the fact that while the title is *Comedia de Cornelia*, the lady's name, except in three cases, appears as *Carmelia*, and furthermore, while Valencia is supposed to be the setting, the local color is almost exclusively Castilian. He suggests that a play with Castilian background, probably based on Italian materials, fell into Timoneda's hands and was revised by him and published as his own work. For my part, I doubt whether we have sufficient evidence to deny to Timoneda its authorship. The confusion of names is not important, and so far as the local color is concerned, it might be argued that Timoneda wrote it for some traveling company and adapted his local allusions to a Castilian audience. The play seems to me to give evidence of the same skill in construction and dialogue that we find in some of the original scenes of the *Amphitrión* and the *Menemnos*.

The title-page of the *Comedia de Amphitrión* states that the play contains *graciosos passos*, but Timoneda evidently used the term in the sense of "incident," as it had been used by Villalobos in the preface to his version of *Amphitruo*, since neither *Amphitrión* nor the *Menemnos* includes irrelevant comic episodes with dramatic unity. In the *Carmelia*, there is a *paso de comedia* about the unfortunate Cornalla which recalls Rueda's piece *Cornudo y contento*, included in the third of *El Deleitoso*.

In 1565 a volume entitled *Turiana*, containing six plays, namely, *Comedia Filomena*, *Farça Paliana*, *Comedia Aurelia*, *Farça Trapacera*, *Farça Rosalina* and *Farça Floriana*, and a number of *entremeses*, was published at Valencia by Joan Diamonte, an obvious anagram of Timoneda. The printing of the volume was delayed for some reason, since the first three plays bear the date 1564. All these plays are in verse and, with the possible exception of the *Farça*

Trapacera, are far inferior to any dramatic work published by Timoneda under his own name.   We have no right, and it would be manifestly unjust, to ascribe to him authorship which he himself did not claim.

The prologue to the *Comedia Filomena* promises us an unfamiliar theme, which turns out to be the well-known story of the violation of Philomela, narrated by Ovid.   The impertinence of the inevitable simpleton fails to relieve the gruesome details of the play which is, from every point of view, ridiculous.

The impression created on the reader of the *Farça Paliana* is akin to the nightmare of the first scene, the consequences of which are developed throughout the play.   The action covers some twenty years, beginning with the exposure of a newly born baby by its parents, and ending with its ultimate recovery under preposterous circumstance.   It has not a single redeeming quality.

The influence of Torres Naharro is seen in the division into five acts of the *Comedia Aurelia,* which on internal evidence may be ascribed to the early part of 1560.   The exposition is given in the first act, the *dénouement* in the fifth, and the interval is filled up with wholly irrelevant matter.   The plot, which deals with the recovery of the missing half of a ring, thus enabling a brother and sister to gain possession of their patrimony, is highly fantastic and hardly deserves notice.   A *paso* in which a Portuguese, Spaniard, Basque, and a Frenchman discuss in an almost unintelligible jargon questions of national honor recalls a similar incident in the *Tinellaria,* and there are also minor resemblances with the *Aquilana* and *Jacinta* of Naharro.

By far the best of the plays included in *Turiana* is the *Farça Trapacera,* which unfortunately is extant only in an incomplete form.   This is a close adaptation of Ariosto's *La Lena,*[1] and owes most of its interest to its diverting original.

The *Farça Rosalina* is essentially undramatic.   In the first scene, two friends who have suffered much from the

hand of Fate determine to renounce the world and, toward
the end of the play, reach a monastery after resisting successfully the assaults of the world. The few pages that
have been preserved of the *Farça Floriana,* the last play
included in the *Turiana,* are not sufficient for us to form
any judgment concerning its nature or value.

The same volume contains five *passos y entremeses* in
verse, which the editor declares were intended as introductory scenes or curtain-raisers. The *Entremés de un
ciego y un moço y un pobre* presents a blind man asking for
alms, and who blames his non-success upon Hernandillo,
his guide. The latter shows no concern over the threats
of a thrashing, and makes sport of his master when he tries
to pitch his voice in a particularly pathetic key. A com-
petitor appears in the person of another beggar; they begin
to abuse one another and finally come to blows. The influence of *Lazarillo de Tormes* is still more marked in the
Paso de dos ciegos y un moço, which served as a curtain-
raiser to some Christmas play. Palillos enters, saying that
he hopes to find a master in the audience, and telling of his
qualifications. He is not a thief, he declares, but he was
obliged to steal six ducats from his last master, a blind man
who nearly starved him to death. As he describes the
theft, two blind men approach asking for alms, and in one
of them Palillos discovers his late master. The trick that
he plays upon them is not original because Timoneda told
it in his twelfth *patraña,* and in French literature the jest
goes back at least to *Le Garçon et l'Aveugle* (1270), but
in the arrangement of the incidents and in the individuality
given to Palillos, this can stand comparison with any of
Lazarillo's experiences.

The *Passo de dos clérigos, cura y beneficiado, y dos moços
suyos simples* treats, after the fashion of Diego Sánchez, of
a quarrel between two unworthy members of the clergy
concerning their respective duties. In the *Passo de un
soldado, un moro y un hermitaño,* a Moor is the victim of
a clever trick played upon him by a soldier. The *Passo de*

la Razón y la Fama y el Tiempo is a unique example of an
entremés dealing with allegorical and serious material. It
is a free imitation of Petrarch's *Trionfi.*

Timoneda's interest in the stage was likewise responsible
for the preservation of three plays in prose by Alonso de la
Vega, namely, the *Comedia Tholomea, Tragedia Seraphina,*
and *Comedia de la Duquesa de la Rosa,* published by him
in 1566. We know little of this dramatist, save that he
was an actor and died at Valencia between 1560 and 1566.
The *Comedia Tholomea* is based upon the unexplained resemblance between two youths, both named Tholomeo, and
the confusion in identity resulting from the substitution of
one for the other by their nurse. It recalls the 116th tale
of the *Gesta Romanorum.* The *dénouement* is far less
convincing than in the first story of Timoneda's *Patrañuelo*
(1567) which deals with the same story, and which specifically states, *Deste cuento pasado hay hecha comedia, que
se llama Tholomea.* It is impossible to speak with certainty as to the priority of one or the other version, but I
think it reasonable to suppose that Timoneda got his story
from some Italian tale or comedy, and when it was in
manuscript Alonso de la Vega read it and used it in writing
his play, giving it the extravagant ending with its mythological characters and unreal episodes. The comic scenes
clearly show the influence of Lope de Rueda.

The *Tragedia Seraphina* is a completely unsuccessful attempt to give a pastoral and mythological setting to a
comedy of intrigue. As Menéndez y Pelayo said, the
poetical idea of a maiden enamored of Cupid and the death
of the two lovers in a lonely forest contains the elements
of a lyrical drama of real beauty, but the concept was too
fragile to stand the strain of the lumbering nonsense of the
comic figures.

Far superior is the *Comedia de la Duquesa de la Rosa,*
which is introduced by a *caso de amor* with pastoral setting
analogous to the prologues of Timoneda's three comedies.
This play, as well as the seventh *patraña* of Timoneda, is

based upon Bandello's story entitled *Amore di Don Gio-vanni di Mendozza e della Duchessa di Savoja,* or upon some text derived from it. However, Alonso de la Vega attributes to the duchess a dignity and nobility of character which she, does not possess in the other versions. Her passion, as Menéndez y Pelayo says in his excellent appre-ciation, is the chaste recollection of an innocent love of childhood, and her pilgrimage is an act of piety. When she meets Dulcelyrio at Burgos, no sign of recognition is given, save that he offers her a cup containing the ring she had given him years before when he was taking leave of her father's court. Alonso de la Vega rarely rises above mediocrity, but in a few scenes of this play he shows a capacity for poetic feeling and delicate fancy.

The influence of Rueda is apparent in the anonymous *Farsa llamada Rosiela,* printed in 1558, in six-line *coplas de pie quebrado.* The play rests upon a case of mistaken identity, and its theme is that gentility must reveal itself whatever be one's accidental station in life. It bears a certain resemblance to many plays of the following century which have a *príncipe villano* as the central figure. Bonilla y San Martín called attention to the fact that the *Farsa Rosiela* is somewhat similar to Timoneda's thirteenth *patraña,* and the lost play *La Feliciana.*[8]

The well-known story of Griselda was dramatized by a certain Navarro in his *Comedia muy exemplar de la mar-quesa de Saluzia, llamada Griselda,* printed in 1603. An actor, manager, and playwright named Pedro Navarro, contemporaneous with Rueda, was praised enthusiastically by Cervantes, Rojas Villandrando, and Lope de Vega, and while there is nothing in this play to justify such eulogies, his identification with the author of this play is probably correct. Its immediate source is not the *Decameron,* but Foresti's *Supplementum chronicorum orbis ab initio mundi,* which was translated into Spanish by Viñoles in 1510, and also Timoneda's second story of the *Patrañuelo,* based upon

Petrarch's Latin version. The play defies unity of time, for it opens with Galtero's offer of marriage to Griselda, and ends with the restitution of her child twelve years later. It requires Griselda-like patience to read the five *jornadas* of this bungling adaptation of Boccaccio's story. Its strophic form is a loose *copla real*.

A few anonymous *entremeses* have been published from sixteenth-century manuscripts. The most important of these is the *Entremés de las esteras,* contained in the well-known codex of ninety-six plays, of which this is the only secular one, preserved at the Biblioteca Nacional. This describes effectively the possible embarrassments that attend love-making in the kitchen. The *Entremés del Estrólogo borracho*, probably of the year 1583, is a rare example of the use of drunkenness on the early Spanish stage for comic effect. Two *entremeses* without title treat the familiar theme of the deceits practised by a wife upon a stupid husband, and the *Entremés de un viejo que es casado con una mujer moza,* which has a similar popular basis, but is not derived from the *Decamerone* [9] as has been held. A *rufián cobarde* plays the leading part in the *Entremés de un muchacho llamado Golondrino,* and the cunning exploits of thieves are described in the *Segundo entremés del Testamento de los ladrones.* As has been pointed out,[10] the *Segundo entremés de Pero Hernández* must belong to the early seventeenth century. All of these were written in prose.

An early example of improvised farce occurs in the *Entremés de un hijo que negó a su padre* in which the text states, for example, in the course of the dialogue, " The rustic may say whatever occurs to him and then his master says," and " Here the rustic applies to him such abusive epithets as suit him best, and asks permission to sing him a few stanzas, and the other replies to him." Obviously such statements refer to some practice of extempore recitation and acting, and it is probable that we have to do

here with the direct influence of the Italian *commedia dell'*
arte.[11]   As is well known, Ganassa traveled frequently in
Spain with his Italian company between 1574 and 1584,
when he introduced his favorite part of Harlequin; his
performances were successful and Lope de Vega mentions
him with praise.   Unfortunately, his plays or the parts that
he represented have come down only as a memory, and the
somewhat later actors of the *commedia dell' arte* type must
be judged solely by *scenari* or skeleton outlines of the plot,
not the plays themselves.

These short comic scenes were important features of
religious as well as secular entertainments, and in making
contracts for Corpus plays, the municipalities usually took
care to stipulate the number of *entremeses* to be performed
with each *auto*.   In a number of cases, the words *Aquí ha
de haber un entremés* in the manuscript clearly indicate the
independent nature of these compositions.   We have com-
paratively few texts of *entremeses* in the latter part of the
century, but there is no doubt that they continued to be
performed, and they enjoyed the public's favor.   Furthermore, the *entremés* in the early part of the seventeenth
century has more points of contact with the work of the
preceding century than has any other dramatic form.   To
the reader of today, the early *entremeses* are a source of
unfailing pleasure for what we may learn about popular
manners, customs, language, and superstitions of the sixteenth century.

To return to the pastoral drama of the latter half of
the century, the more formal type of dramatic eclogue is
represented by the *Comedia Tibalda* of Perálvarez de
Ayllón, the date of which can only be guessed from the
fact that certain verses of its author were included in the
1511 edition of the *Cancionero General* of Hernando del
Castillo.   It was first printed at Toledo in 1553 under the
title *Comedia de Preteo y Tibaldo,* which consists of the
original composition and an added absurd conclusion of

256 lines by Luis Hurtado de Toledo. It was written in *coplas de arte mayor*, the measure used by Encina in his *Égloga de tres pastores*, with which it offers striking similarities in subject matter. The composition merely serves as a medium for the discussion of two questions that are frequently found in Spanish literature of the early sixteenth century, the remedies for the illness of Love, and the virtues and imperfections of women. For the first of these, the author is indebted to Ovid's *Remedia amoris*, while the inordinately long defense of women is copied almost literally from Juan Rodríguez del Padrón's *Triunfo de las donas.*[12]

Luis Hurtado de Toledo not only attempted to write a more satisfactory ending to the *Comedia Tibalda*, in which he was unsuccessful, but he also composed another pastoral eclogue entitled *Égloga Silviana del galardón de amor*, printed at Valladolid with the second undated edition of the *Comedia Tibalda*. The *Égloga Silviana* follows closely the incidents of the *Égloga de Torino*, and offers little of interest. Like the *Comedia Tibalda*, it should probably be classified as a non-dramatic eclogue.

The earliest dramatic *caso de amor* in Spain is the anonymous *Comedia Fenisa*, written in *quintillas* and first printed in 1540. Three shepherds, enamored of Fenisa, dispute as to which has received the greatest mark of her affection. Their pretensions are ridiculed by a simpleton, who relates how Fenisa had shown her interest in him by laying a mighty blow on his head with her crook. Finally, the three rivals request her to express her preference. This play, in spite of its puerile simplicity, seems to have enjoyed unusual popularity. It was reprinted in 1588 and 1625, and forms the basis of two religious plays of the middle of the sixteenth century, the *Colloquio de Fenisa* and *Fide Ypsa*, in which the theme is treated *a lo divino*. It is likely that Juan de Melgar, to whom the version published in 1625 is attributed, is the *arreglador* and not the author.

The analogy is clear between the *Comedia Fenisa* and the various themes treated in the Italian *dubbi* or *casi d'amore* such as we find in the prologues of Timoneda and Alonso de la Vega.

A return to the circle of unhappy lovers, treated by Lope de Rueda in his *Discordia y qüestión de amor,* is found in the *Comedia Metamorfosea* of Joaquín Romero de Cepeda, printed in 1582 in three *jornadas.* Three shepherds and three shepherdesses suffer the pangs of unrequited love and each blames another for heartlessness. Almost the entire play is occupied with silly proposals, followed by brusque refusals. A sudden change takes place simultaneously in their hearts, and each shepherd or shepherdess expresses his or her love for the person who, a moment before, had been scorned. This leads to as difficult a situation as the previous one, and the author, in despair of reaching a satisfactory conclusion, ends the play. It is written in *quintillas,* but the presence of one sonnet shows a very early combination of native and Italian forms. The play shows no evidence of an acquaintanceship with the metrics of Juan de la Cueva.

The *Comedia Metamorfosea* closes the list of pastoral plays composed in Spain in the period that antedates the dramatic activity of Lope de Vega. With the triumph of Italian comedy in the second half of the sixteenth century and the influence of classical and Italian tragedy, the Spanish drama enlarged its scope. The pastoral drama contained within itself the causes of its inevitable dissolution: it was not original and did not represent actual life. Imitative by its very nature, it could not thrive when the drama was no longer restricted to private performances at the palace of some grandee, but was forced to go out on the village square or into an improvised corral to win the applause of the crowd. Audiences demanded at least a semblance of what was real in life or some human interest, and this demand the pastoral drama failed to supply.

The passion of Philip IV for dramatic entertainments resulted in an active support of the court drama, and explains a revival of pastoral plays in the time of Lope de Vega. By that time, however, the traditions of the sixteenth-century drama were forgotten to a large degree, and Italian subjects, scenery, and elaborate stage devices were in fashion. Except for the combination of recitation and song found in the works of Encina and some of his successors, there is almost a complete break in continuity between the sixteenth-century pastorals and compositions like *La selva sin amor* of Lope de Vega.

THE RELIGIOUS DRAMA IN THE LATTER HALF OF THE SIXTEENTH CENTURY, AND THE SCHOOL DRAMA

THE traditions of the Christmas plays of Encina and Fernández, with the addition of a pronounced tendency toward allegory and preaching which we have already found in the works of Diego Sánchez, were continued in a few compositions of the latter half of the sixteenth century. A play of this type consisting of three *autos* or scenes, is included in an edition of *Las Obras* of the Portuguese poet Jorge de Montemayor, which was first published at Antwerp in the year 1554. It was performed at Christmas matins before Prince Philip, probably between 1545 and 1547. The allegorical figure of Time binds together in a sequence these three scenes. The first presents the disobedience of Adam and Eve who fall victims to the wiles of Sensuality, and the promise made by Hope of the birth of the Redeemer who will restore to humanity its lost estate. This prophecy is fulfilled in the second scene, and after an explanation of the doctrine of Redemption, Time goes off to limbo to inform Adam of Christ's birth. The third scene contains more popular elements, and ends with the visit of three shepherds to the manger. Comic elements are introduced without success in an attempt to enliven these theological discussions. The play is totally lacking in inspiration or interest, and it is hard to believe that the author of the *Diana* could have written a work so devoid of merit.

Still more primitive is the *Danza del santíssimo nacimiento de Nuestro Señor Jesucristo*, composed in *quintillas* and occasional *villancicos*, by Pedro Suárez de Robles, a cleric of Ledesma. It was printed at Madrid in 1561. A copy of it was seen by Moratín, and a second edition of 1606 has been recently reprinted. Singing, and more particularly dancing, were prominent features about this play which was probably presented in church and resembles in a sense the *Danza de los pecados* of Diego Sánchez and other plays where ritual dancing had the chief part. The stage directions tell us that the play was introduced by a procession in which eight shepherds, angels, Joseph and the Virgin with the Christ Child, probably represented as a doll, marched to the high altar where the Christ was placed in a manger. An angel mounts the pulpit and announces the birth of Jesus. After the shepherds recover from their surprise, they draw near to the manger and each one offers a gift to the Christ Child. The Virgin promises them her protection, and the play ends with a song by the angels and the shepherds.

The first two editions of Bartolomé Aparicio's *El Pecador* bear no date, and the third known edition printed in 1611 is too late to be of aid, but judging from its general character, it seems to belong to the middle of the sixteenth century. The didactic purpose to teach theology is apparent in the dispute between Justice and Mercy regarding the punishment of Sinner for his transgression, and then the doctrine of Redemption is explained by Hope. Mercy announces the incarnation of God in a Virgin, and the play ends with the Nativity scene. Composed in *quintillas*, it is a pleasing play which kept its popularity for a long time. The author, otherwise unknown, also wrote the *Misterio de la bienaventurada Santa Cecilia,* a short fragment of which was printed in Milá y Fontanals' *Los orígenes del teatro catalán.*

To approximately the same period belongs the *Comedia a lo pastoril* which has been reprinted from a manuscript at the Biblioteca Nacional. Written in *quintillas*, the play is introduced by an expository prologue recited by a *Faraute,* who recalls the same figure in Carvajal's *Tragedia Josephina.* It is divided into three *estancias* or stations, which refer to the place of performance. The third *estancia* is divided into two *nocturnos,* a liturgical term that does not occur in any other Spanish play so far as I know. The manuscript contains interesting information about the costumes worn by the various characters. Music played an important part, and a number of songs were introduced which were doubtless already familiar to many of the listeners.

The play shows an interesting combination of the dispute of the four Virtues—Mercy, Peace, Truth, and Justice—with the Nativity scene. The allegory of the Four Daughters of God, or *Procès de Dieu,* based upon Psalm 84: 11, *Misericordia et Veritas obviaverunt sibi; Justitia et Pax osculatae sunt,* enjoyed extraordinary popularity throughout the Middle Ages. The author followed closely the version of the allegory that is found in a sermon of Bernard de Clairvaux entitled *In festo Annuntiationis Beatae Mariae Virginis,* upon which nearly all of the dramatic forms of the story in other literatures are based. In the Spanish play, however, the dispute serves to introduce the Nativity rather than the Annunciation, which is found in most other versions.

The anonymous *Farsa del Sordo* shows the same tendency toward the complete secularization of the Christmas story as Encina's *Égloga de las grandes lluvias.* After a prologue which recalls both in meter and incidents the *introito* of Naharro's *Diálogo del Nascimiento,* the rest of the play, written in octosyllabic *coplas,* consists of a series of disconnected scenes without semblance of plot, which serve to introduce the announcement by a shepherd of Christ's birth. The earliest dated edition contains a license to print of the year 1568. The ascription of this play to Lope de Rueda, on the authority of an edition of 1616, in which his name appears as author, must be regarded as exceedingly doubtful. Both by its contents and metrics it seems to be earlier than Rueda.

Another Christmas play, preserved only in manuscript, is the *Representación hecha en la Santa Iglesia de Sevilla* by Pedro Ramos,[1] a notary. According to the summary, the allegorical figures Temperance and Humility eventually save Holiness from prison where she has been placed by three of the deadly Sins, and this is followed by the announcement of Christ's birth.

Juan Timoneda printed an *Auto del Nascimiento* included in the newly discovered *Ternario Spiritual*, Valencia, 1558, which has been reprinted by Padre Olmedo. The play is an early work: unquestionably earlier than any other religious play by Timoneda. Both in the prologue and in the composition itself he followed Naharro's *Diálogo del Nascimiento* in utilizing three pilgrims who talk with a shepherd; and in the process of asking and answering questions, the doctrine of the Nativity is explained.

In the same *Ternario Spiritual* Timoneda also is mentioned as the author of the *Auto de la quinta angustia, nuevamente compuesto y añadido y mejorado.* The play was anonymously printed at Burgos in 1552 with the title *Auto de la quinta angustia que Nuestra Señora passó al pie de la Cruz*, which has been republished,[2] and another edition was published also at Burgos in the same year by another printer. After an introductory scene, in which Joseph of Arimathaea secures permission from Pilate to place in a sepulchre the body of the Crucified One, it presents the grief of the friends of Jesus and the anguish of the Virgin as preparations are made for the burial. While it lacks dramatic power, its lyrical qualities imbue it with a truly devotional spirit.

As for the relationship between the anonymous play of 1552 and Timoneda's play included in the *Ternario Spiritual*, it is impossible to answer definitely. The version of 1558 contains an added Prologue of forty lines, a new introductory scene between Joseph and Nicodemus, and other additions and corrections have been made. It might not be unwarranted to conjecture that Timoneda, hearing of the popularity of the play of which two editions had been printed at Burgos in 1552, decided to reprint it in his own *Ternario Spiritual,* in which, Timoneda-like, he made a few additions and corrections, and with this explanation he printed it as his own. Also, the play is included in the Llabrés manuscript of sixteenth-century dramatic compositions in Catalan and Castilian,[3] and it would seem likely that it went back to a version earlier than either the Burgos or the Timoneda texts.

The *Auto llamado Lucero de nuestra salvación, que trata del despedimiento que hizo Nuestro Señor Jesucristo de su bendita madre,* by Ausías Izquierdo Zebrero, written in *quintillas,* was first printed probably in 1582 and has been incorrectly attributed to Inocencio de Salceda. It offers more human interest than the preceding play in its portrayal of the efforts of the Virgin to dissuade Jesus from going to Jerusalem to meet his death. An angel presents to her five letters written by Adam, David, Moses, Jeremiah, and Abraham in which all prophesy the death of Christ. He entrusts her to the care of John, and she is then left alone with the symbols of the Passion. The author undoubtedly knew the two excellent plays contained in the celebrated codex published by Rouanet, the *Auto del Despedimiento de Christo de su madre* (LIV) and the *Aucto de las donas que embió Adán a Nuestra Señora* (LIII), and he wrote his own play as a connecting link between them.

The most elaborate Easter play in Spanish known to us is the *Auto que trata primeramente cómo el ánima de Christo decendió al infierno,* etc., by Juan de Pedraza or Pedreza, a weaver of Segovia. Besides this play, which was printed in 1549, he was the author of the *Farsa llamada Dança de la muerte* (1551) and the *Comedia de Sancta Susaña,* printed in the same year. The play is introduced by a prologue in the manner of Diego Sánchez which here bears the name of *entrada* or *entremés,* the earliest use of the word for a distinct and separate dramatic presentation, and is written in *coplas de pie quebrado.* The rest of the play—over a thousand lines—portrays the Harrowing of Hell, the Resurrection with its attending circumstances, ending with Christ's appearance to Mary Magdalene and to Peter, and is attractively written, mainly in *redondillas*. It was evidently performed in church on Easter morning, and follows liturgical or scriptural narrative.

In its combination of themes derived from the Old and New Testaments, the *Victoria de Christo* of Bartolomé Palau appears at first sight as an example of the cyclic type of composition with which we are familiar in English and French literature, but in reality it must be regarded as an Easter play, with a rather detailed exposition of Old Testament history, interpreted in the light of the Resurrection. Its division on a chronological basis into six parts, with a varying number of *autos* or scenes, is unique in the Spanish drama. The general subject is the spiritual captivity of mankind as a consequence of the original sin, and extends from the disobedience of Adam and Eve to the Last Judgment with the redemption of mankind through Christ. There is no reason to suppose that it was written any considerable time before 1570, the year of its earliest dated edition. Its popularity is attested by the publication of no less than nine editions, and it is still performed occasionally in Catalonia and Aragon.

By far the most important monument of the Spanish religious drama is a codex of ninety-six plays preserved at the Biblioteca Nacional, written from 1550 to 1575 approximately, and edited by Léo Rouanet. All but one of these, namely, the *Entremés de las esteras,* treat sacred themes, and all are anonymous, with the exception of the *Auto de Caín y Abel,* which bears the signature of Maestro Jaime Ferruz. In the opinion of their editor, three of these plays, namely, the *Auto del robo de Digna, Auto de los desposorios de Moysén* and *Auto de Naval y Abigail,* were written by Lope de Rueda. All but three are in verse, with the *quintilla* as the favorite measure. The manuscript copy of the *Auto de la Resurreción de Christo* (LX) contains a license for performance at Madrid in 1578, and a number of the compositions may probably be identified with plays performed at Seville. With the exception of two *coloquios*, derived from the pastoral *Coloquio de Fenisa*, and the *Entremés de las esteras*, these plays bear the name *auto* or *farsa*, the latter being used to designate allegorical compositions in honor of the Sacrament, while the former was apparently applicable to any type of religious play.

The similarity in the structure and spirit of these plays indicates that their authors were following an established tradition. They begin with a *loa* or *argumento*, in prose or in verse, which usually includes a greeting to the audience, a summary of the plot, and a request for silence. The term *loa* as the equivalent of dramatic monologue going back to the prologue of Pedraza's *Farsa llamada Danza de la muerte* (1551) is not laudatory as the name would suggest, but a characteristic *introito* in rustic dialogue. The word *loa* was first used in religious plays, probably at the outset in reference to the Sacrament, and in the course of time it was employed in secular plays as we find it in the prologue to *Alejandra* by Lupercio Leonardo de Argensola.

They generally end with a *villancico*, and occasionally are divided into two parts by an *entremés*, which is sometimes merely indicated in a stage direction. It is the comic elements that are chiefly responsible for their air of similarity. In almost all of them a clown appears, designated indiscriminately as *pastor, bobo, villano*, or *simple*, whose dull understanding provokes explanations about theological doctrines, and whose silly chatter, impertinence, and fondness for food afford comic relief after serious scenes.

It is by no means easy to classify accurately the ninety-five religious plays of this codex, nor to determine on what festivals they were performed. The *Aucto del rey Nabucdonosor cuando se hizo adorar* (XIV) is inspired by the spirit of penitence which is characteristic of Advent, and the *Auto del sueño de Nabucdonosor* (XV), with Daniel's prophecy of the Incarnation as its central point, refers to the same season. *La justicia divina contra el peccado de Adán* (XLIII) presents a version of the allegory of the Four Daughters of God, already found in the *Comedia a lo pastoril,* and frequently employed as an introduction to Christmas plays. In this case only two sisters appear, Justice and Mercy, and the dispute takes place shortly after the disobedience of Adam. The theme, therefore, is not the immediate, but the ultimate, redemption of man. The *Aucto de los hierros de Adán* (XLIV) presents the release of Adam and his sons as a consequence of the Redemption. The *Aucto de la culpa y captividad* (XLV) describes the imprisonment by Guilt and Captivity of various characters who secure their freedom through the announcement of the birth of Christ. This shows the influence of Palau's *Victoria de Christo,* except that these incidents are here related to Christmas instead of Easter. A shepherd who has heard the angel's song serves to connect the *Aucto de la circuncisión de Nuestro Señor* (LI) with the Christmas festival, and another post-Christmas play is the *Aucto de la huída de Egipto* (LII), to which the prophecies of Christ's destiny, pronounced ingenuously by a band of gypsies, impart a real charm. While in subject matter these plays are related to the Advent and Christmas seasons, we cannot definitely state that they were performed on Christmas day, with the exception of the *Aucto de la culpa y captividad,* which on internal evidence may be called a Christmas play.

Five plays, namely the *Aucto de la degollación de Sant Juan Baptista* (XXXV), *Aucto del hijo pródigo* (XLVIII), *Auto de la entrada de Cristo en Jerusalén* (XLVI), *Aucto de la conversión de la Madalena* (LXIV) and *Auto del hospedamiento que hizo Sancta María a Christo* (LVI) deal with incidents of the Ministry of Christ. The first presents with unusual dramatic power the execution of John the Baptist. The *Aucto del hijo pródigo* sketches only in briefest outline the Prodigal's downfall, and is far inferior to Luis de Miranda's *Comedia Pródiga*. The third describes with simple dignity the scene of Christ's entry into Jerusalem and the driving of the money changers from the temple. The transformation of a sinful woman into a devoted disciple of Jesus is pleasingly described in the *Aucto de la conversión de la Madalena*. Less interesting is the last play of the group which deals with undramatic material.

Five plays deal with Christ's Passion and Resurrection, and were presumably performed on Easter, while two others are also related to the Easter festival. The *Auto del despedimiento de Christo de su madre* (LIV) emphasizes the element of physical horror in Christ's description to the Virgin of the sufferings he must endure on the Cross. It is one of the sources of Izquierdo Zebrero's *Lucero de nuestra salvación*. The *Aucto del descendimiento de la cruz* (XCIII) closely resembles, even in minor details, the *Auto de la quinta angustia* already discussed. The *Aucto de la Resurreción de Nuestro Señor* (XCV) is a regrettable attempt to popularize an Easter play by the introduction of trivial incidents. The *Auto de la Resurreción de Christo* (LX) performed in Madrid on Easter 1578, contains popular and allegorical figures, and centers about the Harrowing of Hell, recited by Time. Even less dramatic is the play of like name (LXI) which consists of a conversation between the four Evangelists and two allegorical figures concerning the doctrine of Redemption. The *Aucto de la destruición de Jerusalén* (XXX) treats in a spirited way the legend of the destruction of Jerusalem by Vespasian in return for his miraculous cure from leprosy. The *Aucto de la redención del género humano* (XCIV) presents with allegorical figures the Harrowing of Hell, and with the exception of a few additions and changes, is identical with the sixth part of Palau's *Victoria de Christo*.

Three plays entitled *Aucto de la Asunción de Nuestra Señora* (XXXI, XXXII and LXII), to which should be added the *Auto de la Assumptión de Nuestra Señora*, not included in the codex under discussion, but published from a manuscript by Rouanet in the Appendix E to that collection, the *Colloquio de Fenisa en loor de Nuestra Señora* (LXV), and the *Aucto de acusación contra el género humano* (LVII), were all written in honor of the Virgin. The *Colloquio de Fenisa* is an insipid version *a lo divino* of the pastoral composition with the same title already mentioned. The *Aucto de acusación contra el género humano* presents a trial scene in which Satan lays claim to the possession of Mankind, the Virgin acts as his advocate, and Christ serves as judge. Its source is a version of the *Processus Belial,* attributed to Bartolus, which had extraordinary vogue throughout the Middle Ages. The theme recalls the Catalan *Mascarón* and analogues in other European literatures.

Twelve plays contained in this same manuscript deal with the lives of Saints, namely, the *Auto de Sant Jorge quando mató la serpiente* (XXVI), *Aucto de Sant Christóval* (XXVII), *Aucto de un milagro de Sancto Andrés* (XXVIII), *Aucto de quando Sancta Elena halló la cruz de Nuestro Señor* (XXXIII), *Auto del martyrio de Sancta Bárbara* (XXXVII), *Aucto del martyrio de Sancta Eulalia* (XXXVIII), *Aucto de Sant Francisco* (XXXIX), *Aucto de la prisión de Sant Pedro* (XLVII), *Aucto de la visitación de Sant Antonio a Sant Pablo* (LXXVI), two plays *Aucto de la conversión de Sant Pablo* (XXV and LXIII), and the *Auto del martyrio de Sant Justo y Pastor* (XXIX). The last was probably written by Alonso de Torres, and performed at the University of Alcalá in 1568. In honor of the same festival, a *Representación de los mártires Justo y Pastor* was composed by Francisco de las Cuebas. A manuscript of the Biblioteca Nacional which contains the play furnishes valuable information concerning the pageant upon which it was performed. It was given first in the open air at Alcalá de Henares on an elaborate *carro* upon which this three-part performance was to be given at three different places. A week later this itinerant presentation was given inside the church of San Justo.[4]

Twenty-six plays not already mentioned and included in the manuscript published by Rouanet treat Old Testament material, and it appears that those subjects were chosen which would serve to illustrate the close symbolic connection between Christ and the patriarchs of the Old Testament. The *Auto del peccado de Adán* (XL), *Aucto de la prevaricación de nuestro padre Adán* (XLII), and the *Auto de Caín y Abel* (XLI), the latter by the Valencian humanist Jaime Ferruz, treat of the Fall and the story of Cain and Abel, while the *Auto de quando Abrahán se fué a tierra de Canaan* (III), *Aucto de Abrahán quando vençió los quatro reyes* (XXII), *Auto del destierro de Agar* (II), *Auto del sacreficio de Abrahám* (I) and *Auto de los desposorios de Isac* (V and VI) treat incidents in the life of Abraham. The *Aucto de quando Jacob fué huyendo a las tierras de Aran* (IV), *Aucto de la lucha de Jacob con el ángel* (XI), *Auto del robo de Digna* (VIII), and *Aucto del finamiento de Jacob* (XII) deal with the story of Jacob. The *Auto de los desposorios de Joseph* (XX) describes Joseph's marriage, and the *Auto de los desposorios de Moysén* (XLIX) and the *Aucto del Magna* (X) deal with Moses. It will be seen that these subjects correspond to the *lectiones* and *responsoria* in Septuagesima, Sexagesima, and the Quadragesima season. It is probable that most, if not all, of these plays were written for the Corpus Christi festival.

The remaining plays of this manuscript treating Old Testament subjects, namely, the *Aucto de la ungión de David* (XIX), *Auto de Naval y Abigail* (LIX), *Auto de la muerte de Adonias* (XXXVI), *Auto de Sansón* (XIII), *Aucto del rey Asuero quando desconpuso a Basti* (XVI), *Auto del rey Assuero quando ahorcó a Aman* (XVII), *Aucto de la lepra de Naaman* (XVIII), *Auto del sacrificio de Jete* (XXIV), *Aucto de la paciencia de Job* (XCVI), and *Aucto de Tobias* (XXI), represent a widening of the scope of Old Testament material for use in Corpus Christi plays.

The tendency toward allegory and symbolism, fore-
shadowed in the *Farsa Sacramental* of López de Yanguas
and in certain plays of Diego Sánchez, prevailed in the second half of the sixteenth century, and these elements served
as a basis for the further development of the *autos sacramentales* in the following century. Thirty-three plays of
this type are included in the codex under discussion, and all
of these refer to the Eucharist and the festival of Corpus
Christi.

The *Farsa sacramental de la residencia del hombre* (IX)
and the *Auto de la residencia del hombre* (L) recall by their
juristic setting the *Auto de acusación contra el género humano,* but here it is not original sin, but sin in general, which
must be expiated by contrition and penitence, and the author's aim is to explain the Eucharist rather than the doctrines of the Incarnation and Redemption. The *Aucto de
la verdad y la mentira* (LV), *Farsa del triunpho del sacramento* (LXXXI), *Farsa del sacramento de las tres coronas*
(LXXXII), *Farsa sacramental de la fuente de la gracia*
(LXXXVI), and *Farsa sacramental llamada Desafío del
honbre* (XC), describe the victory of the forces of good
over evil. The *Farsa del sacramento de Moselina*
(LXXVII), *Farsa del sacramento de los tres estados*
(LXXXIII), and *Farsa del sacramento de la entrada del
vino* (LXXXVIII), contrast the Christian and Jewish dis-
pensations. Both types of plays—*auto* and *farsa*—were
suitable for performance on Corpus Christi celebrations,
but the term *Farsa del sacramento* was also used when the
author wished to emphasize the doctrine of the Real
Presence.

There is little evidence to support the theory that the
religious plays were frequently employed in the sixteenth
century as a weapon against Protestantism. Rarely do we
find in these doctrinal plays even a reference to heresy.
Only three in this codex are devoted primarily to a refuta-
tion of heterodoxy. The *Farsa del sacramento de las cortes
de la yglesia* (LXVIII) is a glorification of the Church

militant as represented by the tribunal of the Inquisition, while hatred of Luther and his teachings finds expression in the *Farsa del sacramento de Peralforja* (LXXII) and *Farsa sacramental de la moneda* (LXXXIV).

The symbolism of the Eucharist is described in the *Farsa del sacramento del Amor divino* (VII), *Farsa del sacramento de los sembradores* (LXX), and *Farsa del sacramento llamada Premática del pan* (LXXV). The last mentioned was abridged and rewritten by Timoneda with a title *Aucto de la fee* or *La pragmática del pan,* and was printed at Valencia in 1575. Transubstantiation is the subject of the *Farsa del sacramento* (LXIX), and the Evangelists and various saints are employed in the *Farsa del sacramento* (LXXXVII) and *Farsa del sacramento de los quatro Evangelistas* (LXXXIX) to explain the Eucharist. The *Colloquio de Fide ypsa* (LXVI) is still another version *a lo divino* of the *Coloquio de Fenisa,* and the fragmentary *Auto* (LXVII) also has a pastoral setting.

Less obvious is the relationship to the Corpus festival of the *Aucto del emperador Juveniano* (XXIII), which is derived from a story of the *Gesta Romanorum.* The *Aucto de los triunphos de Petrarca* (LVIII) gives a theological setting to the *Trionfi* of Petrarch, and the *Farsa del sacramento llamada La esposa de los cantares* (LXXIII) derives its inspiration from the *Song of Songs.* The *Farsa del sacramento de la fuente de Sant Juan* (LXXI) explains the Sacraments. It was rewritten by Timoneda, was performed at Valencia in 1570 and was printed in the *Segundo Ternario* with the title *Aucto de la fuente de los siete sacramentos* (1575). The *Farsa del sacramento del engaño* (LXXVII) is derived in part from the *Farsa del mundo y moral* of López de Yanguas. The *Farsa del sacramento del pueblo gentil* (LXXIV) treats of the conversion of the sinner; the *Farsa del sacramento del entendimiento niño* (LXXXV) teaches that understanding is vain without a knowledge of God, and the *Farsa del sacramento de Adán* (XCI) treats of Redemption through faith.

The *Farsa del sacramento llamada de Los lenguajes* (LXXX) is a linguistic medley that reminds us of a scene in Torres Naharro's *Comedia Tinellaria,* and the *Farsa del sacramento de los cinco sentidos* (LXXIX) anticipates Calderón in the symbolical use of the five senses in Corpus plays. The *Farsa sacramental de las bodas de España* (XCII) presents Spain as the champion of Catholicism. It was performed at Toledo on Corpus Christi day, 1570, and its title refers to the coming marriage of Philip II to Anne of Austria. The *Aucto de las donas que embió Adán a Nuestra Señora* (LIII) is attractively presented, and recalls Gómez Manrique's *Representación del nacimiento de Nuestro Señor* in its use of the symbols of the Passion, which we find in other Peninsular plays, notably in Gil Vicente's *Auto da Alma* and in Timoneda's *Desposorios de Cristo.*

So far as Timoneda's religious plays are concerned, mention has already been made of the *Auto del Nascimiento* and the *Auto de la quinta angustia* included in the *Ternario Spiritual* (1558). The third play of the *ternario* is the *Aucto de la oveja perdida* or *Obra llamada La pastorella* which was " added to and improved by Juan Timoneda," and performed on Corpus Christi in 1557. It was reprinted with slight variations in 1575 from which Pedroso republished it in his collection of *Autos Sacramentales;* a sixteenth-century manuscript with variants is preserved in the Academia de la Historia, and it has been performed by students at the University of Salamanca in 1920. Whether the credit is due to Timoneda or to the unknown playwright who furnished him the original draft, the Parable of the lost sheep is tenderly and simply told in the *auto* which is generally considered the best religious play with which the name of Timoneda is connected.

In 1575 Timoneda published at Valencia a volume entitled *Ternario Sacramental* with the following *autos: de la Oveja perdida, del Castillo de Emaús,* and *de la Iglesia.* As we have just seen, the first was printed in 1558 and was not original, but the other two were presumably Timoneda's own work. The *Aucto del Castillo de Emaús* begins with a scene in Castilian between an innkeeper, his wife, and his stepson, which recalls Rueda's device of introducing a *paso* at the start, while Valencian is spoken by most of the serious figures. The play proper is based upon the twenty-fourth chapter of St. Luke where Christ appeared after his Resurrection to two disciples, and it ends with an explanation of the Eucharist. The *Aucto de la Iglesia* is written wholly in Valencian and deals with the Church, banished from England, which is defended by the two stalwart defenders of Catholicism, Pope Gregory XIII and Philip II. On internal evidence it was performed on Corpus Christi in 1573.

It was due to the interest in Corpus plays which the newly appointed archbishop of Valencia, Juan de Ribera, showed, that Timoneda took up again the writing of religious compositions after a lapse of ten or eleven years. Religious plays had been performed at Valencia for many years on Corpus Christi, but these had been limited to scenes from the Old and New Testaments, and were not used specifically for an explanation of the Eucharist. The Archbishop Ribera knew thoroughly the latter kind of play owing to his long residence in Badajoz and Seville, and under his patronage Timoneda's work, in which the doctrines of the Eucharist were explained and emphasized, constituted an innovation in that city.

In the same year 1575 and dedicated to the Archbishop Ribera, as the preceding volume, Timoneda published his *Segundo Ternario Sacramental* which included *Aucto de la fuente de los siete sacramentos, Aucto de los desposorios de Cristo,* and *Aucto de la Fee.* The Valencian bookseller and printer nowhere states that he has written these plays: *puestos en su perfección y representados por Ioan Timoneda* is as far as he can go in claiming their authorship. As we have seen, the *Aucto de la fuente de los siete sacramentos* and *Aucto de la Fee* are reworkings of the *Farsa del sacra-*

mento de la fuente de Sant Juan and *Farsa del sacramento llamada Premática del pan,* both of which are found in the codex published by Rouanet. *Los desposorios de Cristo,* which presents the Parable of the marriage of the king's son, is a revision of earlier plays that are not known to be extant.

Another play of which Rafael Floranes possessed an original copy at the end of the eighteenth century and which Muñiz mentions briefly in his *Biblioteca Cisterciense Española* is the *Triunpho de Llaneça* by Fr. Ignacio de Buendía,[5] a Cistercian monk. The play, apparently the work of a copyist under the supervision of the author, was included in the manuscript entitled *Obras poéticas* which was written in 1577 and contains religious verse of some merit. The *Triunpho de Llaneça* is a closet-play with a varied metrical scheme of Italianate and Spanish measures. Repose, a simple peasant, and Simplicity, avoiding the lures which Curiosity and Care hold out to them for greater joy in life, keep to the straight and narrow path, a decision which Justice commends. The author was more successful as a lyric poet than as a dramatist.

The use of the familiar *Dance of Death* theme combined with an explanation of the Eucharist is found in Juan de Pedraza's *Farsa llamada Danza de la Muerte,* written in *coplas de arte mayor,* and printed in 1551. The prologue, composed in double *redondillas,* is called a *loa,* which is the earliest datable use of the word in its dramatic sense. The play proper introduces a pope, a king, and a beautiful lady who are confronted by Death, and are carried away by him in spite of their protests. The shepherd is in danger of following suit in his altercation with Death, but she tells him that her appearance was only a warning, and after she disappears, his questions elicit from Reason an explanation of the mystery of the Eucharist. Pedraza also published the same year (1551) the *Comedia de Sancta Susaña,* a pleasing dramatization in double *redondillas* of the familiar story found in the thirteenth chapter of the Book of Daniel.

The *Auto de las Cortes de la Muerte* recalls Pedraza's *Danza de la Muerte* and Diego Sánchez' *Farsa de la Muerte,* as well as the Sorrowful Knight's encounter with a troupe of strolling players who had just performed a play with the above named title, as told in the eleventh chapter of the second part of *Don Quixote.* However, the play to which Cervantes referred was not the same as the composition under consideration. In 1557 Luis Hurtado de Toledo finished the play which had been begun by Michael de Carvajal, the author of the *Tragedia Josephina.* What part of the composition of nearly eight thousand lines can be attributed to Carvajal, and what to his successor? Judging from the proven habits of the latter with respect to literary dishonesty, we can agree with Dr. Gillet [6] that Luis Hurtado de Toledo is responsible probably for the *introito* and for two or three scenes which are out of harmony with the rest of the composition while Carvajal is the author of most of the play. Reasonable conjectures have been made to explain why Carvajal, who was living in 1557, permitted a plagiarist to stand as author of his work.

Las Cortes de la Muerte, written in *quintillas,* is divided into twenty-three scenes or *cenas.* The play has much in common with the *Dance of Death* theme with all persons coming to the Court of Death, with representatives of the clergy, military class, the rich and the poor, celibates and married persons, the legal and medical profession, the peasants and so on, but as Miss Whyte [7] has aptly said, the author is possessed by moral and ethical rather than social concepts. Besides, Death is not called upon for an immediate decision, but a court scene is represented with the World, the Flesh, and Satan as the prosecution assisted by Luther, and the lawyers for the defense are the saints, Jerome, Augustine, and Francis. The play is too long and is at times dull, but many passages occur which remind one of the *Tragedia Josephina.*

The same undramatic quality is found in an early play of Bartolomé Palau entitled *Farsa llamada Custodia del hombre* in five *jornadas,* written in 1541 or after, in six-line *coplas de pie quebrado* and printed in 1547. Composed in honor of the Corpus festival, it contrasts in allegorical fashion the paths of virtue and evil, and contains in the first *jornada* a combination of the *Processus Belial* and the Four Daughters of God themes, which we have met in other plays. Far more important is another early play by Palau, *Historia de la gloriosa Santa Orosia,* in six *autos,* and written in almost the same meter as the *Custodia.* It has peculiar interest as the earliest dramatic composition in Spain dealing with national history. Palau was an Aragonese and he chose to write upon a devout story which was very familiar in Aragon, and it was doubtless intended for performance on the day of Santa Orosia. Palau conceived the idea of combining the experiences of Orosia culminating in her martyrdom at the hands of the Moors as told in the missals and breviaries of Aragon with the story of La Cava, Count Julián, and Roderic as was told in the *Crónica General.*[8] Tirso de Molina used this play in writing *La joya de las Montañas y verdadera historia de santa Orosia.* Palau wrote another play entitled *Historia de santa Librada y sus ocho hermanas* which is not extant.[9]

The development of the Corpus festival into a great civic holiday and the supervision exercised by the municipal authorities over dramatic performances gave increased importance to the Corpus plays during the latter half of the century at the expense of Christmas, Passion, and Easter plays which did not receive official support. Documents discovered, particularly in the archives of Seville, Madrid, Valladolid, Valencia, and Badajoz attest the vogue attached by the municipal authorities to these performances, and we may assume that in other cities and even in small towns the celebration of Corpus was not considered complete without the procession of movable *carros* upon which members of the guilds or a company of strolling players presented a play or plays, more or less directly related to the mystery of the Eucharist. This practice even crossed the seas for we know that religious plays were written and performed in the colonies, both in the native languages and in Castilian.

The history of the School drama [10] in Spain is imperfectly known and its study is rendered particularly difficult because of the scarcity of printed texts. As in other countries, the performance of Latin plays was regarded in Spain as an important feature of the instruction in Latin and rhetoric. These performances were encouraged by the university authorities because it was realized that they served the pedagogical purpose of familiarizing students with colloquial Latin. We know, for example, that between 1531 and 1539 five performances of Latin plays were given by students of the recently organized Studi General of Valencia, including a presentation of a play by Plautus in 1532. Occasionally the old Roman comedies were replaced by Latin translations of well-known contemporaneous plays or by original compositions that represented a compromise between classical practice and modern taste. The Statutes of the University of Salamanca, in 1538, mention performances before the students of comedies of Plautus and Terence, or tragicomedies.

The earliest of these plays of which we have any record is the *Hispaniola* by the Erasmist, Juan Maldonado, composed in Latin prose, and in five acts. It was written about 1519, was performed in Portugal and with great applause at Burgos. It was printed at Valladolid in 1525 and again at Burgos in 1535. Plautus was the author's model, and the play deals with the rivalry of two young men for a girl's love.

Of greater significance is the dramatic activity of Juan Pérez who occupied the Chair of Rhetoric at the University of Alcalá from about 1537 until his death in 1545 at the age of thirty-three years. We are told that he often entertained the students with his comedies, four of which, the *Necromanticus, Lena, Suppositi,* and *Decepti,* were published by his brother in 1574. The first three were

translated from Ariosto, and the last from the anonymous
Gl' Ingannati. It is likely that Pérez was also the author
of a brief Latin comedy performed at Alcalá before Prince
Philip in 1539 or 1540 with the title *Ate relegata et
Minerva restituta*.[11] Here the author attempts to reconcile the privileges of the University with the rights of the
archbishop, and to win for the University the sympathy
of Archbishop Juan Tavera who already showed a disposi-
tion to insist upon what he considered to be his prerogative.
This little play did not, apparently, aid in the settlement of
the dispute in question, but it gives a good idea of the
special purpose that might be served by a school play. He
was also the author of a Latin play entitled *Chrysonia*,
taken from the *Golden Ass* of Apuleius, of which only the
prologue has been preserved.

The most prominent figure in the Spanish School drama
was the Aragonese Juan Lorenzo Palmyreno (1514?–
1579) who, as professor at the Studi General of Valencia,
attempted by means of dramatic performance to make
classical studies popular. Selections from three of his plays,
namely, the *Comœdia Lobenia* (1546), the *Comœdia
Sigonia*, and the *Comœdia Octavia* were published in 1566.
These are too fragmentary to allow us to form a definite
opinion as to their value, but it is evident that by his use
of prose, occasional dialogues in Castilian, and conventional
incidents of the comedy of intrigue, he tried to give a classical setting to modern material. There is still less of
Plautus and Terence, and a predominance of Castilian over
Latin in his *Fabella Ænaria*, performed in 1574. The
action is laid during the reign of Vespasian, but the vicissitudes of the Prince Alberto, who falls in love with the
daughter of a king of Denmark, effects his escape from
prison with her aid and wins her hand by his courage in
single combat, are thoroughly romantic. We cannot doubt
the author's explanation that he had imitated Spanish plays,
and not the serious art of Terence, in order to please his
audience.[12]

As elsewhere in Europe, religious plays were performed in Jesuit schools [13] in Spain from the latter half of the sixteenth century to celebrate important academic exercises and Church festivals, particularly Corpus Christi.   A pioneer in plays of this kind was the gifted Padre Pedro Pablo de Acevedo who wrote twenty-five plays which were presented in the Jesuit schools of Cordova and Seville from 1556 to 1572.   They have not been printed, but are preserved in manuscript form in the Academia de la Historia of Madrid.   A few were composed entirely in Latin and a few wholly in Spanish, but most of these plays were bilingual with the serious characters speaking Latin and the rest Spanish.   Of the twenty-five so-called plays, nearly half were written either to welcome some illustrious guest, or to celebrate some important academic or literary exercise, but the others were real plays of ascetic and moral type. *Metanea* (1556), *Lucifer furens* (1563), and *Occasio* (1564) deal with theological problems, and *Philautus* (1565), *Caropus* (1565), *Athanasia* (1566), and *Bellum virtutum et vitiorum* treat of moral questions. Three were written for the Corpus festival, and four plays were composed to be represented on Christmas and other holy days.[14]   In the same codex, there is a five-act inedited tragedy entitled *Iudithis,* written mainly in Latin verse, but in part in Spanish.   The author is known only as Padre Joseph who composed it in 1578.   Following the model of Seneca, the experiences of Judith and her murder of Holofernes are tragically told.[15]

The Jesuits built a new college at Seville in 1580 and the students performed the *Tragedia de San Hermenegildo* [16] in honor of the martyrdom of the patron saint of the college.   The authorship is unfortunately unknown. The five-act play is chiefly in Spanish verse—*octavas, tercetos, quintillas,* and *redondillas*—of a high order, while a few characters speak Latin and Italian.   The plot deals with the conflict of paternal love and religion in Visigothic Spain.   Ermengild, a son of the Arian king Leovgild, is

persuaded by Bishop Leander to turn his back upon his.
father and embrace Catholicism, and there are many dramatic scenes culminating in his martyrdom. Between the
various acts of this tragedy the author intercalated a composition in Spanish divided into three parts which might
be called *Hércules vencedor de la ignorancia.* Science, a
slave of Ignorance, is released finally by Hercules who
fights and vanquishes her enemies. These plays are also
preserved in the library of the Academia de la Historia
of Madrid.

In the same library there is a codex of seventeen plays [17]
written to be performed in the Jesuit colleges of Salamanca,
and more particularly of Medina del Campo and Avila
from 1560 to 1575 or 1580, only two of which have been
printed, namely, the *Parábola Cœnae* and the *Examen
Sacrum* which were included in the collection of *Autos
Sacramentales* by González Pedroso.[18] The author of
these plays was probably Padre Juan Bonifacio who joined
the Jesuit Society in 1557; he was appointed the following
year teacher of Grammar at Medina, and in 1567 he went
to teach Humanities at Avila. Most of these plays were
written in Latin and Spanish with a mingling of prose and
verse, and usually included a *præfatio jocularis* or *loa;* the
play proper often divided into five acts; the *actio interca-
laris* or *entremés,* and choruses and occasionally some dancing. While, of course, the religious and moral teaching
was uppermost in the author's mind, he felt the necessity
of introducing some popular characters which are often
delightful.

VIII

TRAGEDY AND LATER COMEDY

WHILE in general outlines the development of comedy in Italy and Spain followed parallel paths in the first half of the sixteenth century, Italy anticipated Spain by nearly sixty years in the composition of tragedies based upon classical models. Eight of the ten plays of Seneca were freely translated by Vilaragut [1] into Valencian in the latter part of the fourteenth century, and the first Castilian version was made at the beginning of the fifteenth, but there is no evidence that they awakened any desire to perform Latin tragedies at that time, either in the original or in translation. Spanish poets seem to have cared little about the traditions of classical tragedy, and they were slow to follow the example of Trissino and Giraldi, who introduced into Italy the theories and practices of Greek and Latin playwrights.

Even the incidents of Roman history offered little attraction to Spanish dramatists of the first half of the century, and only two extant plays of that period deal with such material. The *Farsa o Tragedia de la castidad de Lucrecia* by Juan Pastor, author of an *Auto nuevo del santo nacimiento de Cristo Nuestro Señor,* was printed in 1528 according to Moratín, and we may assume that his play on Lucrece, which is not dated, belongs approximately to the same period. This composition is written in six-line *coplas de pie quebrado,* without division into acts or scenes, and has nothing in common with classical tragedy, although the material has been taken from the well-known incident told in the fourth book of the *Roman Antiquities* of Dionysius of Halicarnassus. The scenes of the violation of Lucrece and her self-inflicted death are not without interest, but the attempt to relieve so many tragic incidents by the incessant

impertinences of the simpleton is wholly unsuccessful. The
play should be considered as one of a long line of compositions which extolled the virtues of women, using Lucrece as
model. It deserves attention only as a precursor of the
plays of Juan de la Cueva on Roman history. He wrote
also two *farsas* called *Grismaltina* and *Clarina* which the
author mentions at the close of the tragedy of Lucrece, but
of which nothing further is known.

The other early play dealing with Roman history is the
Tragedia de los amores de Eneas y de la reyna Dido, one
of the earliest instances of the word " tragedy " in the Spanish drama. The author's name is not given on the title-
page, but it has been discovered by means of an acrostic [2]
that he was Juan Cirne, a Portuguese and a friend of
Montemayor. The date 1536 appears on the single known
copy extant, but the editors believe that it was printed a
little later. It is an immature work, as the author frankly
confesses in the preface, and while using freely the fourth
book of Virgil as the main source, he knew so well most
of the plays of the *Propalladia* of Torres Naharro, especially the *Comedia Aquilana,* not to speak of his non-dramatic verse, that he incorporates reminiscences of these,
strangely enough, in a play about Dido and Aeneas. He
gives proof of having been familiar with the story of Dido
related in the *Primera Crónica General,* and of having
imitated the account of Melibea's death in the *Celestina* in
writing of the death of Dido.[3] Following Torres Naharro,
he divided his play into five *jornadas,* but instead of imitating him in versification, he preferred a form used by Gil
Vicente and other Portuguese dramatists, six lines of eight
syllables with the *quebrado.*

The Spanish translations of Greek tragedies in the sixteenth century seem to have had no influence upon the development of the drama. Hernán Pérez de Oliva made a
free adaptation in prose of the *Electra* of Sophocles, printed
in 1528 and again in 1531 with the title *La vengança de
Agamenón,* the earliest version of Sophocles in any modern

language, and a free rendering of Euripides' *Hecuba,* with the title *Hécuba Triste,* which was not printed until his collected works in 1586.   It is likely that these translations were based upon Latin versions, since Pérez de Oliva nowhere refers to a knowledge of Greek.   His purpose was not to make an accurate rendering of these masterpieces, but to prove that their lofty ideas might be adequately expressed in Castilian.   He wished to communicate to his contemporaries the inspiration which he himself felt, and did not hesitate to alter the form in order to make his own versions more intelligible.   He suppresses and adds to the original text when he thinks it desirable, changes the order of scenes, and too often substitutes their dramatic power with mere eloquence.   On the other hand, both plays, particularly *Hécuba Triste,* are excellently written, and are well able to stand comparison with the best works of the time. The *Vengança de Agamenón* was translated into Portuguese verse by Anrique Aires Vitória, and was printed between 1536 and 1555, but without even making any references to Pérez de Oliva.

His innovations had little effect upon the development of humanistic drama in Spain.   When Boscán died in 1542, he left a translation of a play by Euripides which was never printed, and Pedro Simón Abril, the translator of Terence, is said to have translated the *Plutus* of Aristophanes and the *Medea* of Euripides in 1570.   In view of the interest shown throughout Europe in the revival of Greek and Latin studies, it is surprising that not a single tragedy on classical lines is known to have been printed in Spain before 1577, the date of publication of *Nise Lastimosa* and *Nise Laureada,* for which their author, Fr. Jerónimo Bermúdez, justly claimed the title of *primeras tragedias españolas.*

The long controversy regarding the originality of *Nise Lastimosa* may be regarded as settled since it is now generally conceded that Bermúdez read in manuscript a play entitled *Dona Ignez de Castro* by the Portuguese poet and dramatist, Antonio Ferreira (1528–1569), and translated it almost line for line. Ferreira studied at the University of Coimbra, and besides two comedies, *Bristo* and *Cioso*, based upon classical and Italian comedy, he wrote excellent lyric verse. At that time Coimbra had become the center of classical influence, chiefly owing to the presence there of the famous Scotch humanist, George Buchanan, who encouraged the students to represent classical plays, and it is to these college performances that we owe Ferreira's *Dona Ignez de Castro*, the first Portuguese tragedy written according to classical models. In composing it, he did not seek his material from classical history, but chose an incident from Fernão Lopes and other Portuguese chroniclers who told the sad story of Inés de Castro who suffered cruel death (1355) because of her love for the Infante Pedro, and who *despois de ser morta, foi Rainha*, in the words of Camoens who immortalized the story in the third canto of *Os Lusiadas*. Ferreira's tragedy was written between 1553 and 1567, and it was performed by students at Coimbra under his personal direction. It was not published until 1587, although it had circulated freely in manuscript before that time, and it appeared in a revised version in 1598 where the title is merely given, *Castro*.

Dona Ignez de Castro gives evidence of an intimate acquaintance with both Greek and Latin tragedy. The function of the chorus seems to be a compromise between the practice of Seneca and of the Greek dramatists. Stichomythia is frequently employed, and the rôle of the attendant of Inés shows a classical origin. There are also a number of textual borrowings from Seneca, especially in the choral odes. However, Ferreira had the good taste to avoid the worst faults of the Latin dramatist, and he obtains his effects by simplicity, restraint, and poetic diction rather than by declamation and brutality. The prevailing verse form is the *verso solto* of eleven syllables, with occasional lines of seven syllables, a measure which probably shows the influence of Trissino, and heptasyllabic *soltos* and sapphic strophes in the choral odes.

Bermúdez's version of *Dona Ignez de Castro* entitled *Nise Lastimosa,* together with *Nise Laureada,* its continuation, was printed at Madrid in 1577 under the pseudonym of Antonio de Silva. The plays were composed while Bermúdez was a reader in theology at the University of Salamanca, and they were completed by the year 1575, the date of their dedication to the Count of Lemos.

The Spanish version, in which the heroine appears as Nise, an anagram of Inés, follows the Portuguese text and adds no new incidents. The rôle of the chorus is restricted in the main to the recitation of choral odes between the acts. A few changes were also made in the arrangement of scenes and there is evidence of independent borrowing from Seneca, especially from *Phaedra.* No line-by-line comparison, however, can give an adequate idea of the great superiority of the original over the translation. The work of the Portuguese scholar, inspired by a love for the classics, is generally attractive, but the Galician student of theology too frequently replaces the poetry and grace of the original by moralizing platitudes and vapid rhetoric. Early in the following century Mejía de la Cerda used this play in composing his own *Doña Ynés de Castro,* published in 1612.

In *Nise Laureada,* Bermúdez displays his shortcomings as a dramatist when obliged to rely upon himself for inspiration. The theme is the disinterment and coronation of Inés de Castro after Pedro's accession to the throne and the ghastly death inflicted by him upon her murderers. The fate of the latter is a foregone conclusion, and each act is filled with wearisome monologues and interminable dialogues until we reach the *exitus horribilis* at the close. Like the preceding, the play is divided into five acts but with a richer variety of verse measures, and the chorus not only serves to fill in the intermissions with choral recitations, but also declaims during the action and occasionally engages in dialogue with other characters. Lack of restraint in expressing grief or anger, far-fetched figures of speech, sententiousness, the stoicism of the prisoners when faced with death, and the atrocious murders committed on the stage all indicate the influence of Seneca.

So far as we know, only one other tragedy definitely based upon classical models, the *Elisa Dido* of Virués, was written in Spain during the sixteenth century, and this was not published until 1609. The experiment made by Bermúdez is of historical interest, but apparently contributed little to the development of the drama. Spanish playwrights refused to obey blindly classical precepts, and other dramatists created new types of plays which carried the Spanish drama along untrodden paths.

Juan de la Cueva is an important figure in this period of transition before Lope de Vega. Born at Seville in 1543, he tried nearly all sorts of verse, but it was not until after his return to his native city in 1577, after a residence of over two years in Mexico, that he wrote for the stage. His fourteen comedies and tragedies, printed in 1583 and again in 1588, were performed in various playhouses in Seville from 1579 until 1581, and he also applied for authorization to print a second series in 1595. Nothing further is known of this volume; perhaps he realized, or perhaps the publisher did, that his plays were old-fashioned and could not compete successfully with the new pattern created by Lope.

In his *Exemplar Poético,* completed in 1606 but not printed until our own day, he attempts no defense of his own plays, written nearly thirty years before, but quite properly claims a share in the triumphs of his successors. While we must regard as unfounded his statements that he was the first to bring kings and gods on the comic stage, that the name *jornada* was his own invention, and that he had reduced the conventional five acts to four, there can be little doubt that he contributed to the establishment of the vogue of the four-act play between 1580 and 1585, that he preferred to use a variety of meters in his plays, and that he first used, so far as we know, Italian meters for dialogue in public drama.

So little is known concerning the immediate predecessors of Juan de la Cueva on the Sevillan stage that it is impossible to determine whether these innovations are due to him alone. In his *Exemplar Poético,* he mentions Guevara, Gutierre de Cetina, Cozar, Fuentes, Ortiz, Mexía, and Mal Lara as dramatic poets who had followed the older traditions of plays at Seville. With respect to their dramatic work we know practically nothing, and Cueva gives us specific information only concerning Juan de Mal Lara who, we are told, composed a thousand tragedies in which he altered ancient practice to conform with modern requirements. From his well-known *Filosofía Vulgar* we learn that while still a student at Salamanca Mal Lara wrote first in Latin and later in Castilian a comedy called *Locusta,* performed in 1548, and a tragedy entitled *Absalón,* and from other sources we have records of two other plays. These, apparently, were School or religious plays, and seem to have little relationship with the dramatic compositions of Cueva. It is significant of the interest taken in the drama that when Cueva began to write, there were three playhouses at Seville, the Corral de Don Juan, the Corral de las Atarazanas, and La Huerta de Doña Elvira, and in these theatres his comedies and tragedies were performed by the well-known actors Alonso Rodríguez, Alonso de Capilla, Pedro de Saldaña, and Alonso de Cisneros.

Of the fourteen plays, three deal with epic material of Spain. The *Comedia de la muerte del rey don Sancho y reto de Zamora* presents one of the most celebrated incidents related in the chronicles and ballads. This story is a part of the Cid legend, and while the Cid himself plays a very secondary part, his spirit permeates the whole composition. The play consists of a series of scenes taken from the chronicles; the siege of Zamora by King Sancho and his death at the hands of the traitor Vellido Dolfos, who escapes to the city; the challenge of Diego Ordóñez to the defenders of Zamora; the acceptance of the challenge by the aged Arias Gonzalo; the death of the three sons in single combat; the death-struggle between Arias Gonzalo and Diego Ordóñez; and the final award. The dramatist merely limits himself to arranging his material and introducing dialogue. These characters of heroic mold win our sympathy and interest, and we can imagine the delight of an audience in seeing on the stage a story with which they were familiar and in hearing verse recited which recalled ballads which they had known from childhood, as for example, the famous challenge of Don Diego to the defenders of Zamora.

Even better known was the story dealt with in the *Tragedia de los siete infantes de Lara,* derived from *La estoria del noble cauallero el conde Fernán González con la muerte de los siete infantes de Lara.*[4] Cueva failed to reproduce the somber beauty of the legend, and its violation of the unities is glaring. It is probable that Cervantes had this in mind when he spoke in *Pedro de Urdemalas* of a play in which twenty-odd years elapsed between the first and second acts, unless he had already read a similar criticism in López's *Filosofía antigua poética.* Instead of concentrating the interest upon the vengeance taken by Mudarra for the death of the seven infantes, three-fourths of the play is taken up with the exposition. The story was a favorite one with later dramatists, and in *El moro expósito* (1834) the Duque de Rivas won the first decisive victory of Romantic poetry.

The third of the chronicle plays is the *Comedia de la libertad de España por Bernardo del Carpio,* which follows closely the account given in the *Crónica de España* by Alfonso X, printed by Ocampo. The figure of Bernardo del Carpio, the national hero who was credited with having turned back the invading French knights at the battle of Roncesvalles, has ever been popular in Spain, and his exploits were sung in ballads and related in many a long-drawn-out epic poem. First brought upon the stage by Cueva, he appears again in the *Casa de los celos y selvas de*

Ardenia of Cervantes, and in two plays by Lope de Vega, *Las mocedades de Bernardo* and *El casamiento en la muerte*.

Juan de la Cueva was the first dramatist, so far as we know, to make use of the legendary lore of Spain, to bring Spanish heroes on the stage and to avail himself to any considerable extent of the rich treasure offered by the ballads.   In his use of historical material Cueva is a true precursor of Lope de Vega.   His chief fault was the failure to distinguish clearly between the nature of dramatic and epic poetry.   Some observance of the unities would have forced him to knit his scenes more closely together.   Many scenes have dramatic power, but he often failed to realize their relationship to each other or to a play as a whole. The dialogue is too often forced, and never creates the illusion of ordinary conversation.

Cueva also wrote three plays dealing with early Greek and Roman history.   The first is the *Tragedia de la muerte de Ayax Telamón sobre las armas de Aquiles,* which describes in disconnected scenes the departure of Aeneas from Troy and the contest between Ajax and Ulysses for the arms of Achilles as is narrated in the thirteenth book of the *Metamorphoses*.   The *Tragedia de la muerte de Virginia y Appio Claudio,* based upon the story familiar to us in the third book of Livy, has far more dramatic interest.   The scenes are arranged so as to form a real plot, and the *dénouement* which presents the heroism of Virginius to save his daughter's honor is effective.   The *Comedia de la libertad de Roma por Mucio Cevola* lacks dramatic unity.   The play was written merely as a setting for the scene in which Scævola proves to Porsenna the sort of courage possessed by the defenders of Rome, whom he proposes to enslave.

His inability to realize the difference between a series of dramatic incidents and a plot with dramatic unity is well illustrated by the *Comedia del saco de Roma,* which offers the novelty of dealing with modern history.   The action extends from the sack of Rome by the Duke of Bourbon in May 1527 until the arrival of the Emperor for his corona-

tion at Bologna in February 1530. The author's purpose
seems to have been to arouse a feeling of righteous horror
at this unholy undertaking.

The *Comedia del Príncipe tirano* presents the Prince
Licimaco, whose jealous hatred of his sister, Eliodora, is
stirred to action by the Fury Alecto and by the suggestions
of his counselor, Trasildoro. He determines to kill her,
and this brotherly act is performed in the garden of the
palace, while the Fates spin and then cut the thread of her
life. Trasildoro is also put to death in order that the
secret of his death may be guarded. The Prince and his
father are pursued by gruesome visions at night, and finally
the ghosts of Eliodora and Trasildoro reveal to the King
the bloody deeds of the Prince. The latter is condemned
to death, effects his escape, and is finally pardoned by the
King. The second part, entitled *Tragedia del Príncipe
tirano,* is a perfect riot of bloodshed and crime. The es-
timable young Prince develops into a monster incarnate
after his father's abdication. He burns the books of the
Law, demands of reputable citizens the surrender of their
daughters, executes anyone who ventures to oppose him,
buries two of his adversaries alive, and finally meets his
death at the hands of two women whom he had sought to
injure. All of the imitators of Seneca reveled in excesses
of this sort, but this play passes the bounds of propriety
and credibility.

The *Comedia del tutor* is an insignificant comedy of intrigue, dealing with the rivalry of two students, and the
guardian of one of them, for the love of a young Sevillan.
Through the aid of one of his servants, Otavio plays a trick
upon his rivals and completely discredits them. Otavio is
another Calisto; Licio plays the part of a resourceful
Sempronio, and Astropo, an engaging braggart, also recalls the *Celestina.*

The *Comedia de la constancia de Arcelina* is an extravagant play, made up of characters and incidents that never
existed except in a distorted imagination. One ridiculous

situation follows another until an absurd *dénouement* is reached which violates every law of probability. The plot of the *Comedia del viejo enamorado* has certain dramatic possibilities, but is marred by extravagant incidents. The intrigue by which old Liboso seeks to win the love of Olimpia is good material for a farce, but the later scenes, with the intervention of a magician and the Furies, are preposterous.

Far superior to these is the *Comedia del Degollado,* which has interesting points of similarity with Whetstone's *Historye of Promos and Cassandra* and with Shakespeare's *Measure for Measure.*[5] Its source seems to be the well-known fifth story of the eighth Decade of Giraldi Cinthio's *Gli Hecatommithi,* or the latter's dramatization of the same story entitled *Epitia,* but the romantic incidents of the capture of Arnaldo and Celia create an original setting. In Giraldi's story, in his *Epitia* and in *Promos and Cassandra,* the young woman actually sacrifices her honor to save her brother's life. This sacrifice is avoided in *Measure for Measure* by the substitution of Mariana for Isabella, and in *El Degollado* by the rather tardy repentance of the Prince. Arnaldo is more courageous than his counterpart in the other versions, for he refuses to live at the cost of Celia's virtue. In Giraldi's story, his *Epitia* and *Promos and Cassandra,* the heroine not only marries her violator but saves him from the death he so richly merited. Judged from modern standards, a satisfactory solution was found only by Shakespeare and by Cueva. It is probable that Cueva was familiar also with the sixth novel of the second Decade of Giraldi's book in writing this play.

The *Comedia del Infamador* is a play which later would be called *de capa y espada,* with the addition of extravagant mythological and supernatural elements. While it is unlikely that it served as a model for the composition of Tirso de Molina's *El burlador de Sevilla,*[6] as was claimed by Schack, Leucino is a forerunner and has contributed materially to the Don Juan type. There is interest in the early part which deals with the efforts of the dissolute Leucino to secure possession of Eliodora, and the latter's defense of her honor. The conclusion, however, brought about by Diana's assertion of the girl's innocence and her command that Leucino be buried alive after the river Guadalquivir refuses to receive his body, is ridiculous. As in the case of the *Comedia del viejo enamorado*, a plot with dramatic possibilities was spoiled by the introduction of absurd incidents.

In regard to versification Cueva was the first to use the single *redondilla* extensively; he discarded the *quintilla* completely, and he showed a greater preference for the octaves, *tercetos, sueltos* and *estancias* in his later plays.

A desire to protect Spanish tragedy from the restrictions imposed by classical traditions is apparent in *Los amantes*, by the Valencian poet Andrés Rey de Artieda (1549– 1613), printed at Saragossa in 1581. A soldier by profession who spent many years in the armies of Philip II and Philip III, and a comrade in arms of Cervantes at Lepanto, where he was also wounded, he devoted his leisure time to writing verse. In addition to *Los amantes*, he is said to have written two plays, *El príncipe vicioso* and *Amadís de Gaula*, of which nothing is known; and another play, *Los encantos de Merlín*, ascribed to him by Rojas Villandrando, is not extant.

In an epistle which precedes *Los amantes*, he contrasts the magnificence of the theatres of ancient times with the meager stage setting of his own day. While aware of the beauties of the classical drama, he does not resign himself to follow blindly its traditions, but he believes that tragedy has the right to adapt itself to modern conditions. The date of writing *Los amantes* is uncertain because while he refers in the epistle to having recently read the two plays by Bermúdez (1577), he may have composed it after the year of their publication. The play shows no definite influence of Juan de la Cueva.

Its subject is the well-known legend of the lovers of Teruel which was especially familiar to a Valencian audience. About the year 1555, Pedro Albentosa had printed in *redondillas* the *Historia lastimosa y sentida de los dos tiernos amantes Marcilla y Segura, naturales de Teruel,* and in 1562 Diego Ramírez Pagán mentioned the two persons among the celebrated lovers in a composition included in his *Floresta de varia poesía,* printed at Valencia. Whatever the origin of this story, whether based upon popular traditions, or upon a real occurrence, or upon a tale of the *Decameron,* this pathetic couple had become completely identified with Teruel when Rey de Artieda composed his play. Thanks to *Los amantes,* to the pretentious epic of Juan Yagüe de Salas, and to the plays of Montalbán, Tirso de Molina, and Hartzenbusch, the couple have become paragons of frustrated love which finds an issue only in death.

The originality of Rey de Artieda does not lie, therefore, in the invention of the plot and in the arrangement of dramatic situations, but in his choice of a story replete with romantic incidents. His play is a tragedy but, as he writes in his dedication, it does not deal with kings and princes. He presents " only a man and woman who strive to win Laura's laurel," a reference not without interest because he shows his admiration for Petrarch by translating, in the third scene of the second act, a well-known sonnet by him. The earlier Spanish drama offers us no serious portrayal of love with its fatal consequences when thwarted. Here is represented the painful conflict between duty and will in the lady's heart, and the grief of the lovers, gradually intensified throughout the four acts. In the *comedias* of Tirso and of Montalbán, the biographical method is used, while in *Los amantes* emphasis is laid upon the crisis, and our sympathy is awakened by the moral struggle of the lovers against fatality.

With all these commendable qualities, the play cannot be regarded as a success. Tragic and commonplace elements too often stand side by side, and the scenes and characters employed to give comic relief frequently mar the unity of impression. The style is sometimes obscure, and the author unfortunately conceived of each act as a separate entity. He was conscious that Spain needed a new form of dramatic art, and his attempt to meet this need has historical interest, but he was lacking the originality to indicate definitely the path that the new drama must take.

The consuming love of Antony for Cleopatra, a favorite theme for dramatists for four hundred years, is portrayed in *Marco Antonio y Cleopatra,* a tragedy by the Licentiate Diego López de Castro, printed from an autograph manuscript of the year 1582. The first two acts, which present the jealousy of Flaminio, his betrayal of Antony, and the madness of Marcela appear to be original, but the last two acts are derived from Plutarch, and offer interesting analogies with Shakespeare's *Antony and Cleopatra.* The suicide of Heros is dramatically and tenderly presented, and there is almost a Shakespearian note in Cleopatra's anguish when she sees the lifeless body of Antony. "Surely he is dead," she cries, "since he hides from me his face." Cleopatra's death follows immediately upon this scene, and the play ends with Octavian's tender tribute to her beauty and charm.

It has a human interest which is absent from the tragedies of Cueva. Antony is not a pseudo-heroic type, but merely a weak man dominated by an unscrupulous and vacillating woman, and the sinister influence of Cleopatra upon his life is intelligible and awakens our sympathy. We may criticize the constant shifting of the scene from Rome to Alexandria, and we may find that the first two acts are unconvincing and unnecessary, but in his use of Plutarch's story in the last two acts, we must credit López de Castro with true dramatic sense, and he had lyrical talent of a high order. The influence of Juan de la Cueva may be seen in the division of the play into four acts and a tendency, as well, to imitate him in the metrical forms.

A far less successful attempt to imitate the methods and
verse forms of Cueva is found in an anonymous romantic
comedy entitled *Los cautivos*, printed from an undated
manuscript. The youth Ylioneo has abducted his sweetheart Lucela, and the maiden adopts the disguise of a man
in order to escape detection. They are captured by high-
waymen and sold to corsairs who carry them off to Carthage. Since they have different masters, they can see each
other only with great difficulty, and to make matters worse,
the daughter of Lucela's master falls in love with her, be-
lieving her to be a man. In the fourth act Rosiana persists
in her advances to Lucela and, angered by the latter's indifference, charges her with attempting to do her violence,
and Lucela is consigned to prison. When the latter appears for trial, she succeeds in proving her innocence by
revealing her identity, the lovers are promised their release,
and are forgiven by their fathers who arrive opportunely
on the scene.

The theme of a young girl masquerading as a man, either
from choice or necessity, was a favorite one in sixteenth-
century fiction and plays, and the ingenuity of novelists and
dramatists was taxed to contrive new complications arising
from this disguise. In many cases the disguised lady awakened love in the heart of another woman, as in the love of
Phebe for Rosalind, but rarely did this situation have tragic
possibilities. This central incident in *Los cautivos* bears
a marked resemblance to a scene in Calderón's *El José de
las mujeres*, and another analogue is found in Lope de
Vega's *Las Batuecas del Duque de Alba*. *Los cautivos*
contains the elements of a good play, of which the author
signally failed to take advantage except in parts of the
fourth act. The style is mediocre, even when due allowance is made for the lamentably incorrect text that we
possess.

The *Comedia Salvaje* of Joaquín Romero de Cepeda,
printed at Seville in 1582, is the last of the sixteenth-century dramatizations of the *Celestina*.[7] The author was a

native of Badajoz, and wrote the *Comedia Metamorfosea,* already mentioned, as well as lyrical verse. The *Comedia Salvaje* consists of four short acts, written in simple *redondillas,* and in this verse measure he may have been influenced by Juan de la Cueva. The first two acts, which deal with the abduction of Lucrecia by Anacreón with the aid of the bawd Gabrina, faithfully reproduce familiar incidents of the *Celestina* and are acceptable, but the attempt to show the consequences of wrongdoing in the last two acts cannot be taken seriously. The play represents an unsuccessful effort to combine the comedy of manners with the pastoral drama.

In discussing the predecessors of Lope de Vega in his *Loa de la comedia,* Rojas Villandrando mentions Francisco de la Cueva as the author of *El bello Adonis.* This play has been lost, but the Biblioteca Nacional preserves an undated autograph manuscript of the same writer's *Tragedia de Narciso.* He also wrote an inedited manuscript play of three acts (1587), preserved in the Biblioteca del Palacio, entitled *Farsa del obispo D. Gonzalo.* Don Gonzalo was a bishop, famous in the ballad of *Un día de San Antón,* who led four hundred knights from Jaen to recover cattle belonging to Don Diego de Haro from the Moors. Don Rodrigo cautions them about proceeding any further because the enemy was too numerous, but the bishop, unwilling to listen to reason, attacks them and is taken prisoner. We know little of the play, except in the portions derived from the ballad.[8] Francisco de la Cueva y Silva was a playwright, was praised by his friend Lope de Vega in his *Dorotea,* and was one of the foremost jurists of his time.

The *Tragedia de Narciso* treats the familiar story of Echo and Narcissus as told in the third book of the *Metamorphoses.* It is divided into four acts and belongs to the school of Juan de la Cueva. The author seems to have possessed greater lyrical than dramatic talents, but it is marked by good taste, and the description of the death of Narcissus is well done. It is also interesting as a unique example of the dramatic use of mythological material which attained such favor in the court plays of the following century.

The anonymous *Gran comedia de los famosos hechos de Mudarra,*[9] written in 1583 or 1585, and preserved in a manuscript at the Biblioteca Nacional, deals with the legend of the Infantes de Lara, already brought upon the stage by Juan de la Cueva. The author avoids the multiplicity of incidents which formed the basis of the latter's play, and restricts the action to Mudarra's vengeance. Familiar ballad materials were skilfully introduced to supplement the narrative of the chronicles, and truly dramatic situations are not lacking. It is divided into three acts, and the *redondilla* is the prevailing measure. Another playwright of the school of Juan de la Cueva is the anonymous author of an inedited *Segunda parte de las Hazañas del Cid,* mentioned by Don Ramón Menéndez Pidal in his *L'Épopée castillane.*[10]

In a conversation introduced into Chapter XLVIII of the first Part of *Don Quixote,* Cervantes discusses with some resentment the infatuation of theater-goers for nonsensical plays that violate all the laws of art, and mentions enthusiastically three tragedies, *La Isabela, La Filis,* and *La Alejandra,* which had found favor with their audiences in spite of the fact that they had observed the principles of art. These plays, written by Lupercio Leonardo de Argensola in his youth, were not included in the edition of the poet's works published at Saragossa in 1634, and were known only from the above-mentioned reference in *Don Quixote* until 1772 when two of them, *Isabela* and *Alejandra,* were included in his *Parnaso Español* by López de Sedano, who preserved the division into three acts found in the manuscript which he used. The Conde de la Viñaza followed López de Sedano's text in his edition of these plays, but he also printed variants from a manuscript preserved at the Biblioteca Nacional in which they are divided into four acts. That the latter was the original form is proved by the prologue to *Alejandra,* in which Tragedy

mentions among the innovations of modern drama the reduction of the five acts of the Latin theatre to four.   They
were probably written between 1581 and 1585 for presentation at Saragossa.   The prologue to *Alejandra* contains
a specific reference to that city, and *Isabela* has Saragossa
as its scene of action, and contains numerous appeals to local
patriotism.   *Filis,* the third play mentioned by Cervantes,
has been lost.

The prologues to the plays, written in *verso suelto,* furnish conclusive proof that while Argensola was not a strict
classicist in his conception of tragedy, he had little sympathy
with the Spanish popular drama.   *Isabela* is introduced by
the allegorical figure of Fame who, after apologizing for
violating the laws of tragedy by appearing in a public
theatre, congratulates the audience upon its good judgment
in preferring pitiful tragedies with a moral lesson to lewd
nonsense that pleases the masses.   The prologue to *Alejandra* is called *loa,* the first example of the word in a secular
play, and is recited by Tragedy herself who explains her
ancient and honorable lineage.   The learned Aristotle had
made rules for her adornment, but time had intervened, de-
priving her of one of her five acts, and of the choral songs
as well.   She expresses her surprise at seeing the spectators
so attentive, and bids them prepare for the war, deaths, and
tears that are to follow.   The *loa* to this play, while echo-
ing certain parts of the prologue to Lodovico Dolce's
Marianna (1565), the principal source of the play, is
largely borrowed from the prologue of *Orbecche* [11] (1541)
of Giraldi Cinthio, one of the earliest Italian imitators of
Seneca.

The action of *Isabela* is laid at Saragossa sometime between the battle of Alcoraz (1096) and 1104, the year of
the death of Peter I of Aragon.   The conflict between
Moors and Christians forms the background, and the plot
revolves about the passion of the Moorish king, Alboacén,
for the Christian maiden, Isabel.   It is a romantic tragedy,
conceived after the manner of the Italian followers of

Seneca rather than based on a close study of the Latin dramatist himself. The unities of place and time are observed, but no attention seems to have been given to unity of action. The central point is the determination of Isabel to die with her lover Muley, a convert to Christianity, rather than to yield herself to the enemy of her people. The generous attempt of Isabel to sacrifice herself for her lover recalls the episode of Olindo and Sofronia in the *Gerusalemme Liberata,* which Argensola may possibly have known, and a few similes and other material have been translated from the *Orbecche,* Virgil, and Horace. *Isabela* is a martyr of the type that has made Saragossa famous, and it is this spirit of Christian devotion, joined with national inspiration, which constitutes one of the chief beauties and merits of the play.

The tragedy of *Alejandra* has two well-defined actions: the desire of a prince to avenge his father's death, and the insane jealousy of a king which finds its satisfaction in the death of his queen, thus combining the themes of *Hamlet* and *Othello.* The latter part of the play, including the jealously of King Acoreo and his bloody revenge upon the queen and an innocent courtier, is based upon Lodovico Dolce's *Marianna,* a dramatization of the world-famous story of Herod and Mariamne, as related by Josephus. The court of one of the Egyptian Ptolemies, which the author chose for a background, was well adapted to the gruesome incidents here presented. After being obliged to wash her hands in the blood of the man she loves, Alejandra drinks poison, bites off her tongue in her agony and spits it at the king; children are ruthlessly murdered; Acoreo is assassinated by members of his own escort, who offer his head to Orodante, and are themselves executed as traitors; Sila stabs Orodante and then commits suicide, and although the ghastly execution of Lupercio is mercifully described by a messenger, Argensola even surpasses Dolce in the element of physical horror.

In adapting this Italian play, Argensola made a number of important changes. Marianna is entirely innocent of infidelity; Alejandra is unfaithful, at least in thought. The cup-bearer, who is merely an instrument in the conspiracy in Dolce's tragedy, becomes a prominent character in *Alejandra* as claimant to the throne. *Marianna* ends with the repentance of Herod for the execution of Soemo, Marianna, Alessandra, and his two sons. In *Alejandra*, the death of Acoreo at the hands of the conspirators furnishes the *dénouement*. The sub-plot, including the love of Lupercio and Orodante for Sila, as well as the conspiracy of Ostilo and Rémulo, seems to be entirely of Argensola's invention.

It is easy to ridicule the horrors of this play, but we should not forget that the romantic tragedy of the sixteenth century was a natural outgrowth of imitation of Seneca. *Alejandra*, therefore, should not be compared with the plays of Lope de Vega and Tirso, but with *The Spanish Tragedy* of Kyd, with Giraldi Cinthio's *Orbecche* and with the tragedies of Robert Garnier, all of which represent approximately the same stage of dramatic development as the plays of Argensola. With respect to versification, they both belong to the school of Juan de la Cueva, showing a preference for *tercetos*.

A tyrant play belonging to about the same period is the anonymous *Comedia del Tirano Rey Corbanto*, edited from a manuscript in the Biblioteca Nacional and written mainly in *redondillas*. It is in four acts and belongs in general to the manner of Juan de la Cueva. While the play is elementary in its simplicity, the author had the good judgment to present only such scenes and episodes which were necessary for the unity of the plot.

In the prologue to his *Ocho comedias y ocho entremeses* (1615), Cervantes chats half playfully and with a touch of sadness about his early plays before Lope de Vega directed the Spanish drama along new paths. He tells us that at first he composed from twenty to thirty plays, of which he mentions specifically *Los tratos de Argel, La destrucción de Numancia,* and *La batalla naval,* written for the theatres of Madrid, and he adds whimsically that all of these were performed without any offering of cucumbers or other sign of disapproval from the audience.

In the *Adjunta al Parnaso,*[12] published the preceding year, Cervantes mentions among his early plays *Los tratos de Argel, La Numancia, La gran Turquesca, La batalla naval, La Jerusalém, La Amaranta o la del Mayo, El bosque amoroso, La Única,* and *La bizarra Arsinda,* " and many others which I have forgotten," and expresses preference for still another, *La Confusa,* which is also referred to in the *Viaje del Parnaso.* With respect to the latter, we know, thanks to a discovery of Pérez Pastor, that while residing at Madrid in 1585 Cervantes contracted with a theatrical manager to write two plays called *La Confusa* and *El trato de Constantinopla y muerte de Selín.* We do not know whether the latter was ever performed or even written since Cervantes did not include it in either list. Of these early plays, only two have been preserved in their early form, *El trato* (or *Los tratos*) *de Argel* and *El cerco* (or *La destruyción*) *de Numancia,* which were first printed in 1784, and which, on the basis of their order in the two above-mentioned lists, were probably the first dramatic compositions of Cervantes.

" Of the captivity and deeds of Miguel de Cervantes a separate history might be written," says Padre Diego de Haedo in his *Topografía e historia general de Argel* (1612). Quite as interesting as such a history, had it been written, are the three *novelas* and the two plays, *El trato de Argel* and *Los baños de Argel,* in which Cervantes drew largely upon his own experiences during his five years of slavery. With the memories of his own hardships fresh in his mind, he attempted to describe in *El trato de Argel* the sufferings of the Christian captives in Algiers, and drew a picture that must have been painful to his audience. One could not see with equanimity the courageous efforts to escape that were rewarded only by death; the apostasy of men of weaker stuff; the ruthless disregard of Christian womanhood, and the martyrdom of Christian priests; nor could one witness without righteous anger the scene of the slave-market where members of the same family were sold to the highest bidders and separated from each other, condemned to a living death. The purpose of Cervantes was to prick the conscience of Philip II, and in an eloquent outburst in the first act he pleads for those captives, introducing verses which he had directed to the Secretary of State, Mateo Vázquez, in 1577.

The plot and characters are completely overshadowed by the absorbing interest of the background. The trials of the lovers, Aurelio and Silvia, which recur in *Los baños de Argel* and in *El amante liberal,* become insignificant when compared with the misery of their companions in slavery. Cervantes did not understand at that time the art of arranging dramatic scenes. The construction is loose and, as a play, it cannot be accorded high rank. However, as a picture of some of his own experiences during five years, as a cry of anguish from the heart of a brave man, and as an appeal to remedy conditions that were a disgrace to Christendom, it deserves our respect and admiration. Of the two manuscripts of the play which have been preserved, the chief difference is that in one of these it is divided into four acts, and in the other, into five. The original version was undoubtedly in four acts. The play was written for performance in some theatre of Madrid, not during the author's captivity in Algiers as has been claimed,[13] and the date may be fixed at 1582 or 1583.

The *Comedia del cerco de Numancia,* in four acts, presents the heroic defense made by the city of Numantia against the Romans, culminating in its capture in 133 B.C. by Scipio Æmilianus. Cervantes may have read the details of this famous campaign in the histories of Appian or Florus, or in the continuation of Florián de Ocampo's *Crónica* by Ambrosio de Morales. He showed good judgment and secured a semblance of dramatic unity by focusing his attention upon the death agony of the city that dared defy the might of Rome.

The play begins with the arrival of Scipio as commander-in-chief, his refusal to discuss peace terms with the Numantians, and his determination to starve them into submission and to destroy the city. The gradual exhaustion of the defenders in their struggle against hunger is painfully described, and when Scipio finally succeeds in entering the city, he finds himself deprived of the chief fruits of his victory. Only heaps of corpses and desolation meet his eyes. He offers wealth and liberty to a youth who has mounted a tower of the wall with the keys of the city, but the brave Numantian hurls himself from it, thus robbing Scipio of the glory of taking a captive to Rome as a symbol of his victory. This last scene is borrowed by Cervantes from a ballad by Timoneda which was included in the *Rosa Gentil* and was derived from an account in the absurd *Corónica de España abreviada* (1481) by Diego de Valera in which reference is made to the last survivor of Zamora, not of Numantia.[14]

Many of the incidents, such as the love of Marandro and Lira, and the bold attempt of Marandro and Leonicio to secure food in the Roman camp, claim our interest and sympathy, but it must be admitted that the play has epic rather than dramatic qualities. The introduction of the personified figures of War, Famine, Spain, the Duero River and others which in a way take the place of a chorus and upon which Cervantes later prided himself, detracts from the impression of reality he sought to create. It is the somber background that enlists our respect and admiration. To Cervantes the Numantians were the forbears of his own people, and their bravery represented the defense of Spain against a foreign invader. The play is the best literary expression that we possess of Spanish patriotism at the close of the sixteenth century.

The two early plays of Cervantes show the imitatiun of Juan de la Cueva with respect to versification. *El trato de Argel* shows about an equal number of *redondillas* and *coplas reales* on the one hand, and Italian meters on the other, while in the *Cerco de Numancia,* owing to the tragic theme and the chorus-like allegorical figures, the predominant strophic measure is *octavas.*

Concerning the other early plays written by Cervantes from the year 1582 to 1587, it has been proved, I think, by Professor Schevill and the late Señor Bonilla y San Martín in their notable edition [15] that the volume of *Ocho Comedias* was made up of plays composed at different periods of the author's life, and that the manuscripts of the older plays appeared probably in 1615 with new titles; with a semblance of a more up-to-date versification, marked principally by the addition of verses in *romance;* and divided somewhat awkwardly at times, in three acts instead of four. *La casa de los celos y selvas de Ardenia,* based upon incidents from Boiardo and Ariosto, is an early play and may be identified as *El bosque amoroso* which was referred to in the *Adjunta al Parnaso.* *El laberinto de amor,* taken from the *Orlando Furioso,* by internal evidence must have been originally written as *La Confusa,* the favorite play of Cervantes, as he tells us in the *Viaje del Parnaso.* *Los baños de Argel* also belongs in part to the first *fórmula estética* of Cervantes.

Like Rey de Artieda a veteran of Lepanto, and like him a native of Valencia, Cristóbal de Virués spent many years fighting in Tunis, Italy, and Flanders, and at the close of his life published five tragedies at Madrid in 1609. We have little evidence for determining the date of their composition, but the fact that they were undoubtedly earlier than the first plays of Lope de Vega, and show an acquaintance with the theatre of Juan de la Cueva, allows us to conjecture that they were written between 1580 and 1585. Four of these plays were composed in three acts, an innovation for which he claimed priority in the prologue to his

La gran Semiramis, and this claim was supported by Lope de Vega in his *Arte nuevo de hacer comedias en este tiempo.* It is true that Avendaño's *Comedia Florisea,* in three acts, was printed in 1551, but the Spanish plays with which Virués was acquainted were written in four or rarely five acts, and he had good reasons to believe himself the inventor of a new form.

In the tragedy of *Elisa Dido,* he proposed to write a play " entirely after the manner of the Greeks and Romans, with care and study." So far as the Greek drama is concerned, Virués probably knew it only by the pale reflections that we find in Trissino's *Sofonisba,* but the moral declamation comes from Seneca. Unity of time is observed, and the division into five acts, the use of the chorus, and the exclusion of comic elements are also, superficially at least, characteristic of a classical play. In common with Trissino and most of the Italian dramatists of his time, and Bermúdez as well, he adopted hendecasyllabic *verso suelto* as the basis of his verse with *estancias* of various forms in the choruses. While the main outlines of this play on Dido are derived from the historical account contained in Justin's *Historiae Philippicae,* the poetical narrative of Virgil also contributed a few incidents.

At the beginning of the play, Dido is aware of the ambitious plans of Iarbas and accepts the proposal of marriage made by his emissary. Her reply is a diplomatic lie, and the interest is concentrated upon this fallacious answer and her suicide in the presence of her suitor. Iarbas himself does not appear until the *dénouement,* and the heroine's rôle occupies only about one hundred lines. Unfortunately, after the manner of Giraldi with his liking for romanesque intrigue, Virués preferred a more complex plot by introducing two Carthaginian chiefs, Seleuco and Carquedonio, who are enamored of Dido, and who in turn have awakened love in the hearts of Ismeria and Delbora. He attempted to heighten the interest by the introduction of irrelevant episodes, and was totally unable to focus his attention upon a logical sequence of incidents.

We do not know the date of *Elisa Dido,* probably it was the first, judging from the evolution of his dramatic technique, but it is certain that *La gran Semiramis* is the first of his three-act plays. He tells us in his preface that in these four tragedies he attempted to reconcile classical art and the practice of contemporaneous writers, taking from each its best elements, and thus satisfying the requirements of modern art. It is charitable to assume that this preface was written many years before its publication in 1609, for it is inconceivable that Virués could have expressed himself with such complacency had he been acquainted with the *comedias* of Lope de Vega, or even with the development of the drama in his native city of Valencia.

"In all my plays," wrote Virués, "although written for my own amusement and in my youth, heroic and grave moral examples are shown, as befits their grave and heroic style," as the author did in his poem *El Monserrate.* He shared Giraldi Cinthio's conception of the moral function of tragedy, and followed his example by trying to deter men from sin by showing its terrible consequences. He did not concern himself, however, with the petty sins that are within the reach of any man. In order to strengthen the force of his moral lesson, he deals with crime on a heroic scale, of such extravagant proportions that the reader of today, instead of trembling at the consequences of misdoing, merely smiles incredulously.

La gran Semiramis presents the familiar story as narrated by Justin and other classical historians. The action covers some twenty-two years, but unity of time is kept in each one of the three acts. It describes the triumphant progress of this monster of vice who, through the betrayal of her husband, becomes consort of Ninus, king of Assyria whom, in due time, she poisons, and her assassination by her son Ninias, for whom she had an incestuous love, ends the play. The theme is the rise and fall of a queen and of her court, due to the destructive power of ambition.

La cruel Casandra presents another woman who is an artist in crime. Her fury is directed against a prince and princess of Leon, and also against a lady of the court, named Fulgencia. In order to encompass their death, Cassandra has no scruples in sacrificing her own brother, and finally dies as a penalty for her treachery. In this most complicated play, the author makes good use, at times, of dramatic suspense.

Delirium reaches its limit in Atila Furioso, the protagonist of which is not Attila himself, but Flaminia, a woman dressed as a page whose identity is known only to him. The play is made up of scenes of crime and bloodshed, culminating in the madness of Attila in his own wedding festivities caused by a poison given to him by Flaminia; the latter is strangled by Attila, and the king dies from poison she had given to him. The historical basis of part of the plot was found in Foresti's Supplementum Chronicorum ab initio mundi which was translated by Viñoles with the title Suma de todas las crónicas del mundo, and also probably the Crónica General, but Virués did not follow his sources closely and invented many of the incidents. The influence of Seneca is found particularly in this play, and the madness of Attila is based upon Hercules Furens and Hercules Œtaeus.

The experiences of Marcela in La infelice Marcela are directly based upon the story of Isabel in five Cantos of the Orlando Furioso. Virués was pitiless with his principal characters, and refused to allow a protagonist to survive the last act, thereby altering Ariosto's story because in the original, Isabel was rescued by Orlando. The play, to be sure, ends tragically, but the atmosphere is that of a romance of chivalry, far removed from the horrors of his earlier compositions.

With respect to the versification of the three-act plays, La cruel Casandra has no Spanish meters, but it has a wide variety of Italian forms, while the other three plays use both Spanish and Italian meters. In these four tragedies, each act presents a fairly complete action, a method of procedure to which he approvingly refers in the prologue to *La gran Semíramis*. He applied to his plays the same principles of composition that he later employed in his epic poem, *El Monserrate,* and it would not be unfair to consider them as tragedies in three cantos. His intense imagination and his ignorance of the meaning of moderation, either in fancy or in language, led to a complete disregard of the principle of unity of action. According to his conception, playwriting consisted in the accumulation of horrible scenes.

Two plays by Gabriel Lobo Laso de la Vega, well known as epic poet and ballad writer, and printed at Alcalá de Henares in 1587, might have been written by Virués in a gentle mood. Composed in three acts with *redondillas,* octaves, and *tercetos* as the favorite meters, they represent a completely unsuccessful attempt to adapt epic material with lyrical incidents, to dramatic form. The *Tragedia de la honra de Dido restaurada* proposes to correct the false opinion concerning Dido derived from Virgil, and, following Justin's account, describes the murder of Sichaeus by Pygmalion, Dido's flight across the seas and arrival at Carthage, and her suicide to escape the unwelcome attentions of the neighboring king Iarbas. He apparently conceived of drama as a series of disconnected lyrical scenes. The same faults are found, to an even greater degree, in the *Tragedia de la Destruyción de Costantinopla* which deals with the defeat of the Emperor Constantine and the capture of Constantinople by Mahommed II in 1453 in spite of the valiant efforts to defend the city by the Genoese Justiniani. The use of allegorical figures such as Discord, Envy, Ambition, and Fame recalls the first tragedies by Cervantes and a few other contemporaneous plays. It was published again in a collection of *Seis comedias de Lope de Vega,* printed at Lisbon in 1603, of which only the last, *El Perseguido,* is by Lope.

A reference by Lope de Vega in his *Laurel de Apolo* to Miguel Sánchez Requejo, well-known author of the *Canción a Cristo crucificado*, as " the first master that the Muses of Terence have had in Spain," were explained by Baist, Rennert, and others as recognition by Lope that Sánchez had preceded him in writing plays.   When we turn to other references to Miguel Sánchez, we find that he is mentioned after Lope de Vega in Rojas Villandrando's *Loa de la comedia*, in Cervantes' prologue to his *Ocho Comedias* and in Suárez de Figueroa's *Plaza Universal*.   He was mentioned as living, in a book printed in 1620, although when Lope referred to him in his *Arte nuevo de hacer comedias* (1609), it is apparent that by that time he had given up writing plays.   It is clear, therefore, that Lope de Vega and Sánchez were contemporaries, and besides, as Stephenson [16] has pointed out in an unpublished thesis, that Lope's words are literally true with reference to the influence of Terence on Sánchez.

In the above-mentioned citation from the *Arte nuevo*, Lope speaks of Sánchez as the dramatic poet who employed the device *engañar con la verdad* in all of his plays.   Morel-Fatio explained this as a premature disclosure of the *dénouement*, but Northup [17] has proved that to his contemporaries " deceiving with the truth was a veracious statement couched in plain language with the intent that it be not believed," and that it was far from original with Sánchez. He finds one example of this in Sánchez's play *La guarda cuidadosa*, first published, so far as we know, in 1615.

Going a step forward, Stephenson finds an undeveloped and episodic form of the device in question in the *Heautontimorumenos* and *Andria* of Terence, that there are examples of *engañar con la verdad*, not only in *La guarda cuidadosa* but also in *La isla bárbara*, that Lope learned from Sánchez the trick of " deceiving with the truth," and used it in many of his plays.

The second play ascribed to him, *La isla bárbara*, was first printed in 1638 and attributed to Lope de Vega, but there are three manuscripts of the play, one of which assigns it to Miguel Sánchez, and another contains licenses for performances in 1611 and 1614. The critics agree that *La isla bárbara* is earlier than *La guarda cuidadosa,* and in the opinion of Alonso Cortés,[18] in view of its mediocre workmanship it was not written either by Lope or by Sánchez. On the basis of versifrcation, Morley [19] said speaking of *La guarda cuidadosa,* that " aside from the *romance,* there is nothing in Sánchez's strophic formula which might not be derived from Cueva."

About the year 1587 has been fixed by most critics as the end of the first period of Spanish dramatic history. Of the plays of Lope de Vega that have come down to us and can be dated approximately, three were written before 1585 and possibly two or three more by 1587. Bataillon has said justly: *Peut-être faudrait-il conclure que le théâtre espagnol du dernier tiers du xvie siècle, période décisive où prend forme la comedia à laquelle Lope a attaché son nom, ne nous est connu que par des vestiges très insuffisants pour reconstituer cette création dramatique dans son ensemble et dans son progrès.*[20] He was speaking of the dearth of material in the Spanish drama not only in the days of Juan de la Cueva but also when Lope de Vega began to write and to attract notice from the public.

It is possible that no amount of study can fill in satisfactorily the gap which exists between the precursors of Lope and Lope himself. On the other hand, great progress has already been made with respect to the chronology of the Spanish drama, and notably of Lope's plays. Due to the pioneering work of Buchanan, Morley, Hämel, and others, a chronological basis has been laid. It is possible that a further study of Lope's carly plays as compared with those of his contemporaries would produce valuable results.

However, although the lines connecting Encina to Lope may never be drawn exactly, many of the forerunners of the master mind are interesting in themselves, and a few of them are notable examples of what the sixteenth century could accomplish in the writing of plays.

ABBREVIATIONS

ARom —Archivum Romanicum
BAE —Biblioteca de Autores Españoles
BHi —Bulletin Hispanique
BRAE —Boletín de la (Real)Academia Española
EEB —Estudios eruditos in memoriam de Adolfo Bonilla
       y San Martín
Hisp —Hispania
HMP —Homenaje ofrecido a Menéndez Pidal
HR   —Hispanic Review
MLN —Modern Language Notes
MLR —Modern Language Review
PQ   —Philological Quarterly
PMLA—Publications of the Modern Language Associa-
       tion of America
RABM—Revista de Archivos, Bibliotecas y Museos
RBAM—Revista de la Biblioteca, Archivo y Museo del
       Ayuntamiento de Madrid
RFE —Revista de Filología Española
RHi —Revue Hispanique
RR   —The Romanic Review
ZRPh —Zeitschrift für romanische Philologie

NOTES

CHAPTER I

1. Karl Young, *The Drama in the Medieval Church*, 1933, I, 577, 569; II, 427.
2. R. Menéndez Pidal, *Cantar de Mio Cid*, 1908, I, 25–26.
3. Winifred Sturdevant, *The Misterio de los Reyes Magos*, 77–79; 43.
4. Schack, *Historia de la literatura y del arte dramático en España*, I, 219–220.
5. The development of the Catalan and Valencian drama as opposed to pageantry is obscure, chiefly owing to lack of texts. In his interesting article *Notes on the Religious Drama in Mediæval Spain*, MLR, 1935, XXX, 176, Mr. A. A. Parker after giving an outline of pageantry in Valencia and Catalonia, says: "It is evident . . . that real miracle plays only came into being in Valencia between 1500 and 1550." Dr. H. Corbató who has recently edited the *Misteri de Sant Christofol*, the *Misteri de Adam y Eva* and the *Misteri del rey Herodes* in his volume *Los Misterios del Corpus de Valencia*, University of California, Berkeley, 1932, says that these three plays (p. 67) were probably written in the latter part of the fifteenth or early sixteenth century.
6. *Memorial histórico español*, VIII, 75–76.
7. E. K. Chambers, *The Mediæval Stage*, 1903, I, 274–335; J. Sánchez-Arjona, *El teatro en Sevilla en los siglos XVI y XVII*, 1887, 3–24; J. P. W. Crawford, *A Note on the Boy Bishop in Spain*, RR, 1921, XII, 146–54.
8. A. Bonilla y San Martín, *Las Bacantes, o del origen del teatro*, 1921, 48–61 and R. Menéndez Pidal, *La poesía juglaresca y juglares*, 1924, 1–142.
9. J. Alenda y Mira, *Relaciones y fiestas públicas de España*, 1903.
10. *Memorial hist. esp.*, VIII, 50–51.
11. A. Cortina, *Rodrigo Cota*, RBAM, 1929, VI, 165.
12. Rudolph Schevill, *Ovid and the Renascence in Spain*, Berkeley, 1913, 65.

CHAPTER II

1. Included in *El viaje entretenido*, 1603, which may be read conveniently in *Orígenes de la novela*, IV, 1915 (NBAE, XXI), by Menéndez y Pelayo.
2. E. Giménez Caballero, *Hipótesis a un problema de Juan del Encina*, RFE, 1927, XIV, 59–69.
3. Joseph E. Gillet, *Notes on the Language of the Rustics in the Drama of the Sixteenth-Century*, HMP, I, 443.
4. G. Lozinski, *La Bataille de Caresme et de Charnage, Bibl. des Hautes Études*, CCLXII.
5. R. M. Macandrew, *Notes on Juan del Encina's Églogas trobadas de Virgilio*, MLR, 1929, XXIV, 454–58.
6. C. Michaëlis de Vasconcellos, *Nótulas sobre cantares e vilhancicos peninsulares e a respeito de Juan del Encina*, RFE, 1918, V, 346–50. This song, which is not included in the Asenjo Barbieri edition of the plays of Encina, may be read in Menéndez y Pelayo, *Antología*, IV, 373.

7. Michaëlis de Vasconcellos, *ibid.*, 351–54. R. Espinosa Maeso, *Ensayo biográfico del Maestro Lucas Fernández*, BRAE, 1923, X, 403, conjectures that a play given at Salamanca on Corpus Christi day, 1505, called *Auto del Dios de Amor* might have been Encina's *Representación del Amor*. It might be objected that Encina's play ill accords with the devotional spirit that characterizes the Corpus festival.

8. R. E. House, *A Study of Encina and the Égloga interlocutoria*, RR, 1916, VII, 458–69.

9. J. P. W. Crawford, *The Source of Juan del Encina's Égloga de Fileno y Zambardo*, RHi, 1916, XXXVI, 475–88 and *Encina's Égloga de Fileno, Zambardo y Cardonio and Antonio Tebaldeo's Second Eclogue*, HR, 1934, II, 327–33.

10. P. Mazzei, *Contributo allo studio delle fonti italiane del teatro di Juan del Enzina e Torres Naharro*, Lucca, 1922.

11. A. Miola, *Un testo drammatico spagnuolo del XV secolo*, in *Miscellanea Caix-Canello*, 1886, 175–89.

12. J. A. Meredith, *Introito and Loa in the Spanish Drama of the Sixteenth Century*, 17–21.

13. W. S. Jack, *The Early Entremés in Spain: The Rise of a Dramatic Form*, 9–21.

14. S. G. Morley, *Strophes in the Spanish Drama before Lope de Vega*, HMP, I, 508.

15. J. B. Trend, *The Music of Spanish History*, Oxford University Press, 1926, 133–41.

16. M. Gauthier, *De quelques Jeux d'Esprit*, RHi, 1915, XXIII, 388–93.

CHAPTER III

1. Meredith, *ibid.*, 11–17.

2. I do not agree with Dr. Queirós Veloso that Vicente in the first part imitated Encina's *Auto del Repelón*. The resemblances of the two plays are not striking. See A. Forjaz de Sampaio, *Historia da literatura portuguesa ilustrada*, Lisboa, 1930, II. Queirós Veloso, *Gil Vicente*, 31.

3. C. Michaëlis de Vasconcellos, *Notas Vicentinas*, IV in *Rev. da Univ. de Coimbra*, IX.

4. G. G. King, *The Play of the Sibyl Cassandra*, New York, 1921. The play has been edited separately by Álvaro Giráldez, 1921. See also A. H Krappe, ARom, 1924, VIII, 178.

5. A. F. G. Bell, *Four Plays of Gil Vicente*, Cambridge, 1920, xxi–xxii.

6. Morley, *Strophes etc.*, HMP, I, 512–13.

7. For certain of these riddles, see R. Schevill, *Some Forms of the Riddle Question*, Univ. of California Pub. in Mod. Phil., II, 1911.

8. Morley, *Strophes etc.*, 510.

9. E. Cotarelo y Mori, *Fragmentos de una farsa*, Rev. Esp. de Lit. y Arte, 1901, I, 140.

10. A. Bonilla y San Martín, *Las Bacantes*, 1921, 117n.

11. J. P. W. Crawford, *The Catalan Mascarón and an Episode in Jacob van Maerlant's Merlijn*, PMLA, 1911, XXVI, 31–50.

12. Meredith, *ibid.*, 57–77.

13. See J. P. W. Crawford, *The Pastor and the Bobo in the Spanish Religious Drama of the Sixteenth Century*, RR, 1911, II, 376–401.

14. J. P. W. Crawford, *The Devil as a Dramatic Figure in the Spanish Religious Drama before L. de V.*, RR, 1910, I, 302–12.

15. See J. P. W. Crawford, *The Braggart Soldier and the Rufián in the Span. Drama of the Sixteenth Century*, RR, 1911, II, 186–208.

16. W. S. Hendrix, *Some Native Comic Types in the Early Span. Drama*, Columbus, Ohio, 1924.

17. S. G. Morley, MLN, 1923, XXXVIII, 298.

18. J. E. Gillet, *Apuntes sobre las obras dramáticas de Vasco Díaz Tanco de Fregenal*, RABM, 1923, XLIV, 352–56.

19. R. Espinosa Maeso, *Ensayo biográfico del maestro L. F.*, BRAE, 1923, X, 403–04 and 406–08.

20. Morley, *ibid.*, 509.

21. *La vida de Lazarillo de Tormes*, edición y notas de Julio Cejador y Frauca, 1914, 35–68. See A. H. Krappe, ARom, 1924, VIII, 178–79.

22. W. H. Shoemaker, *The Multiple Stage in Spain during the Fifteenth and Sixteenth Centuries*, Princeton, 1935.

CHAPTER IV

1. Professor J. E. Gillet will print shortly in the *Hispanic Review* this *Égloga* with introduction.

2. A. Pellizzari, *Strenne di Leone Decimo*, publ. in *Portogallo e Italia nel secolo XVI*, Napoli, 1914.

3. E. Cotarelo y Mori, RABM, 1902, VII, 267–72 and A. Bonilla y San Martín, *Rev. Crít. Hispano-Americana*, 1915, I, 44–51.

4. J. Hutton, *The First Idyl of Moschus in Imitations to the Year 1800*, *American Journal of Philology*, 1928, XLIX, 105–25. See also on the folktale of the rejuvenating smithy, A. H. Krappe, ARom, 1924, VIII, 179.

5. Óscar de Pratt, *G. V. Notas e Comentários*. Lisboa, 1931, 221–37.

6. Pratt, *ibid.*, 239–44.

7. R. Schevill, *Cuatro palabras sobre " Nadie,"* *Rev. Crít. Hispano-Americana*, 1915, I, 30–37 and P. Lehmann, *Die Parodie im Mittelalter*, 1922, 40–44.

8. E. Cotarelo y Mori, *La historia de la zarzuela*, 1934, 21.

9. Rev. of Adam Darowki, *Bona Sforza*, Rome, 1904. *Archivio Storico Ital.*, Ser. 4, VI, 1906, 504–507.

10. *Cancionero Musical*, ed. Asenjo Barbieri, 197–201.

11. J. P. W. Crawford, *Echarse Pullas, a Popular Form of Tenzone*, RR, 1915, VI, 150–64.

12. E. Kohler, *Sieben span. dram. Eklogen*, 172–73.

13. J. P. W. Crawford, *The Relationship of Castillejo's Farsa de la Constanza and the Sermón de Amores*, HR, 1936, IV, 373–75.

CHAPTER V

1. J. E. Gillet, *The Date of T.N.'s Death*, HR, 1936, IV, 41–46.

2. J. A. Meredith, *Introito and Loa in the Span. Drama of the Sixteenth Century*, 46–47.

3. A. Luzio, *Isabella d'Este ne' primordi del papato di Leone X e il suo viaggio a Roma nel 1514–1515*, *Arch. Stor. Lomb.* 1906, Ser. 4, 147 ff. and H. M. Vaughan, *The Medici Popes*, London, 1908, 185–91.

4. J. P. W. Crawford, *Two Notes on the Plays of T.N.* I. *Who is the Character of Divina in the Comedia Jacinta?* HR, 1937, V, 76–77.

5. M. Romera-Navarro, *Estudio de la Comedia Himenea de T.N.*, RR, 1921, XII, 50–62.

6. J. P. W. Crawford, *Two Notes on the Plays of T. N.* II. *Terence's Andria and the Comedia Serofina*, HR, 1937, V, 78.

7. Mazzei, *ibid.*, 97–103.

8. See Barbara Matulka, *The Main Sources of Scudéry's Le Prince Déguisé, the Primaleón*, RR, 1934, XXV, 1–14; C. Mazzi, *La Congrega dei Rozzi di Siena*, Firenze, 1882, II, 46–48; Mazzei, *ibid.*, 117–122; A. H. Krappe, ARom, 1924, VIII, 179.

9. J. E. Gillet, *T.N. and the Span. Drama of the Sixteenth Century*, EEB, II, 437–68. A second part was published in the HR, 1937, V, 193–207.

10. Pratt, *ibid.*, 217–20.

11. Pratt, *ibid.*, 209–15.

12. J. E. Gillet, *Micael de Carvajal*, xxix–xxxii.

CHAPTER VI

1. W. S. Jack, *ibid.*, Chap. II.

2. N. Alonso Cortés, *El teatro en Valladolid*, 12–16.

3. Cervantes, *Comedias y entremeses*, edición pub. por R. Schevill y A. Bonilla, 1915, I, 315; 318–319; 380.

4. J. P. W. Crawford, *Analogues to the Story of Selvagia in Montemayor's Diana*, MLN, 1914, XXIX, 192–94.

5. J. P. W. Crawford, *Again the Cuestión de amor in the Early Span. Drama*, HR, 1933, I, 310–22.

6. Henri Mérimée, *L'Art dramatique à Valencia*, 149–55.

7. W. Creizenach, *Geschichte des neueren Dramas*, 1923, III, 91.

8. A. Bonilla y San Martín, *Las Bacantes o del origen del teatro*, 1921, 137n.

9. A. Giannini, *Una creduta fonte boccaccesca di un intermezzo spagnolo anonimo del secolo XVI*, RHi, 1933, LXXXI, pte. I, 526–29.

10. W. S. Jack, *ibid.*, 115–16.

11. See G. T. Northup, *Ten Spanish Farces of the 16th, 17th and 18th Centuries*, Boston, 1922, Introduction ix–xiv. Professor E. B. Place has recently written an article *Does Lope de Vega's Gracioso siem in part from Harlequin?* Hisp., 1934, XVII, 257–270, in which he answers the question affirmatively.

12. J. P. W. Crawford, *The Spanish Pastoral Drama*, 1915, 83–90.

CHAPTER VII

1. Jenaro Alenda, *Catálogo de autos sacramentales*, BRAE, 1921, VIII, 268–69.

2. J. P. W. Crawford, ed. RR, 1912, III, 280–300.

3. W. H. Shoemaker, *The Llabrés Manuscript and its Castilian Plays*, HR, 1936, IV, 243–46.

4. W. H. Shoemaker, *The Multiple Stage in Spain during the Fifteenth and Sixteenth Centuries*, 1935, 45–48, 116–18.

5. Owing to the courtesy of my friend, Dr. H. J. Chaytor of St. Catharine's College, Cambridge, I possess an edition of this play in manuscript.

6. J. E. Gillet, *Micael de Carvajal, Tragedia Josephina*, xv–xviii.

7. Florence Whyte, *The Dance of Death in Spain and Catalonia*, 111.

8. R. Menéndez Pidal, *El rey don Rodrigo en la literatura*, 1924, 120–21.

9. M. Serrano y Sanz, *B.P. y su historia de Santa Librada*, BRAE, 1922, IX, 301–10.

10. See A. Bonilla y San Martín, *El teatro escolar en el renacimiento esp. y un fragmento inédito del toledano Juan Pérez*, HMP, III, 143–55.

11. A. Morel-Fatio, *Ate relegata et Minerva restituta*, BHi, 1903, V, 9–24.

12. For his plays see H. Mérimée, *L'Art dramatique à Valencia*, 250–71.

13. For plays given in the Jesuit schools in Spain in the sixteenth century see an incomplete study by J. García Soriano, *El teatro de colegio en España*, BRAE, 1927, XIV; 1928, XV; 1929, XVI and 1932, XIX.

14. García Soriano, *ibid.*, BRAE, 1927, XIV, 374–409.

15. García Soriano, *ibid.*, BRAE 1927, XIV, 409–11.

16. García Soriano, *ibid.*, BRAE, 1927, XIV, 535–65.

17. García Soriano, *ibid.*, BRAE, 1928, XV, 406–46; 651–80; XVI, 80–104.

18. González Pedroso, *Autos Sacramentales*, BAE, LVIII.

CHAPTER VIII

1. Antoni de Vilaragut, *Les Tragedies de Séneca*, ed. M. Gutiérrez del Caño, Valencia, 1914.

2. N. Alonso Cortés, *El autor de la Tragedia de los amores de Eneas y de la reyna Dido*, RFE, 1931, XVIII, 162–64.

3. C. Eyer, *Juan Cirne and the Celestina*, HR, 1937, V, 265–268.

4. R. Menéndez Pidal, *La leyenda de los Infantes de Lara*, 1934, 126 and 353–80.

5. J. P. W. Crawford, *A Sixteenth-Century Spanish Analogue of Measure for Measure*, MLN, 1920, XXXV, 330–34.

6. J. E. Gillet, *Cueva's Comedia del Infamador and the Don Juan Legend*, MLN, 1922, XXXVII, 206–12.

7. Menéndez y Pelayo, *Orígenes de la novela*, III, cclxviii–cclxx.

8. R. Menéndez Pidal, *L'Épopée Castillane*, 1910, 210–11, and RFE, 1915, II, 112–36.

9. R. Menéndez Pidal, *La leyenda de los Infantes de Lara*, 126–27; 353–80.

10. Page 210.

11. J. A. Meredith, *Introito and Loa in the Spanish Drama of the Sixteenth Century*, 116–22.

12. Miguel de Cervantes, *Obras completas*, ed. R. Schevill y A. Bonilla, *Viaje del Parnaso, Adjunta al Parnaso*, 124.

13. Cervantes, *ibid.*, *Comedias y entremeses*, VI, 5–8.

14. Cervantes, *ibid.*, *Comedias y entremeses*, VI, 40–52.

15. Cervantes, *ibid.*, *Comedias y entremeses*, VI, 73–84, 107–123.

16. R. C. Stephenson, *Miguel Sánchez: A Contemporary Terentian Influence upon Lope de Vega*, University of Texas unpublished thesis, Austin, 1930.

17. G. T. Northup, *The Rhetorical Device of Deceiving with the Truth*, MP, 1930, XXVII, 492–93.

18. N. Alonso Cortés, *Miscelánea Vallisoletana (Tercera Serie)*, 1921, 125.

19. Morley, *Strophes in the Span. Drama*, HMP, I, 524.

20. M. Bataillon, *Simples Réflexions sur J. de la C.*, BHi, 1935, XXXVII, 335.

SELECTIVE BIBLIOGRAPHY

I. General

Bonilla y San Martín, Adolfo, *Las Bacantes, o del origen del teatro español,* 1921.

Cañete, Manuel, *Teatro español del siglo XVI,* 1885.

Crawford, J. P. W., *The Spanish Pastoral Drama,* Philadelphia, 1915.

Creizenach, Wilhelm, *Geschichte des neueren Dramas,* vol. III, 2nd ed., revised by Adalbert Hämel, Halle, 1923, 1–92.

Kohler, Eugen, *Sieben spanische dramatische Eklogen,* Dresden, 1911.

Jack, W. S., *The Early Entremés in Spain: The Rise of a Dramatic Form,* Philadelphia, 1923.

Meredith, J. A., *Introito and Loa in the Spanish Drama of the Sixteenth Century,* Philadelphia, 1925.

Mérimée, Henri, *L'Art dramatique à Valencia,* Toulouse, 1913.

Milá y Fontanals, Manuel, *Los orígenes del teatro catalán,* Barcelona, 1895.

Moratín, Leandro F. de, *Orígenes del teatro español,* BAE, vol. II.

Morley, S. G., *Strophes in the Spanish Drama before Lope de Vega,* in HMP, vol. I, 505–31.

Rennert, H. A., *The Spanish Stage in the Time of Lope de Vega,* New York, 1909.

Schack, Adolfo Federico Conde de, *Historia de la literatura y del arte dramático en España,* translated by E. de Mier, vol. I, 1885.

Schmidt, Erich, *Die Darstellung des spanischen Dramas vor Lope de Rueda,* Berlin thesis, 1935.

Shoemaker, W. H., *The Multiple Stage in Spain during the Fifteenth and Sixteenth Centuries,* Princeton, 1935.

Valbuena, A., *Literatura dramática española,* 1930, I–III.

II. Individual Dramatists and Anonymous Plays

Altamira (Pedro), *Auto de la Aparición que Nuestro Señor Jesucristo hizo a los discípulos que iban a Emaús,* ed. J. E. Gillet, RR, 1922, XIII, 228–51.

Aparicio (Bartolomé), *El Pecador,* reprinted Gallardo, *Ensayo de una biblioteca,* Vol. I, cols. 221–34. See J. E. Gillet, *A Note on B. A.,* HR, 1936, IV, 272–76; W. H. Shoemaker, *The Llabrés Manuscript and its Castilian Plays,* HR, 1936, IV, 246–55.

Auto de Clarindo, ed. A. Bonilla y San Martín in *Cinco obras dramáticas anteriores a L. de V.,* RHi, 1912, XXVII, 390–498.

Auto de los Reyes Magos, ed. R. Menéndez Pidal, RABM, 1900, IV, 453–462, reprinted in *Poema de Mio Cid y otros monumentos,* 1919; ed. J. D. M. Ford, *Old Spanish Readings,* Boston, 1911. See Winifred Sturdevant, *The Misterio de los Reyes Magos,* Baltimore, 1927; A. M. Espinosa, *Notes on the Versification of El Misterio de los Reyes Magos,* RR, 1915, VI, 378–401.

Avendaño (Francisco de), *Comedia Florisea,* ed. A. Bonilla y San Martín in *Cinco obras anteriores a Lope de Vega,* RHi, 1912, XXVII, 390–498. See L. Pfandl, *Die Comedia Florisea von 1551,* ZRPh, 1919, XXXIX, 182–99.

Ávila (Diego de), *Égloga Interlocutoria,* ed. E. Kohler, with introduction in *Sieben span. dram. Eklogen.*

Bermúdez (Jerónimo), *Nise Lastimosa and Nise Laureada,* ed. López de Sedano, *Parnaso esp.,* VI, 1772; ed. Ochoa, *Tesoro del teatro esp.,* vol. I, Paris, 1838. See J. P. W. Crawford, *The Influence of Seneca's Tragedies upon Ferreira's Castro and B.'s Nise Lastimosa and Nise Laureada,* MP, 1914, XII, 171–186; S. G. Morley, *Strophes in the Span. Drama before Lope de Vega, Postscript,* RFE, 1925, XII, 398–99.

Carvajal (Micael de), *Tragedia Josephina,* ed. with an important introduction by J. E. Gillet, Princeton, 1932; ed. Cañete, 1870 (*Biblióf. Esp.,* VI); *Cortes de la Muerte,* completed by Luis Hurtado de Toledo, ed. Justo de Sancha, BAE, XXXV. See M. Cañete, *Teatro esp. del siglo XVI,* 105–247; A. Morel-Fatio, *Romania,* 1886, XV, 462–68; Florence Whyte, *The Dance of Death in Spain and Catalonia,* Baltimore, 1931, 100–16.

Castillejo (Cristóbal de), *Farsa de la Constanza,* Moratín's description and extracts, ed. by R. Foulché-Delbosc, *Deux œuvres de C. de C.,* RHi, 1916, XXXVI, 489–502. See J. P. W. Crawford, *The Relationship of Castillejo's Farsa de la Constanza and the Sermón de Amores,* HR, 1936, IV, 373–75.

Cervantes Saavedra (Miguel de), *Obras completas,* ed. R. Schevill y A. Bonilla, *Comedias y entremeses,* V–VI, 1920–22. See A. Cotarelo y Valledor, *El teatro de C.,* 1915.

Cirne (Juan), *Tragedia de los amores de Eneas y de la reyna Dido,* ed. J. E. Gillet and E. B. Williams, PMLA, 1931, XLVI, 353–431. See N. Alonso Cortés, *El autor de la Tragedia de los amores de Eneas y de la reyna Dido,* RFE, 1931, XVIII, 162–64; H. Serís, *Unos documentos sobre J. C.,* RFE, 1931, XVIII, 252–54; C. Eyer, *J. C. and the Celestina,* HR, 1937, V, 265–68.

Comedia a lo pastoral para la noche de Navidad, ed. J. P. W. Crawford, RHi, 1911, XXIV, 497–541.

Comedia Fenisa, ed. Gallardo, *El Criticón,* 1858, No. 8, 29–46; ed. Bonilla y San Martin, RHi, 1912, XXVII, 488-97.

Comedia yntitulada del Tirano Rrey Corbanto, ed. I. G. Probst Laas, Iowa City, Iowa, 1933.

Comedia Ypólita, ed. P. E. Douglass with an introduction, Philadelphia, 1929.

Coplas de la Muerte, reprinted in Florence Whyte, *The Dance of Death in Spain and Catalonia,* Baltimore, 1931, 163–71. The text is discussed in pages 52–67.

Coplas de una doncella y un pastor, ed. by Gallardo, *Ensayo de una biblioteca,* vol. I, 1863, cols. 703–711 and E. Cotarelo y Mori, *Farsas y Églogas por Lucas Fernández,* 1929, Apéndice, 1–16.

Cota (Rodrigo), *Diálogo entre el amor y un viejo* in *Cancionero de Hernando del Castillo,* 1882, vol. I, 297–308; Menéndez y Pelayo, *Antología de poetas líricos cast.,* vol. IV, 1–20; (text of a little later date), ed. A. Miola, *Miscellanea Caix-Canello,* Firenze, 1886, 175–89. See Menéndez y Pelayo, *Antología* etc., VI, ccclxxvi–ccclxxxiv; A. Cortina, *Rodrigo Cota,* RBAM, 1929, VI, 151–65.

Cuebas (Francisco de las), *Representación de los mártires Justo y Pastor,* ed. J. P. W. Crawford, RHi, 1908, XIX, 431–53. See M. Cañete, *Teatro esp. del siglo XVI,* 297–354; W. H. Shoemaker, *The Multiple Stage in Spain etc.,* 45–48, 116–18.

Cueva (Juan de la), *Comedias y tragedias,* ed. F. A. de Icaza, 2 vols., 1917 (Biblióf. esp., XI); *El infamador, Los siete infantes de Lara y el Exemplar poético,* ed. F. A. de Icaza, 1924 (Clás. cast. LX). See A. Hämel, *J. de la C. und die Erstausgabe seiner " Comedias y tragedias,"* ZRPh, 1923, XLIII, 134–53; M. Bataillon, *Simples Réflexions sur J. de la C.,* BHi, 1935, XXXVIII, 329–36; E. S. Morby, *The Plays of Juan de la Cueva,* unpublished thesis, University of California, Berkeley, 1936.

Cueva y Silva (Francisco de la), *Tragedia de Narciso,* ed. J. P. W. Crawford, Philadelphia, 1909.

Díaz (Fernando), *Farsa nuevamente trobada,* reprinted in Kohler, *Sieben span. dram. Eklogen,* and by Cronan, *Teatro. esp. del siglo XVI.*

Durán (Diego), *Égloga nueva,* ed. with introduction by E. Kohler, *Sieben span. dram. Eklogen,* and also in U. Cronan, *Teatro esp. del siglo XVI,* 367–89.

Égloga de Torino, included (67–73) in the anonymous *Qüestión de Amor,* ed. Menéndez y Pelayo in *Orígenes de la novela,* vol. II, 1907. See Menéndez y Pelayo, *Orígenes de la novela,* vol. I, cccxxvii–cccxxx; Benedetto Croce, *La Spagna nella Vita italiana durante la Rinascenza,* Bari, 1917, 122–48.

Égloga pastoril, ed. E. Kohler, *Sieben span. dram. Eklogen,* and U. Cronan, *Teatro esp. del siglo XVI.* See Kohler, *ibid.,* and H. Mérimée, *L'Art dram. à Valencia,* 104–111.

Égloga sobre el molino de Vascalon, ed. J. E. Gillet, PQ, 1926, V, 87–9.

Encina (Juan del), *Cancionero,* facsimile of princeps, ed. with important introduction by E. Cotarelo, 1928; *Teatro completo,* ed. Cañete and Asenjo Barbieri, 1893; *Aucto del Repelón,* ed. A. Álvarez de la Villa, Paris; *Égloga interlocutoria,* ed. U. Cronan, in RHi, 1916, XXXVI, 475–488. See Menéndez y Pelayo, *Antología,* vol. VII, i–c; R. Espinosa Maeso, *Nuevos datos biográficos etc.,* BRAE, 1921, VIII, 640–56; R. Mitjana, *Nuevos documentos etc.,* RFE, 1914, I, 275–88; E. Díaz-Jiménez, *J. del E. en León,* 1909; R. E. House, *A Study of Encina and the Égloga Interlocutoria,* RR, 1916, VII, 458–69; G. Boussagol, *La deuxième Eglogue de J. del E., Revue de l'Enseignement des Langues Vivantes,* 1929, XLVI, 193–98; J. P. W. Crawford, *Encina's Égloga de Fileno, Zambardo y Cardonio and Antonio Tebaldeo's Second Eclogue,* HR, 1934, II, 327–33.

Entremés de las esteras, ed. Rouanet, *Colección de autos etc.,* vol. II, 43–48.

Entremés de un hijo que negó a su padre, ed. J. P. W. Crawford, PMLA, 1910, XXV, 268–74; ed. Cotarelo, *Colección etc.,* No. 12.

Entremés de un muchacho, llamado Golondrino . . . , ed. G. L. Lincoln, RR, 1910, I, 41–49; Cotarelo, *Colección etc.,* No. 18.

Entremés de un viejo que es casado con una mujer moza, ed. G. L. Lincoln, RHi, 1910, XXII, 427–36; Cotarelo, *Colección etc.,* No. 14. See A. Giannini, *Una creduta fonte boccaccesca di un intermezzo spagnolo anonimo del secolo XVI,* RHi, 1933, LXXXI, Première Partie, 526–29.

Entremés del Estrólogo borracho, ed. Cotarelo, *Colección etc.,* No. 10.

Farça a manera de tragedia, ed. H. A. Rennert, RHi, 1911, XXV, 283–316; rev. version, Valladolid, 1914.

Farsa del Sordo, ed. Cotarelo, *Obras de Lope de Rueda,* vol. II, 1908, 399–434. See S. G. Morley, *Strophes in the Spanish Drama before Lope de Vega,* HMP, vol. I, 516.

Farsa llamada Rosiela, ed. Cronan, *Teatro esp. del siglo XVI,* 1913.

Farsa sacramental, ed. M. Serrano y Sanz, RABM, 1904, X, 67–71, 447–50.

Fernández (Lucas), *Farsas y Églogas,* facsimile of princeps, ed. with introduction by E. Cotarelo, 1929; *Farsas y Églogas,* ed. by Manuel Cañete, 1867. See R. Espinosa Maeso, *Ensayo biográfico del maestro L. F.,* BRAE, 1923, 386–424, 567–603.

Fernández de Heredia (Juan), *Obras,* reprinted Martí Grajales, Valencia, 1913. See H. Mérimée, *L'Art dramatique à Valencia,* Toulouse, 1913, 65–82.

Ferruz (Jaime), *Auto de Caín y Abel,* ed. L. Rouanet, *Colección,* vol. II, No. XLI, 150–66. See H. Mérimée, *L'Art dramatique à Valencia,* 228–39.

Güete (Jayme de), *Comedia Tesorina* and *Comedia Vidriana,* ed. U. Cronan in *Teatro esp. del siglo XVI.* See Menéndez y Pelayo, *Orígenes de la novela,* vol. III, cxlviii.

Horozco (Sebastián de), *Cancionero,* ed. *Bibl. Andaluces,* 1874, containing his plays. See E. Cotarelo y Mori, *El licenciado S. de H. y sus obras,* 1916.

Izquierdo Zebrero (Ausías), *Auto llamado Lucero de nuestra salvación, que trata del despedimiento que hizo Nuestro Señor Jesucristo de su bendita madre,* publ. in BAE, XXXV, no. 910. See J. E. Gillet, *The Sources of Izquierdo's Lucero de nuestra salvación,* MLN, 1923, XXXVIII, 287–90.

Leonardo de Argensola (Lupercio), *Isabela* and *Alejandra,* pub. in *Obras sueltas,* ed. Conde de la Viñaza, vol. I, 1889. See O. H. Green, *The Life and Works of L. L. de A.,* Philadelphia, 1927, 104–25; J. P. W. Crawford, *Notes on the Tragedies of L. L. de A.,* RR, 1914, V, 31–44.

Lobo Laso de la Vega (Gabriel), *Primera parte del Romancero y Tragedias* (1587). There is a copy of this rare book in the Library of the Hispanic Society of America.

López de Castro (Diego), *Marco Antonio y Cleopatra*, ed. H. A. Rennert, RHi, 1908, XIX, 184–237.

López de Yanguas (Hernán), *Égloga en loor de la Natividad de Nuestro Señor*, ed. with an introduction by E. Kohler, *Sieben span. dram. Eklogen*, 1911. *Farsa del mundo y moral*, edition of 1528, printed by U. Cronan, *Teatro esp. del siglo XVI*, 1913 and edition of 1551 printed by L. Rouanet, *Colección de Autos, Farsas, y Coloquios del siglo XVI*, vol. IV, 396–433. *Farsa sacramental*, see E. Cotarelo y Mori, *El primer auto sacramental del teatro esp. y noticia de su autor el Bachiller Hernán L. de Y.*, RABM, 1902, VII, 251–72. *Farsa sobre la felice nueva de la concordia etc.*, reprinted by U. Cronan, *Teatro esp.* See A. Bonilla y San Martín, *Fernán L. de Y. y el Bachiller de la Pradilla*, *Rev. Crít. Hispano-Americana*, 1915, I, 44–51.

López Ranjel (Pero), *Farsa a honor y reverencia del glorioso Nascimiento de Nuestro Redemptor Jesuchristo y de la Virgen gloriosa madre suya*, ed. by J. E. Gillet, PMLA, 1926, XLI, 860–90.

Los Cautivos, ed. A. Paz y Melia, RABM, 1909, XXI, 536–54.

Manrique (Gómez), *Cancionero*, ed. A. Paz y Melia, 1885, vols. I–II; ed. R. Foulché-Delbosc, *Cancionero del siglo XVI*, vol. II. See M. Menéndez y Pelayo, *Antología de poetas líricos cast.*, vol. VI, lv–ciii.

Martín (or Martínez), Esteban, *Auto cómo San Juan fué concebido*, ed. J. E. Gillet, RR, 1926, XVII, 41–64.

Mendoza (Fr. Íñigo de), *Vita Christi*, pub. by R. Foulché-Delbosc, *Cancionero del siglo XVI*, vol. I, 8–22. See M. Menéndez y Pelayo, *Antología de poetas líricos cast.*, vol. VI, ccvi–ccxiv.

Milán (Luis), *El Cortesano*, reprint in *Colección de libros esp. raros o curiosos*, VII, 1874. See H. Mérimée, *ibid.*, 88–100; J. B. Trend, *Luis Milán and the Vihuelistas*, London, 1925.

Miranda (Luis de), *Comedia Pródiga*, ed. J. M. de Alava, Sevilla, 1868 (Biblióf. Andaluces, XIX). See Menéndez y Pelayo, *Orígenes de la novela*, vol. III, cl–cli.

Montemayor (Jorge de), *Three Autos*, ed. Florence Whyte, PMLA, 1928, XLIII, 953-89.

Natas (Francisco de las), *Comedia Tidea*, ed. U. Cronan in *Teatro esp. del siglo XVI*. See M. Romera-Navarro, *Observaciones sobre la Comedia Tidea*, MP, 1921, XIX, 187–98.

Navarro, *Comedia muy exemplar de la marquesa de Saluzia, llamada Griselda*, ed. Caroline B. Bourland, RHi, 1902, IX, 331–54.

See C. B. Bourland, *Boccaccio and the Decameron in Castilian and Catalan Literature*, RHi, 1905, XII, 175–81.

Negueruela (Diego de), *Farsa llamada Ardamisa*, ed. Léo Rouanet, *Bibl. Hisp.*, 1900.

Ortiz (Agustín), *Comedia Radiana*, ed. R. E. House, with introduction, MP, 1910, VII, 507–556.

Ortiz (Andrés), *A Spanish Play on the Battle of Pavia* (*1525*), ed. J. E. Gillet, PMLA, 1930, XLV, 516–31.

Palau (Bartolomé), *Farsa llamada Salamantina*, ed. A. Morel-Fatio, BHi, 1900, II, 247–304; *Victoria de Cristo*, extracts in Rouanet, *Autos, etc.*, vol. IV, 365–394; *Historia de Santa Orosia*, ed. A. Fernández-Guerra, 1883; *Farsa llamada Custodia del hombre*, ed. with important introduction by Rouanet in *Archivo de invest. hist.*, 1911, vol. I–II. See R. E. House, *Sources of B. P.'s Farsa Salamantina*, RR, 1913, IV, 311–22; M. Serrano y Sanz, *B. P. y su historia de Santa Librada*, BRAE, 1922, IX, 301–10.

París (Juan de), *Égloga*, ed. with introduction by E. Kohler in *Sieben span. dram. Eklogen*, and U. Cronan, *Teatro esp. del siglo XVI*, 391–414. See R. E. House, *The 1536 Text of the Egloga of J. de P.*, MLN, 1913, XXVIII, 28–29.

Pastor (Juan), *Farsa o Tragedia de la castidad de Lucrecia*, ed. Bonilla y San Martín in *Cinco obras dramáticas anteriores a Lope de Vega*, RHi, 1912, XXVII, 437–54.

Pedraza (Juan Rodrigo Alonso de), *Comedia de Sancta Susaña*, ed. Bonilla y San Martín, RHi, 1912, XXVI, 423–36. *Auto que trata primeramente cómo el ánima de Christo decendió al infierno . . .*, ed. J. E. Gillet, RHi, 1933, LXXXI, 550–607. *Farsa llamada Danza de la Muerte*, publ. in BAE, LVIII, 41–46.

Perálvarez de Ayllón, *Comedia Tibalda*, ed. Bonilla y San Martín, 1903 (*Bibl. Hisp.*, XIII). See H. Serís, *Comedia de Preteo y Tibaldo por P. de A. y L. H. de T.*, EEB, vol. II, 1930, 507–33.

Pérez de Oliva (Hernán), *Teatro*, ed. Wm. Atkinson, RHi, 1927, LXIX, 521–659; *Vengança de Agamenõ*, 1528, facsimile ed. Bonilla y San Martín, in *Obras dramáticas del siglo XVI*, 1914; *Venganza de Agamemnón and Hécuba triste*, in Sedano, *Parnaso esp.*, vol. VI; Karl von Reinhardstoettner, *Der spanische Amphitrion des F. P. de O.*, München, 1886. See Wm. Atkinson, *H. P. de O. A Biographical and Critical Study*, RHi, 1927, LXXI, 309–484; P Henríquez Ureña, *Cuba contemporánea*, 1914, VI, 19–55.

Pradilla (Bachiller de la), *Égloga Real,* ed. E. Kohler with a critical study in *Sieben span. dram. Eklogen.* See E. Cotarelo y Mori, RABM, 1902, VII, 267–72; A. Bonilla y San Martín, *Rev. Crít. Hispano-Americana,* 1915, I, 44–51.

Prado (Andrés), *Farsa llamada Cornelia,* reprint by C. Pérez Pastor, *La imprenta en Medina del Campo,* 1895, 330–337.

Rey de Artieda (Andrés), *Los Amantes,* ed. E. Juliá Martínez in *Poetas dramáticos Valencianos,* vol. I, 1929. See H. Mérimée, *L'Art dramatique à Valencia,* 290–324; E. Cotarelo y Mori, *Sobre el origen y desarrollo de la leyenda de Los amantes de Teruel,* 1907.

Romero de Cepeda (Joaquín), *Comedias,* ed. E. de Ochoa, *Tesoro del teatro esp.,* vol. I, 1838. See Gallardo, *Ensayo,* vol. IV, cols. 254–59.

Rouanet (Léo), *Colección de autos, farsas y coloquios del siglo XVI,* 4 vols., 1901. See L. Sorrento, *I " Trionfi" del Petrarca a lo divino e l'allegoria religiosa negli autos,* EEB, vol. II, 397–435.

Rueda (Lope de), *Obras,* ed. Fuensanta del Valle, 2 vols., 1895–1896 (*Libros raros o curiosos,* XXIII–XXIV); ed. E. Cotarelo y Mori, 2 vols., 1908; *Teatro,* ed. J. Moreno Villa, 1924 (*Clás. Cast.,* LIX). *Entremés del mundo y no nadie,* ed. R. Foulché-Delbosc, RHi, 1900, VII, 251–55. *Comedia llamada Discordia y qüestión de amor,* ed. F. R. de Uhagón, RABM, 1902, VI, 341–54. *Registro de representantes,* ed. A. Bonilla y San Martín, 1917. See A. L. Stiefel, *L. de R. und das italienische Lustspiel,* ZRPh, 1891, XV, 183–216, 318–43; W. S. Jack, *The Early Entremés in Spain: the Rise of a Dramatic Form,* Philadelphia, 1923, Chap. III; J. Warshaw, *The Popular Riña in Lope de Rueda,* MLN, 1936, LI, 363–69.

Salaya (Alonso de), *Farsa,* ed. J. E. Gillet, PMLA, 1937, LII, 16–67.

Salazar, *Égloga de Breno y otros pastores compañeros suyos,* ed. H. C. Heaton, RHi, 1928, LXXII, 76–99. See J. P. W. Crawford, *The Date of Salazar's Égloga de Breno,* HR, 1936, IV, 280–82.

Sánchez (de Badajoz) (Diego), *Recopilación en metro,* ed. Barrantes, 1882–1886, 2 vols. (*Libros de Antaño,* XI–XII); ed. J. López Prudencio, Badajoz, 1910, one vol. only has appeared. See *Diego S. de B.,* by J. López Prudencio, 1915.

Sánchez Requejo (Miguel), *La isla bárbara* and *La guarda cuidadosa,* ed. H. A. Rennert, Boston, 1896; *La guarda cuidadosa,* ed. Mesonero, BAE, XLIII. See N. Alonso Cortés, *Miscelánea Vallisoletana, 3ª serie,* Valladolid, 1921, 123–31; G. T. Northup, *The*

Rhetorical Device of "Deceiving with the Truth," MP, 1930, XXVII, 487–93; R. C. Stephenson, *Miguel Sánchez: A Contemporary Terentian Influence on Lope de Vega,* unpublished thesis, Univ. of Texas, 1930.

Segundo entremés de Pero Hernández, ed. Cotarelo, *Colección etc.,* No. 30.

Segundo entremés del Testamento de los ladrones, ed. A. Paz y Melia, RABM, 1902, VII, 371–75; Cotarelo, *Colección etc.,* No. 19.

Sepúlveda (Comedia de), ed. Cotarelo y Mori, *Revista esp. de lit., hist. y arte,* 1901, vol. I. See J. P. W. Crawford, *Notes on the Sixteenth Century Comedia de Sepúlveda,* RR, 1920, XI, 76–81; W. S. Jack, *The Early Entremés in Spain,* 60–63.

Suárez de Robles (Pedro), *Danza del santíssimo nacimiento de Nuestro Señor Jesucristo,* ed. J. E. Gillet, PMLA, 1928, XLIII, 614–34.

Timoneda (Juan), *Obras completas,* ed. Menéndez y Pelayo, vol. I, *Teatro profano,* Valencia, 1911 (contains *Las tres comedias* and *La Turiana;* only vol. published); *Autos,* ed. González Pedroso, BAE, LVIII; F. G. Olmedo, *Un nuevo ternario de J. de T., Razón y Fe,* 1917, XLVII, 277–96, 483–97; XLVIII, 219–27, 489–96; J. E. Gillet, *T.'s (?) Aucto de la Quinta Angustia,* MLN, 1932, XLVII, 7–8; *The Aucto del Castillo de Emaus and the Aucto de la Iglesia,* ed. and translated into English by Mildred E. Johnson, Iowa City, Iowa, 1933. See Henri Mérimée, *L'Art dramatique à Valencia,* 1913, Chaps. III–IV; J. E. Gillet, *A Note on T.,* MLN, 1929, XLIV, 385–89; W. H. Shoemaker, *The Llabrés Manuscript and its Castilian Plays,* HR, 1936, IV, 243–46; J. P. W. Crawford, *Notes on the Amphitrión and Los Menemnos of J. de T.,* MLR, 1914, IX, 248–51.

Torres (Alonso de), *Auto del martyrio de Sant Justo y Pastor,* ed. Rouanet, *Colección,* vol. I, 483–501. See M. Cañete, *Teatro esp. del siglo XVI,* 297–354.

Torres Naharro (Bartolomé de), *Propalladia,* ed. M. Cañete and M. Menéndez y Pelayo, 1880–1900 (*Libros de Antaño,* IX–X) with an important introduction by the latter in the second volume. See J. E. Gillet, *Torres Naharro and the Spanish Drama of the Sixteenth Century,* EEB, vol. II, 1930, 437–68, and two articles *The Original Version of T.N.'s Comedia Tinellaria,* RR, 1923, XIV, 265–75 and *Une Édition Inconnue de la Propalladia de B. de T. N.,* RR, 1920, XI, 26–36; H. C. Heaton, *A Volume of Rare Sixteenth Century*

Span. Dram. Works, RR, 1927, XVIII, 339–45; A. Lenz, *T. N. et Plaute*, RHi, 1923, LVII, 99–107; P. Mazzei, *Contributo allo studio delle fonti ital. del teatro di J. del E. e T. N.*, Lucca, 1922, reviewed by J. E. Gillet in MP, XXI, 101–102; M. Romera-Navarro, *Estudio de la Comedia Himenea de T.N.*, RR, 1921, XII, 50–72; J. E. Gillet, *Torres Naharro and the Spanish Drama of the Sixteenth Century*, II, HR, 1937, V, 193–207.

Tragicomedia alegórica del Parayso y del Infierno, reprinted by U. Cronan, *Teatro esp. del siglo XVI*. See W. S. Hendrix, *The Auto da Barca do Inferno of Gil Vicente and the Spanish Tragicomedia del Parayso y del Infierno*, MP, XIII, 669–80 and a note in MLN, 1916, XXI, 432–34.

Tres Pasos de la Pasión y una Égloga de la Resurrección, ed. J. E. Gillet, PMLA, 1932, XLVII, 949–80.

Uceda de Sepúlveda (Juan), *Comedia Grassandora*, ed. H. C. Heaton in *Two Sixteenth Century Dramatic Works*, RHi, 1928, LXXII, 1–101.

Vega (Alonso de la), *Tres comedias*, ed. Menéndez y Pelayo, Dresden, 1905 (*Gesellschaft f. rom. Lit.*, VI).

Vicente (Gil), *Copilaçam*, facsimile of princeps of 1562, Lisboa, 1928; *Obras*, ed. Mendes dos Remedios, 3 vols., Coimbra, 1907–1917; *Four Plays*, with English translation, and important introduction by A. F. G. Bell, Cambridge, 1920. See Queirós Veloso, *G. V.*, pages 9–96 in the second vol. of Forjaz de Sampaio's handsome *Historia da Literatura portuguesa ilustrada*, Lisboa, 1930; C. Michaëlis de Vasconcellos, four important articles entitled *Notas Vicentinas*, pub. in *Revista da Universidade de Coimbra*, I (1912), 205–93; VI (1918), 263–303; VII (1919), 25–61; IX (1925), 5–394; A. Braamcamp Freire, *G. V., Vida e Obras de*, Porto, 1921; A. F. G. Bell, *G. V.*, Oxford Press, 1921; Ó. de Pratt, *G. V.*, Lisboa, 1931.

Virués (Cristóbal de), *Obras trágicas y líricas*. The five plays have been edited by E. Juliá Martínez in *Poetas dramáticos valencianos*, vol. I, 1929. See C. V. Sargent, *A Study of the Dramatic Works of C. de V.*, New York, 1930; H. Mérimée, *L'Art dramatique à Valencia*, 331–63.

BIBLIOGRAPHICAL SUPPLEMENT

This supplement covers the period from 1951 to early 1967 and contains all the editions and critical works that have come to our notice. Book reviews are not included, as they are easily found in current bibliographies. For earlier studies see W. T. McCready, *Bibliografía temática de estudios sobre el teatro español antiguo* (University of Toronto Press, 1966).

Up to Crawford's time, the attention of scholars was devoted mainly to the discovery and publication of the ancient dramatic texts. In recent years more emphasis has been given to analysis and interpretation of various aspects of the works of the principal dramatists. Editions are still needed, however; especially of Lucas Fernández, Diego Sanchez de Badajoz, and Juan de la Cueva.

ADDITIONAL ABBREVIATIONS

AIUO —Annali dell' Istituto Universitario Orientale di Napoli—Sezione Romanza
BCom —Bulletin of the Comediantes
BEP —Bulletin des Études Portugaises et de l'Institut Français au Portugal
BHS —Bulletin of Hispanic Studies
BHTP —Bulletin d'Histoire du Theatre Portugais
Brot —Brotéria
EEsc —Estudios Escénicos
GilVic —Gil Vicente
HomAlonso —Studia philologica. Homenaje ofrecido a Dámaso Alonso
MP —Modern Philology (omitted from original list)

NRFH   —Nueva Revista de Filología Hispánica
Ocid   —Ocidente
RLit   —Revista de Literatura
RomN   —Romance Notes
RomPhil   —Romance Philology

I. GENERAL

(In alphabetical order of subject-matter)

E. J. Webber, "*Arte mayor* in the Early Spa. Drama," RomPhil, 1951-52, V, 49-60; Manuela Sánchez Regueira, "Los autos esp. del siglo XVI y el *Atto della Pinta*," in *Saggi e ricerche in memoria di Ettore Li Gotti* (Palermo, 1962), III, 144-58; G. H. Lovett, "The Churchman in the Spa. Dr. before Lope de Vega," BCom, 1952, IV, no. 2, pp. [10-13] ; J. V. Falconieri, "Hist. de la 'Commedia dell' arte' en España," RLit, 1957, XI, 3-37 and XII, 69-90; G. Cantieri Mora, "La comedia del arte," EEsc, 1962, VII, 9-53; R. Aguilar Priego, "Autores y comediantes que pasaron por Córdoba en los sig. XVI y XVII," *Bol. R. Acad. de Córdoba*, 1962, XXXIII, 281-314; J. Romeu Figueras, "Notas al aspecto dramático de la procesión del Corpus Christi en Cataluña," EEsc, 1957, II, 29-41; F. G. Very, *The Spa. Corpus Christi Procession: A Lit. and Folkloric Study*, Valencia, 1962 (includes chaps. on the *tarasca* and *gigantones*); W. Sterling Jr., "Carros, Corrales, and Court Theatres: The Spa. Stage in the 16th and 17th Cent.," *Quarterly Journ. of Speech*, 1963, XLIX, 17-22; J. V. Falconieri, "Los antiguos corrales de España," EEsc, 1965, XI; J. de Entrambasaguas, "La lit. dramática esp. en el sig. XVI," in *El Escorial, 1563-1963* (Mad., 1964), I, 603-32; E. Asensio, *Itinerario del entremés desde Lope de Rueda a Quiñones de Benavente*, Mad., 1965; A. M. Pasquariello, "The *entremés* in 16th-Cent. Spa. America," "*Hisp. Am. Hist. Rev.*, 1952, XXXII, 44-58; M. R. Lida de Malkiel, "El fanfarrón en el teatro del Renacimiento," RomPhil, 1957-58, XI, 268-91; J. V. Falconieri, "Más noticias biográficas de Alberto Ganassa," RABM, 1954, LX, 219-22; N. D. Shergold, "Ganassa and the *Commedia dell' arte* in 16th-Cent. Spain," MLR, 1956, LI, 359-68; G. H. Lovett, "The Hermit in the Spa. Dr. before Lope de Vega," *Mod. Lang. Journ.*, 1951, XXXV, 340-55; J. H. Parker, *Breve hist. del teatro esp.*, México, 1957; A. Valbuena Prat, *Hist. del teatro esp.*, Barcelona, 1956; A. Castro, *Le drame et l'honneur dans la vie et dans la litt. esp. du XVIᵉ siècle*, Paris, 1965; F. Yndurain, "Dos comedias inéditas, de hacia 1574," *RLit*, 1955, VII, 181-87 (*La destrucción de Troya* and *Comedia llamada de Torcato*); R. B. Donovan, *The Liturgical Dr. in Medieval Spain*, Toronto, 1958; J. Gómez Pérez, "Un dr. litúrgico medieval en forma rudimentaria," *Archivum*, 1959, IX, 23-37; J. E. Varey and N. D. Shergold, "Datos hist. sobre los primeros teatros de Madrid," *Bol. Bibl. Menéndez Pelayo*, 1963, XXXIX, 95-179; F. Lázaro Carreter, *Teatro medieval*, Valencia, 1958; Manuel R. Pazos, "El teatro franciscano en Méjico durante el sig. XVI," *Archivo Ibero-Amer.*, 1951, XI, 129-89; E. Müller-Bochat, "Mimus, Novelle und span. Comedia," *Rom. Forsch.*, 1956, LXVIII, 241-70; J. E. Gillet, "Valencian *Misterios* and Mexican Missionary Plays in the Early 16th Cent.," *HR*, 1951, XIX, 59-61; Leonard Altman, "Music in the Early Spa. Secular Theatre," *Amer. Record Guide*, 1960-61, XXVII, 542-45, 591-92 (Encina, Fernández, Torres Naharro, etc.); José J. Herrero, *Tres músicos esp.: Juan del Encina, Lucas Fernández, Manuel Doyagüe y la cultura artística de su tiempo*, Mad., 1912; F. Weber de Kurlat, "El tipo cómico del negro en el teatro prelopesco: Fonética," *Filología*, 1962, VIII, 139-68; *ibid.*, "Sobre el negro como tipo cómico en el teatro esp. del sig. XVI," RomPhil, 1963-64, XVII, 380-91; William Davids, *Verslag van een onderzoek betreffende de betrekkingen tusschen de nederlandsche en de spaansche letterkunde in de 16ᵉ-18ᵉ eeuw*, 's-Gravenhage, 1918 (supplements previous works on infl. of Spa. lit. on Dutch); B. W. Wardropper, *Intro. al teatro religioso del Siglo de Oro. La evolución del auto sac.: 1500-1648*, Mad., 1953; J. Fradejas Lebrero (ed.), *Teatro relig. medieval. Auto de los Reyes Magos; Gómez Manrique, "Representación del Nacimiento de Nuestro Señor;" L. Fernández, "Auto de la Pasión,"* Tetuán, 1956; J. L. Flecniakoska, *La formation de l'auto relig. en Espagne avant Calderón (1550-1635)*, Montpellier, 1961; Rainer Hess, *Das roman. geistliche Schauspiel als profane und relig. Komödie, 15. und. 16. Jahrh.* (Freiburger Schriften zur roman. Philol., 4), München. 1965; J. D. Williams, "Juan Bautista de Loyola and the Spa. Relig. Dr. of the 16th Cent.," *HR*, 1956, XXIV, 271-77; J. L. Flecniakoska, "Les rôles de Satan dans les pièces du *códice de autos viejos*," *Rev. des Lang. Rom.*, 1963, LXXV, 195-207; J. Lihani, "Some Notes on sayagués," *Hisp*, 1958, XLI, 165-69; C. Stern, "Sayago and Sayagués in Spa. Hist. and Lit.," *HR*, 1961, XXIX, 217-37; O. T. Myers, "Church Latin Elements in Sayagués," *RomN*, 1963, IV, 166-68; *ibid.*, "Señor in Sayagués," *MLN*, 1965, LXXX, 271-73; C. Bravo Villasante, "Literatura. Teatro esp.," *Consigna*, 1955, XV, 16-21, 23-28 (Juan del Encina; teatro del sig XV); G. Díaz-Plaja, "Una aportación al estudio de la técnica escénica medieval," EEsc, 1957, I, 7-25; J. Lihani, "The Preclassical Meaning of Spa. *Tempero*," RR, 1956, XLVII, 161-65 (in early 16th cent.); E. J. Webber, "The Literary Reputation of Terence and Plautus in Med. and Ren. Spain," HR, 1956, XXIV, 191-206; C. Stern, "Some New Thoughts on the Early Spa. Dr.," BCom, 1966, XVIII, 14-19; A. Hermenegildo, *Los trágicos esp. del sig. XVI*, Mad., 1961; Jean Alexander, "Parallel Tendencies in Eng. and Spa. Tragedy in the Ren.," in *Studies in Comp. Lit.*, (ed. Waldo F. McNeir, Baton Rouge, 1962), pp. 84-101; J. L. Flecniakoska, "L'horreur morale et l'horreur materielle dans quelques tragedies esp. du XVIe siecle," in *Les Tragédies de Sénèque et le théâtre de la Ren.* (ed. J. Jacquot and M. Oddon, Paris, 1964), pp. 61-72; E. Juliá Martínez, "La Asunción de la Virgen y ei teatro primitivo esp.," BRAE, 1961, XLI, 179-334.

II. INDIVIDUAL DRAMATISTS AND ANONYMOUS PLAYS

Alarcon y Rojas (Andrés de). J. Simón Díaz, "Las obras perdidas de Rojas Alarcón," RLit, 1955, VIII, 330-34 (*La hechicera* and *Los graciosos sucesos de Tirsis y Tirseo*).

Aldana (Francisco de). E. L. Rivers, "New Biog. Data on F. de A.," RR, 1953, XLIV, 166-84; O. H. Green, "A Wedding 'Introito' by F. de A. (1537-1578)," HR, 1963, XXXI, 8-21.

Aucto de acusación del género humano. J. M. Castán Vázquez, "El derecho en el *Aucto* . . . ," *Rev. Gen. de Legislación y Jurisprudencia*, Dec., 1959 (offprint of *23 pp.*).

Auto de la huída de Egipto, ed. J. M. Díez Taboada and J. M. Rozas in *Homenajes. Estudios de Filología Española*, 1964, I, 78-89.

Auto de los Reyes Magos, ed. Sebastião Pestana, publ. as supplement to Ocid, 1965-66, nos. 327-34. STUDIES: R. Lapesa, "Sobre el *A. de los R. M.*, sus rimas anómalas y el posible origen de su autor," in *Homenaje a Fritz Krüger* (Mendoza, Arg.), 1954, II, 591-99; G. Díaz-Plaja, "El *A. de los* R. M.," EEsc, 1959, IV, 101-26; E. Aranda, *Teatro medieval en un pueblo murciano* (Reyes en *Churra*), Murcia, 1961; G. J. MacDonald, "*Hamihala*, a Hapax in the *A. de los R. M.*," RomPhil, 1964-65, XVIII, 35-36.

Avendaño (Francisco de). R. Benavides Lillo, "F. de A. y el teatro renacentista esp.," *Bol. de Filología* (Univ. de Chile), 1960, XII, 51-164 (ed. of *Comedia Florisea* on pp. 100-64).

Bermúdez (Jerónimo). M. D. Triwedi, "Notas para una biog. de J. B.," *Hispanófila*, 1967, X, no. 29, pp. 1-9; Marketa L. Freund, "Algunas observaciones sobre *Nise lastimosa* y *Nise laureada* de J. B.," RLit, 1961, XIX, 103-12; M. D. Triwedi, "Notes on B.'s *Nise laur.* and Dolce's Paraphrase of Seneca's *Thyestes*," PQ, 1963, XLII, 97-102.

Cervantes (Miguel de). J. Casalduero, *Sentido y forma del teatro de C.*, Madrid, 1951; R. Marrast, *Michel de C., dramaturge*, Paris, 1957; B. W. Wardropper, "C.'s Theory of the Drama," MP, 1954, LII, 217-21; *La Numancia o La tragedia del cerco de Numancia*, ed. Edit. Gráficas, Barcelona, 1956; *El cerco de Num., El trato de Argel* (Col. "Clásicos y Maestros"), Madrid, 1957; *A destruicão de Num.*, versión poética de José Carlos Lisboa, Rio de Janeiro, 1957; *Numance*, versión française de Robert Marrast et André Reybaz, Paris, 1957; *El cerco de Num.*, ed. R. Marrast, Salamanca, Edics. Anaya, 1961; *La Num.*, ed. F. Yndurain, Madrid, Aguilar, 1964. STUDIES: G. L. Stagg, "Cervantes' 'De Batro a Tile'," MLN, 1954, LXIX, 96-99 (emends a verse of *Num.*); Max Aub, "La Numancia de C.," *Torre*, 1956, IV, no. 14, pp. 99-111; J. Mañach, "El sentido trágico de la *Num.*," *Nueva Rev. Cubana*, 1959, I, 21-40 (also in *Bol. Acad. Cub. de la Lengua*, 1959, VIII, 29-49); R. R. MacCurdy, "The Numantia Plays of C. and Rojas Zorrilla: The Shift from Collective to Personal Tragedy," *Symposium*, 1960, XIV, 100-20; J. B. Avalle-Arce, "Poesía, hist., imperialismo: *La Num.*," *Anuario de Letras* (Mexico, Univ. Nac.), 1962, II, 55-75; W. M. Whitby, "The Sacrifice Theme in C.'s *Num.*," Hisp, 1962, XLV, 205-10; G. L. Stagg, "The Date and Form of *El trato de Argel*," BHS, 1953, XXX, 181-92.

Colloquio de Fenisa. J. L. Flecniakoska, "De cómo un coloquio pastoril se transmuta en dos coloquios a lo divino," *Actas del Primer Cong. Internac. de Hispanistas* (1964), pp. 271-80 (*C. de F. en loor de Nuestra Señora* and *C. de Fide Ypsa*).

Comedia Thebayda. M. R. Lida de Malkiel, "Para la fecha de la *C. T.*," RomPhil, 1952-53, VI, 45-48 (before 1504); D. W. McPheeters, "Comments on the Dating of the *C. T.*," RomPhil, 1955-56, IX, 19-23 (agrees with Lida); G. D. Trotter, "The Date of the *C. T.*," MLR, 1965, LX, 386-90 (*c.* 1519-20).

Consueta del Rey Asuero, intro. y texto de G. Díaz-Plaja, *Bol. Acad. de Buenas Letras de Barcelona*, 1953, XXV, 227-45.

Cota (Rodrigo), *Diálogo entre el amor y un viejo*, ed. Elisa Aragone.

Firenze, 1961; C. H. Leighton, "Sobre el texto del *Diálogo* . . . ," NRFH, 1958, XII, 385-89; R. F. Glenn, "R. C.'s *Diálogo* . . . : Debate or Drama?" Hisp, 1965, XLVIII, 51-56.

Cueva (Juan de la), *El infamador*, ed. José Caso González, Salamanca, Anaya, 1965; P. Verdevoye, "Le poëme *Llanto de Venus en la muerte de Adonis* de J. de la C. dans sa version définitive en partie inédite," in *Mélanges . . . Marcel Bataillon* (1962), pp. 677-89; R. H. Williams, "Francisco de Cáceres, Niccolò Franco, and J. de la C.," HR, 1959, XXVII, 194-99; B. W. Wardropper, "J. de la C. y el drama hist.," NRFH, 1955, IX, 149-56; N. D. Shergold," J. de la C. and the Early Theatres of Seville," BHS, 1955, XXXII, 1-7; *ibid.*, "J. de la C. y los primeros teat. de Sev.," *Archivo Hispalense*, 1956, no. 75, pp. 57-64.

Danza de la muerte. C. Bravo-Villasante, "Literatura. Teatro espanol: *La D. de la m.*," *Consigna*, Feb. 1956, pp. 40-42.

Díaz Tanco (Vasco). A. Rodríguez Moñino, "D. T. en Bolonia durante la coronación de Carlos V," *Filología*, 1962, VIII, 221-40.

Encina (Juan del), *Églogas*, ed. H. López Morales (Vol. I: Texto), New York, 1963; *Égloga de Plácida y Vitoriano, precedida de otras tres*, ed. E. Giménez Caballero, Zaragoza, Ebro, 1960. STUDIES: R. O. Jones, "E. y el Cancionero del Brit. Mus.," *Hispanófila*, 1961, no. 11, pp. 1-21; C. Stern, "J. del E.'s Carnival Eclogues and the Spa. Dr. of the Ren.," *Renaissance Drama*, 1965, VIII, 181-95; J. Caso González, "Cronología de las primeras ob. de J. del E.," *Archivum*, 1953, III, 362-72; Brother Austin (F. S. C.), "J. del E.," Hisp, 1956, XXXIX, 161-74; O. T. Myers, "Lexical Notes on E.: Some Revisions for Recent Additions to the *DCELC*," RomN, 1966, VIII, 143-46; H. López Morales, "Estud. ling. de la obra dr. de J. del E.," *Rev. de la Univ. de Madrid*, 1962, XI, 628-29; R. O. Jones, "An E. Manuscript," BHS, 1961, XXXVIII, 229-37; B. W. Wardropper, "Metamorphosis in the Theatre of J. del E., "*Stud. in Phil.*, 1962, LIX, 41-51; Orlando Martínez, "J. del E. El músico poeta," *Anales de la Acad. Nac. de Artes y Letras* (Havana), 1951, XXXIV, 145-84; J. R. Andrews, *J. del E.: Prometheus in Search of Prestige* (Univ. of Calif. Pub. in Mod. Phil.), Berkeley, 1959; Sira L. Garrido y Marcos, "Nota sobre J. del E. sayagués," *Humanitas* (Tucumán, Arg.), 1953, I, 179-208; O. T. Myers, "E. and Skelton," Hisp, 1964, XLVII, 467-74; Dorothy C. Clarke, "On J. del E.'s *Una arte de poesía castellana*," RomPhil, 1952-53, VI, 254-59; O. T. Myers, "J. del E. and the *Auto del repelón*," HR, 1964, XXXII, 189-201.

Férnández (Lucas), "*Auto de la Pasión*." Noticia literaria: M. Fraile;

notas teatrales: E. Navarro Ramos. Madrid, 1961; J. Lihani, "The Question of Authorship of the *Coplas* Attributed to L. F.," *Ky. For. Lang. Quarterly,* 1965, XII, 238-45; C. Bravo-Villasante, "Literatura. Teatro primitivo: L. F.," *Consigna,* Jan. 1956, pp. 35-36; A. Hermenegildo, "Nueva interpretación de un primitivo: L. F.," *Segismundo,* 1966, II, 9-43; L. J. Cisneros, "Nota," *Mar del Sur,* 1952, VIII, 86 (L. F.'s debt to Encina); J. Lihani, "L. F. and the Evolution of the Shepherd's Family Pride in Early Spa. Dr.," HR, 1957, XXV, 252-63.

Hurtado de Toledo (Luis) and Micael de Carvajal, *"Cortes de casto amor"* y *"Cortes de la muerte."* *Toledo, 1557.* Facs. ed., Valencia, 1963.

Loa entre un cortesano y un villano. J. L. Flecniakoska, "Une épître d'Antonio de Guevara et la *Loa* . . . . ," *Rev. des Lang. Rom.,* 1962, LXXIV, pp. 1-13.

Manrique (Gómez). H. Sieber, "Dramatic Symmetry in G. M.'s *La representación del nacimiento de N. S.,"* HR, 1965, XXXIII, 118-35.

Misterio de Elche, ed. José Pomares Perlasia; pról. del Dr. Carlos Jiménez Díaz (with 43 pp. of musical score), Barcelona, 1957; R. Ramos Folques, *Leyenda del M. de E.,* Mad., 1956; Alberta W. Server, "The Mystery Play of E.," Hisp, 1957, XL, 430-33; J. A. Roig del Campo, "El M. de E.," *Razón y Fe,* 1958, CLVIII, 101-06.

Poliodorus, comedia humanística desconocida, ed. J. M. Casas Homs, Mad., 1953.

Rey de Artieda (Andrés). J. Caruana y Gómez de Barreda, "Los amantes de Teruel," RABM, 1959, LXVII, 35-55 (on anagram of protagonists' names); J. G. Fucilla, "Una scena in *Los amantes* di R. de A. e un sonetto petrarchesco," *Quaderni Ibero-Amer.,* 1951, no. 11, pp. 381-93.

Rueda (Lope de), *Pasos,* ed. Ramón Esquer, Tetuán, Cremades, 1957; *Eufemia,* trans. W. S. Merwin, *Tulane Drama Rev.,* 1958-59, III, no. 2, pp. 57-79. STUDIES: Fred Abrams, "The Date of Composition of L. de R.'s *Comedia Eufemia,"* MLN, 1962, LXXVI, 766-70; *ibid.,* "L. de R.: Una bibliografía analítica en el cuarto centenario de su muerte," *Duquesne Hisp. Rev.,* 1965, IV, 39-55; V. Tusón, *L. de R.: Bibliografía crítica,* (Cuad. Bibliográf., 16), Mad., 1965; Ismael García Rámila, "Una incógnita estancia del gran L. de R. en la ciudad de Burgos," BRAE, 1951, XXXI, 121-25; G. B. Palacín, "¿En dónde oyó Cervantes recitar a L. de R.?" HR, 1952, XX, 240-43; F. Abrams, "¿Fue L. de R. el autor del *Lazarillo de Tormes?"* Hisp, 1964, XLVII, 258-67; R. Hesler, "A New Look at the Theatre of L. de R.," *Educ. Theat. Journ.,*

1964, XVI, 47-54; P. Russell-Gebbett, "Valencian in the 6th *Faso* of L. de R.'s Deleitoso," HR, 1953, XXI, 215-18.

San Pedro (Diego de). A. Pérez Gómez, "*La passión trobada* de D. de S. P.," RLit, 1952, I, 147-82 (facs. ed. and bibl. notes); K. Whinnom, "The First Printing of S. P.'s *Passión trobada*," HR, 1962, XXX, 149-51; Dorothy S. Vivian, "La *Passión trobada* de D. de S. P. y sus relaciones con el dr. medieval de la Pasión," *Anuario de Est. Medievales*, 1964, I, 451-70.

Sánchez de Badajoz (Diego). J. E. Gillet, " 'Las ochavas en cadena': A Proverb in Rodrigo Cota and D. S. de B.," RomPhil, 1952-53, VI, 264-67.

Timoneda (Juan de), *Obras*, ed. E. Juliá Martínez, Madrid, Soc. de Biblióf. Esp., 1947-48, 3 vols. (Drama in vols. 2-3). STUDIES: P. Delgado Barnés, "Contribución a la bibliografía de J. de T.," RLit, 1959, no. 31-32, pp. 24-56; E. Juliá Martínez, "Originalidad de T.," *Rev. valenciana da filol.*, 1555-58, V, 91-151.

Torres Naharro (Bartolomé de). "*Propalladia*" *and Other Works of B. de T. N.*, ed. J. E. Gillet, Bryn Mawr & Philadelphia, 1943-61. Vol. I, *Poems*; vol. II, *Plays*; vol. III, *Notes*; vol. IV, *T. N. and the Dr. of the Ren.*, transcribed, ed. and completed by O. H. Green, Phila., U. of Penn. Press. *Tres comedias: Soldadesca, Ymenea, Aquilana*, ed. H. López Morales, New York, Las Américas, 1965; *Himenea*, ed. Annamaria Gallina, Milano, 1961. STUDIES: M. R. Lida de Malkiel, "Del renacimiento esp.: B. de T. N.," *Sur*, 1952, no. 211-12, pp. 119-23 (on vol. III of Gillet); J. V. Falconieri, "La situación de T. N. en la hist. lit.," *Hispanófila*, 1957, I, 32-40; J. E. Gillet, " 'Escoté la meryenda e party me dalgueua'," HR, 1956, XXIV, 64 (on *dalgueua* in *Libro de buen amor* and similar forms in T. N.); I. S. Révah, "Un tema de T. N. y de Gil Vicente," NRFH, 1953, VII, 417-25; A. Berthelot, "La *Propaladia du Mans*," BHi, 1954, LVI, 167-74; T. Pickering, "A Note on the *Comedia Serafina* and *El Conde Alarcos*," MLN, 1956, LXXI, 109-14. S. Gilman, "Retratos de conversos en la *Com. Jacinta* de T. N.," NRFH, 1963-64, XVII, 20-39.

Vicente (Gil), *Obras dramáticas castellanas*, ed. T. R. Hart (Clás. cast., 156), Mad., 1962; *Poesía*, ed. T. R. Hart, Salamanca, Anaya, 1965; *Teatro y poesía*, ed. Concha de Salamanca (Col. Crisol), 2nd ed., Mad., 1963; *Teatro*, ed. A. J. Saraiva, Lisbon, 1959; *Teatro*, traduzione, intro. e note a cura de Enzio di Poppa Vólture, Firenze, Sansoni, 1957 (2 vols.); *Four Plays*, trans. Jill Booty, *Tulane Drama Rev.*, 1960-61, V, no. 3, pp. 160-86 (*Auto de los Reyes Magos* [The 3 Wise

Men], *Quem tem farelos?* [The Serenade], *Auto da India* [The Sailor's Wife], *Comedia del Viudo* [The Widower's Comedy]):*Auto da Alma de G. V. e Sonetos e canções de Camões,* ed. J. Simão Portugal e Manuel Francisco Catarino, Porto, 1958; *Auto da Alma,* ed. Feliciano Ramos, Braga, 1962; *Amadís de Gaula,* ed. T. P. Waldron, Manchester, 1959; *Trilogie des 'Barques,* trans. Andrée Crabbé, Coimbra, 1958; *Barca do Inferno,* éd. crit. I. S. Révah in *Recherches sur les oeuvres de G. V.,* vol. I, Lisbon, 1951; *Barca da Glória,* ed. P. Quintela, Lisbon, 1958; *Auto de Ines Pereira,* ed. I. S. Révah in *Recherches* . . . , vol. II, Lisbon, 1955 (also publ. in BEP, 1952-54, III-V); *Auto de Mofina Mendes & Diálogo infantil (da Comedia de Rubena),* ed. A. A. Machado de Vilhena, Porto, 1964; *Pranto de Maria Parda,* ed. L. Stegagno Picchio, ˙AIUO, 1963, V, 35-126 (also publ. sep.); *Tragicomédia pastoril da Serra da Estrela,* ed. Álvaro J. da Costa Pimpão, Coimbra, 1963; "Il Trionfo dell' Inverno," trans. Guido Battelli, Ocid, 1965, no. 327, pp. 27-28; *Comedia del Viudo,* ed. A. Zamora Vicente, Lisbon, 1962; I. S. Révah, "Éd. crit. du *romance de Don Duardos et Flérida,*" BEP, 1952, III, 107-39. STUDIES: "Actualidade de G. V.," *Autores,* 1961, IV, no. 14, pp. 25-26; Rebello, Luís F., "Actualidade de G. V.," *Seara Nova,* 1965, XLIV, 208; J. de Oliveira, "A primeira sugestão do mito de Adamastor (G. V. e Luís de Camoes, breve estudo comparativo)," Ocid, 1962, no. 285, pp. 6-25; Nelly Novaes Coelho, "As alcoviteiras vicentinas," *Alfa,* no. 4, Sept. 1963, 83-105; Holger Sten, "G. V. et la théorie de l'art dramatique," in *Études romanes dédiées à Andreas Blinkenberg* . . . (Orbis Litterarum, Supplement 3), 1963, pp. 209-19, J. Lopes Dias, "A Beira Baixa e o seu teatro popular na obra de G. V.," *Memórias da Acad. das Ciências de Lisboa* (Cl. de Let.), 1962, VII, 7-35; F. Pires de Lima, "Jacinto Benavente actualizou Mestre Gil," *Tempo Presente* (Lisbon), 1960, no. 13, pp. 45-56; E. A. Beau, "Sobre el bilingüismo de G.V.," HomAlonso, 1960-63, I, 217-24; A. Monteverdi, "Bilingüismo letterario," *Bol. de Filol.* (Lisbon), 1960, XIX, 87-93 (on G. V.'s use of Spa. & Port.): A. J. Saraiva, "G. V. e Bertolt Brecht," *Vértice* (Coimbra), 1960, XX, 465-75; A. da Costa Ramalho, "Uma bucólica grega em G. V.," *Humanitas* (Coimbra), 1963-64, XV-XVI, 328-47; A Cortez Pinto, "G. V., Camões e os Janotas," *Colóquio,* 1962, no. 18, pp. 61-64; L. Sletsjøe, *O elemento cénico em G.V.,* Lisbon, 1965; Círculo de Cultura Teatral, *Comemorações do quinto centenário de G. V.,* Porto, Edições Divulgação, 1965; J. Mendes, "Comemoração de G. V.," Brot. 1965, LXXXI, 111-20; *Vértice* (Coimbra), 1965, XXV, nos. 264-66 commemorates G. V.'s centenary with 12 arts. (see *Revue*

d'Hist. du Théâtre, XVIII, no. 3 [July-Sept., 1966] , p. 350 for titles);
J. E. Tomlins, "Una nota sobre la clasificación de los dramas de G.
V.," *Duquesne Hisp. Rev.*, 1964, III, 115-31, 1965, IV, 1-16; I.S. Révah.
"La *comedia* dans l'oeuvre de G. V.," BHTP, 1951, II, 1-39; Laurence
Keates, *The Court Theatre of G. V.*, Lisbon, 1962; Álvaro Pinto, "O
culto de G. V.," Ocid, 1953, XLV, 39; P. Groult, "Le diable picard de
G. V.," BEP, 1952, XVI, 79-95; J. Girodon, "Le diable picard," BEP,
1952, XVI, 209-11 (in *Auto das Fadas*); L. Stegagno Picchio, "Diavolo
e inferno nel teatro di G. V.," AIUO, 1959, I, no. 2, pp. 31-59; A.
Pimenta, "O conceito de diabo na Bíblia e em G. V.," Ocid, 1965, no.
332, pp. 231-47; A. Saraiva de Carvalho, "Diálogo com G. V.," GilVic,
1964, XV, 49-54, 75-81, 147-58; Holger Sten, "Uma opinião dinamar-
quesa sobre G.V.," Ocid, 1965, no. 327, pp. 15-16; J. de Sampaio, "Dra-
maturgia mariana em G.V.," *Panorama* (Lisbon), 1964, no. 12, pp. 28-
32; R. de Vasconcelos, "G.V. e a soc. eclesiástica de mil e quinhentos,"
Brot, 1961, LXXIII, 506-33; S. Pestana, "Estudos gilvicentinos," *Rev.
de Port.*, 1951 to 1965, as follows: XVI, 327-28; XIX, 221-24, 241-45;
XX, 13-16; XXI, 121-26, 175-76, 193-96, 221-24, 254-55, 302-12,
XXII, 289-94, XXIII, 501-06; XXIV, 183-86, 410-14; XXV, 362-71;
XXVI, 363-67; XXVIII, 445-54; XXIX, 101-03, 468-73; XXX, 14-18.
R. de Figueiroa Rego, "A familia de G. V., *Arquivo Histór. de Port.*,
1961, I, 311-36; M. Micaela Ramos, "G. V. e a folclore," *Bol. Cult.
da Junta Distrital de Lisboa*, 1962, LVII-LVIII, 191-200; Xosé M.
Álvarez Blásquez, "G. V. Galicia: I. O conto das dúas lousas," *Grial*,
1964, no. 4, pp. 235-39; A. L. de Carvalho, *G. V.; Guimarães sua
terra natal*, Guim., 1959; J. R. Andrews, "The Harmonizing Per-
spective of G. V.," BCom, 1959, XI, no. 2, pp. 1-5; Reis Brasil, "As
determinantes do humanismo na ob. de G. V.," in *Miscelânea de est.
a Joaquim de Carvalho*, 1960, no. 5, pp. 497-517 (comment by H. L.
Johnson, BCom, 1961, XIII, no. 2, p. 9); L. F. Aviz de Brito, "Contrib.
dos notários e guardasmores para a ident. de Mestre G. V.," GilVic,
1965, XVI, 69-73; G. Dolci, "G. V. na língua ital.," *Bol. Cult. da
Câmara Munic. do Porto*, 1958, XX, 292-98; C. Láfer, *O judeu em
G. V.*, São Paulo. 1963; P. Teyssier, *La langue de G. V.*, Paris, 1959
(see HR, XXIX, 269-73); I. S. Révah, "Quelques mots du lexique de G.
V.," *Rev. Bras. de Fil.*, 1956, II, 143-54; J. Cury, "G. V. e a teoria do
livre-arbitrio," Ocid, 1965, no. 330, pp. 158-63; R. Ricard, "Missa
seca chez G. V.," *Colóquio*, 1961, no. 12, pp. 55-56; R. Brasil, *G. V.
e o teatro mod.*, Lisbon, 1965; P. A. Rebelo Bonito, *A música dos
autos de G. V.* (Reprinted from *Rev. de Guim.* and GilVic), Porto, 1958;

ibid., "Aspectos musicales dos autos de G. V.," *Gazeta Musical* (Lisbon), 1958, VIII, 84-85; L. de Pina, *Pecado, culpa e augústia na cena gil-vicentina*, Porto, 1958 (repr. from GilVic and *Rev. de Guim.*); Anon., "G. V. e o Inf. D. Pedro," *Rev. de Port.*, 1963, XXVIII, 400-04; Enzio di Poppa, "G. V., compiuto poeta," *Convivium*, 1952, pp. 216-32; J. Almeida Pavão, *G. V., Poeta*, Ponta Delgada, 1964; Ester de Lemos, "A propósito de G. V., poeta lírico," *Panorama* (Lisbon), 1965, no. 13, pp. 9-14; F. Elias de Tejada, *As idéias políticas de G. V.*, Lisbon, 1945; L. Stegagno Picchio, "Questioni gilvicentine," *Cult. Neolat.*, 1960, XIX, 265-74; Cruz Malpique, "G. V. num relâmpago," GilVic, 1965, XVI, 101-05, 145-50; H. de Castro Guimaraes, "A sátira vicentina," *Bol. da Acad. Port. de Ex-Libris*, 1958, nos. 8-9 (offprint of 42 pp.); L. Stegagno Picchio, "Considerazioni sui testi saiaghesi di G. V.," in *Studi di lett. spa.* (ed. C. Samonà; Roma),1964, pp. 231-41; O. Lopes, "O sem-sentido em G. V.," *Seara Nova*, 1965, XLIV, 275-78; E. A. Pestana, "O sermão de G. V. em Abrantes," *Palestra* (Lisbon), 1959, no. 4, pp. 34-48; Ann Livermore, "G. V. and Shakespeare," in *Proc. Internat. Colloq. on Luso-Braz. Studies (Wash., 1950)*, pp. 158-60; C. M. Bowra, "The Songs of G. V.," *Atlante*, 1953, I, 3-21; J. H. Parker, "G. V.: A Study in Peninsular Dr.," *Hisp.*, 1953, XXXVI, 21-25; M. Martins, "O tempo e a morte em G. V.," *Brot.*, 1965, LXXXI, 186-203; G. C. Rossi, "Il prob. dei testi di G. V.," *Fil. Romanza*, 1956, II, 314-23; *ibid.*, "Text- und Sprach-probleme G. V.'s im Lichte der neuesten Forschung," *Neuphil. Mitt.*, 1957, LVIII, 196-206; S. Reckert, "El verdadero texto de la *Copilaçam.* vicentina de 1562," HomAlonso, 1960-63, III, 53-68; G. de Matos Sequeira, *Tomar e G. V.*, Porto, 1960; Anon., "G. V." *Livros de Port.*, 1965, no. 80, pp. 6-18 (has bibliog.); M. Martins, "G. V.," *Brot.*, 1965, LXXXI, 13-28. STUDIES OF WORK: Solange Corbin, "Les textes musicaux de l'*Auto da Alma* (Identification d'une pièce citée par G. V.)," in *Mélanges d'histoire . . . Louis Halphen*, Paris, 1951, pp. 137-43; J. de Oliveira, *G. V. e "Auto da Al." Estética e ensenação*, Lisbon, 1952; A. F. Gomes, "Caracteristicas do *A. da Al.* e fé de G. V.," Ocid, 1965, no. 327, pp. 17-21; E. Asensio, "Las fuentes de las *Barcas* de G. V.," BHTP, 1953, IV, 207-37; C. Ferreira da Cunha, "Regularidade e irreg. na versificação do primeiro *Auto das Barcas* de G. V.," HomAlonso, 1960-63, I, 459-79; T. R. Hart Jr., "Courtly Love in G. V.'s *D. Duardos*," RomN, 1961, II, 103-06; E. L. Rivers, "The Unity of *D. D.*," MLN, 1962, LXXVI, 759-66; R. Ricard, "Uno piensa el bayo . . . .' Hommage à l'éditeur de la *Tragicom. de D. D.*," HomAlonso, 1960-63, III, 155-60; Anon., ' *O Juiz de Beira* de G. V. e o Direito do seu tempo," *Autores*, 1961, IV, no. 13, pp. 19-21; I. S. Révah, "L'attrib. à G. V. de la *Obra da geração humana*," BHTP, 1950, I, 93-116, 1951, II, 89-106; T. R. Hart Jr., "G. V.'s *Auto de la Sibila Casandra*," HR, 1958. XXVI. 35-51; L. Spitzer "The Artistic Unity of G. V.'s *A. da Sib. Cas.*," HR, 1959, XXVII, 56 77 (Spa. trans. in his *Sobre antigua poesía esp.*, Buenos Aires, 1962 pp. 105-28); I. S. Révah, "L'*Auto de la Sib. Cas.* de G. V.," HR, 1959, XXVII, 167-93; M. R. Lida de Malkiel, "Para la génesis del *A. de la Sib. Cas.*," *Filología*, 1960, V, 47-63; Margit Frenk Alatorre, "Quien maora ca mi sayo," NRFH, 1957, XI, 386-91 (on *Triumpho do inverno*); J. de Oliveira, *Humanidade e grandeza do "Velho da horta,"* publ. as supplements to Ocid, 1963-64, LXIV-LXVI, nos. 297, 301, 304, 306, 309-10; C. Nogueira-Martins, "A propósito de la *Hum. e grand. do 'V. da horta,'*" RomN, 1966, VIII, 96-97; L. Stegagno Picchio, "Il 'Pater noster' dell' *Auto do V. da horta*. Interpretazione di un passo di G. V.," AIUO, 1961, III, 191-98; J. de Oliveira, *A "Visitação" de G. V. à rainha parida dona Maria; ensaios de identificação literária e de encenação,* Lisbon, 1953 (supplement to Ocid, XLIV); A. Zamora Vicente, "Una intro. a la *Comédia do Viuvo,*" HomAlonso, 1960-63, III, 619-34. See also: *"Don Duardos," autos y selección poética,* Sel. e intro. de Mercedes Guillén, Madrid, Taurus, 1966; *Comédia de Rubena,* ed. G. Tavani, Roma, Ateneo, 1965. E. Nunes, "A dimensão histórica na obra de G. V.," Brot, 1966, LXXXII, 50-62; A. F. Gomes, "G. V., D. Diogo Pinheiro e os Judeus," Ocid, 1966, no. 333, pp. 18-24; A. J. Saraiva, *G. V. e o fim do teatro medieval,* Lisbon, 1965; M. dos Remedios Castelo-Branco, "Significado do cómico do Auto da Índia," Ocid, 1966, no. 336, pp. 129-36.

Virués (Cristóbal de). John C. Weiger, "Nobility in the Theater of V.," RomN, 1966, VII, 180-82.

INDEX

219